NO IDENTITY CRISIS

A Father and Son's
Own Story of
Working Together

MELVIN
and MARIO
VAN PEEBLES

A FIRESIDE BOOK
PUBLISHED BY SIMON & SCHUSTER INC.
NEW YORK   LONDON   TORONTO
SYDNEY   TOKYO   SINGAPORE

FIRESIDE
Simon & Schuster Building
Rockefeller Center
1230 Avenue of the Americas
New York, New York 10020

FIRESIDE and colophon are registered trademarks
of Simon & Schuster Inc.

Designed by Bonni Leon
Manufactured in the United States of America

10 9 8 7 6 5 4 3 2 1

Library of Congress Cataloging in Publication Data
Van Peebles, Melvin.
  No identity crisis: a father and son's own story of working to-
gether/Melvin and Mario Van Peebles.
    p. cm.
"A Fireside book."
  1. Van Peebles, Melvin. 2. Van Peebles, Mario. 3. Identity
crisis (Motion picture: 1990). 4. Motion picture producers and
directors—United States—Biography. 5. Motion picture actors
and actresses—United States—Biography. I. Van Peebles,
Mario. II. Title.
PN1998.3.V36A3 1990
791.43'0233'092—dc20
[B]   90-32411
                                                              CIP

ISBN 0-671-67358-0

CONTENTS

NO IDENTITY CRISIS

DEFENDANTS

CHIP	Mario Van Peebles (son)
BLOCK	Melvin Van Peebles (dad)

WITNESSES (in order of appearance)

MOM	Maria Marx (Mario's mother)
RICHARD	Richard Milner (old family gadfly)
ISABEL	Isabel Taylor-Helton (assistant to MVP)
BERNARD	Bernard Johnson (costume designer on *Identity Crisis*)
TOBIE	Tobie Haggerty (Mario's manager)
CHRIS	Chris Michael (Production Assistant on *Identity Crisis*)
MARSHA	Marsha Brooks (lawyer for *Identity Crisis*)
JIM	Jim Hinton (director of photography/co-producer on *Identity Crisis*)
TOMMY	Thomas Jarecki (production assistant on *Identity Crisis*)
VICTOR	Victor Kanefsky (director of postproduction and co-editor of *Identity Crisis*)
JUDY	Judith Norman (production assistant on *Identity Crisis*)
STEVE	Stephen J. Cannell (cameo role in *Identity Crisis*)

BOOK
ONE

GENESIS

CHIP

The desert was mega-hot and my ass had permanent creases in it from sitting on the bike, so I waited, ignoring Dad as he did his Indian Tarzan Scout routine, "hunting up" a place for us to sleep. Outlined against the surrealistic expanse of blue sky, he looked like a throwback to his seventies hit film, *Sweetback,* where Sweetback, escaping from the Man, was roughing his way across the Mojave Desert toward the Mexican border.

Once, as a kid, I had asked him, if he were an animal, which animal would he choose. Much to my disappointment, he replied, "A lizard." Out here, charcoal black, raggedy as a roach, eyelids at half-mast, cigar perched precariously on his lower lip, he sure as shit resembled a lizard.

I was getting bored with this voodoo scout routine, but I refused to be the old man's audience, or as my sixties mom would say, "give it any energy." So I stretched out on the sun-bleached sand, ignoring him.

"What's the big deal, man? Why not just sleep right here?" I thought, We don't have any sleeping bags anyway, 'cause the old man insisted we rough it. Hey, Europe—now that would have been cool, or even the Caribbean, but here we were, somewhere between Nowheresville, Arizona, and Go Home Quick, Utah. This was my you-graduated-from-Columbia-University father-and-son trip. And thus far all I had seen was endless desert and an occasional semi-abandoned Texaco station. I don't mean to come off ungrateful; the desert was exquisite at night and going across it on one motorcycle with your old man was the best—you know,

NO IDENTITY CRISIS

camaraderie, male bonding, all that. But speaking of bonding, what about some females? Or a swimming pool? Even
a plain glass of lemonade would be greatly appreciated. Anything but some hot water from an even hotter canteen, on a
hot-ass desert. Hey, I had been a good son, majored in economics just like he suggested. "Show business is business,"
he had said. So what's the problem? In prep school I had
graduated salutatorian as well as skipping the eleventh
grade. That's a year less in school to pay for. Why not simply
apply some of those fiscal savings to, like, a couple of tickets
to Spain or perhaps Africa. The deal—after graduation, no
more tuition cash. So why should the kid be penalized for an
early graduation? Share the wealth, babe, peace on earth,
get off the wallet. Yeah, I know the drill. He's worried I'll
end up like those wimpy kids with famous parents who can't
negotiate their own way to the toilet solo. But this is a total
overreaction. Unnecessary hardship is simply unnecessary.
Besides, this trip wasn't even hygienic. I hadn't brushed my
teeth since we left L.A., let alone flossed. My *GQ* grooming
routine was definitely suffering.

"How you doing, son?" Dad asked out of nowhere, as if he
could read my thoughts.

"Fine," I replied casually. Hey, if he can tough this out, so
can I. No way I'll wimp first, man, not a chance, *kemosabe*.

"Found the perfect place to make camp," he said and
started scuffing back out across the hot sand, à la *Sweetback* again.

Make camp, my ass, I thought. As I said, we hadn't
brought anything to make camp with unless you count the
Suzuki 550, the leftover water, some old salami, and the one
helmet we took turns wearing.

About one hundred yards from the highway, Dad came to
a stop and gestured to a large hole in the ground that some
tractor must have scooped out ages ago.

"What?" I said.

"There," he said.

"There what?" I asked, bewildered.

"Perfect spot."

"What, sleep in that hole?"

"Yeah," he said, giving me that blank lizard look again as if any second his tongue would leap forward from his mouth, effortlessly zapping a fly.

"Dad, why not just sleep up here on the sand?" I asked.

"Better down here," he mumbled, chewing his unlit cigar and crawling down into the ditch.

What if there's scorpions down there? I thought, or better yet, even snakes. That's all I need, wake up with a snake crawling up my pants leg. No, not the kid.

"I think . . . I think I'll just nod out up here," I said, casually shielding my eyes from the orange glow of the setting sun, "the view's better."

"Suit yourself," he grumbled, lying dead still in the bottom of the pit with his scarf covering his eyes just the way he likes it. Now he looked more like an Egyptian mummy about to be buried.

I ain't sleeping in no grave, I thought to myself as I rolled my funky Columbia University sweatshirt into a makeshift pillow and flipped up the collar on my motorcycle jacket. I figured I looked pretty cool with my jacket collar turned up like Elvis riding the bike, except that when you exceed thirty miles an hour, the wind funnels right down your stylishly cocked-up collar and introduces your buns to some serious wind-chill factor. When we left L.A., Dad had jokingly pointed out that my Elvis look wasn't going to get it on the freeway, which had pissed me off slightly, although I didn't show it.

I took another glance down at my old man stretched out in the pit below, except now he was completely invisible, cloaked in shadow. What if he had vanished? What if the scorpion had bitten the Lizard Dad and he was dead? How would I know? I was twenty years old, but I still enjoyed an occasional round of "self paranoia," a game my younger sister, Megan, and I had perfected during childhood, where one thinks scary thoughts, pumping up the volume until one borders on freaking out.

"Dad," I whispered, "Dad, you asleep?"

NO IDENTITY CRISIS

No reply. Asleep or dead, I guess. Still, I'm not crawling down there to find out. I mean, if he's dead, which he's not, what can I do, and if he's asleep, why wake him? One by one the stars made their entrance like glittering divas on a back-lit stage. Like I said, the desert sky on a clear night is nothing short of breathtaking. I was probably contemplating man's puny existence in relation to the vast and probably expanding universe when I must have dozed off. At any rate, I awoke to the sound of something howling in the distance. It wasn't a coyote. Unfortunately, we had heard them on the first night. This was a longer-drawn-out, drowning sound. I cocked myself up on one elbow as off on the horizon a black wall seemed to be circling toward us. Within seconds, tumbleweeds were hurtling by me at terrific speed, and out of nowhere came this howling wind—I mean it came whipping across the desert like Carl Lewis with fuel injection. The sand was stinging my face. I had to laugh. The sand actually bit into my mug like thousands of tiny needles. I yanked the helmet on, but the wind sucked up underneath it, spewing sand into my ears. I swear I tried to move, but the wind's sheer force kept me pinned. In one mighty effort I managed to dive forward into the safety of the pit. I lay there on my back catching my breath as the storm tore right over the pit. Dad was asleep as I crawled over beside him. It's nice having a lizard dad, I thought.

"Dad, this is like something out of a bad movie," I said aloud. "You know what, we should do a movie together one day, huh . . . you and me."

"Yeah, son," he said without moving, "maybe we will . . . maybe one day we will."

That was several years ago and at the time I had no idea that a few years later we would be doing just that.

BLOCK

Captain's Log 6/18/87 . . .

First there was this ringing, then there was this blackness —that figured, since it was night and the phone had awakened me.

I picked up the receiver.

"Hi, Dad," the voice said. *Dad, huh? . . . That gave me three choices.*

"Mario!" I knew it was him because my other son, Max, had a heavy French accent and my daughter's voice was higher.

"Did I wake you up?" the voice asked.

"No, of course not." I always say that, something to do with the Protestant work ethic, I suppose. "What's up, son?"

"Well, I think I've really got it this time," he bubbled.

"Got what," I snarled.

"A great script, Dad. I've been working on it out here."

"Where are you anyway?"

"L.A. NBC wanted to talk to me. It's really good."

"NBC?"

"No, the script. It's really good."

"So what's so terrific about it?"

"It's just really good, that's all, action, drugs, and lots of tough stuff. Will you take a look at it?" Mario pushed selling hard, totally ignoring my lack of enthusiasm, as I had taught him to do so. "I bet it wouldn't be too expensive to shoot."

"Okay, partner, I'll give it a gander," I drawled.

Mario thanked me and turned solicitous, pouring on the charm. "I sure hope I didn't wake you, sir."

"A little late for that, dontcha think?"

"I suppose so," Mario chuckled and said he'd get the script off to me express the next day.

"Not collect, God damn it," I shouted at the phone. But he was already gone.

NO IDENTITY CRISIS

I hung up and snuggled into my pillow, smiling proud at Mario's aggressive sales pitch.

But, shit, pleased with the kid's persistence or not it was still twelve-thirty at night and I had only been asleep for an hour and a half—just long enough to be wide awake now, but with not enough sleep under my belt to carry me through the rest of the night plus the next day.

I tried to focus my woozy mind. Had this ever happened before? (Concentrate, concentrate.) *Voilà!* Suddenly I re-membered my special wake-up-in-the-middle-of-the-night remedy. I got up and hobbled over to the TV—*long-distance runners over forty tend to start off stiff*—and flicked on the porno channel—*corny sex tends to make me drowsy.*

Usually the screen would simply be running a couple of "escort services" commercials over and over, promising you state-of-the-art-ravishing-executive-caliber females eager to have an intellectual evening in bed with you, or lovely, fresh-off-the-boat-oriental girls trained from childhood to cater to your every sexual whim. Sometimes, if you hit the jackpot, there would be bits of a nude talk show intercut between the commercials with a hairy guy in his birthday suit interviewing some nude lady sitting on a rug or couch with her legs spread, chatting blue-collar-demurely about her childhood.

I would stand staring at the TV for a few minutes, appalled and disgusted at what this world was coming to. Then—being your basic garden-variety hypocrite—I would watch for another couple of minutes just to make sure my eyes weren't deceiving me before turning it off and turn-ing in.

However, that night the porno folks were experiencing one of their frequent "technical difficulties," and the sex chan-nel was only a bunch of squiggly lines with Muzak playing in the background.

Feeling righteous—i.e., betrayed—I shut the damn thing off and went back to bed.

But, suddenly, bingo! Lying there in darkness, aided per-haps by the snatch of Muzak accompanying the squiggly screen, my mind went into reverse and shot back down memory lane to another middle-of-the-night call and, sort of anyway, the beginning of this whole thing.

I flinched at the recollection. Oh God, had I ever been that dumb, that young, that gullible, that stupid?

The truth is YES, I had been!

Of course, we like to think we grow wise with time. Maybe *you* do, but I haven't seen any evidence to support that supposition in my case. This doesn't depress me as much as I suppose it should, because as far as I can see, the nuts of the world have most of the fun.

That long-ago call I suddenly remembered had been for help . . . and there I was beamed back into the past, Sir Galahad, at the wheel of my snazzy new '55 Studebaker, traveling northward through the night, headed for San Francisco. Stars twinkled overhead and the moonscape of the Mojave Desert surrounded me, floating up from the radio embedded in the dash, pop music treated symphonically and classical music treated pop, in short, early Muzak. *Eureka!* The Muzak connection that had started me reminiscing in the first place.

Sometimes the beginning of something is a neat point and sometimes it is like the making of *Identity Crisis*—a piling up of events, like a mound of oily rags in a corner just waiting for a match.

Speaking of that, I guess that call could be considered the original oily rag at the bottom of what turned into the *Identity Crisis* pyre. There I was, chin jutting forward like Jack Armstrong's, a knight in shining armor, urging my faithful car forward up the four-lane highway to my Damsel in Distress.

A background check, synopsis of the plot, would read as follows: This young air-force lieutenant (yours truly) has been reassigned from Sacramento in Northern California to this bomber base in Southern California. He finds a nice room in Frisco for his girlfriend, Wanda, whom he has been sort of living with in Sacramento, to stay in until he gets things squared away at a place near his new base and can send for her.

All I can say is, it didn't seem trite at the time. As the young officer—me—saw it, she would sit in her room, hands folded demurely in her lap, until I came for her.

Cutting to the chase, as they say, my sweet, idyllic, sugary synopsis was short a few facts. That's what the call was about.

Well, it seems while I was flying around down in Southern California keeping the world safe for democracy, Miss pure Wanda was dabbling in promiscuity by the Golden Gate. In fact, she had taken in a poor, homeless Latin boxer. That's what the call was about, at least that was the reason I got. Her roommate had taken to using her head as a punching bag and she had thrown him out and simultaneously realized how much she missed me and would I come and get her immediately. "Well, how could he have been staying in that room with you," I asked, "since there is only one bed?"

"Don't you trust me?" she said. "You're hurting me."

"Of course I do, honey," I stuttered.

Then she explained that the boxer slept on a pallet on the floor. I cursed myself for my filthy, suspicious mind.

To make a long story short, by the next evening I had wangled a twenty-four hour pass. PERFECT. What was so perfect about a twenty-four hour pass, which barely gave me enough time to drive up to San Francisco, grab Wanda and her belongings, and be back at the officers club in Southern California by happy hour? Oh boy, were the guys' eyes going to buck when I walked in with her! She was really a beauty —a twenty-year-old version of Dorothy Dandridge. Unfortunately—*which was where the perfect part came in*—I wouldn't have the time to go looking for the boxer to kick his ass. Actually the not having the time part was true, but pretending to be sorry about it was pure bullshit. Anyway, I've already admitted to being a hypocrite, and, let's face it, sometimes a little self-deception can save you a lot of self-respect and getting your ass kicked.

I arrived at Wanda's building just after midnight. I hadn't

called to tell her I was coming and I can still remember standing there, looking up and smiling to myself as I flashed forward on how happy she was going to be when she came down the stairs to open the door and see me. She would fall in my arms overcome with joy and maybe even swoon.

Finally I realized I had been pushing the buzzer for five minutes or more. At first I panicked, thinking she was dead. He had killed her. Then I calmed down and concluded that I was a complete asshole. Of course she hadn't answered the door, she didn't know I was coming and she thought it was him. I backed myself down the steps and out to the sidewalk so that she could see it was me. I looked, and the window was dark, the curtains teased, wafting back and forth at the street.

Suddenly I knew she was in there sprawled face down, dead, mutilated, mangled, or at least manhandled. With the strength of ten men I actually scaled the outside of the building to her third-floor window and climbed in.

For starters, there was no dead body and not even the signs of a struggle. In fact, the room was as neat as a pin, which wasn't Wanda's style at all.

What the hell is going on? I asked me.

What was going on—you are probably ahead of me on this one—is I was only a pawn in this game. It seems Wanda had acquired a taste for being a surrogate punching bag and had had a change of heart and had run off with the fighter shortly after calling and asking me to come rescue her from the fate worse than death. Not so shortly, however, that she didn't take the time to re-rent the room—for which I had paid in advance—and pocket the money. But I didn't know that at the time. So, getting back to the original oily rag on the pile in the *Identity Crisis* metaphor, I stretched out on the bed and waited for her.

Around three in the morning the key turned in the lock and the girl who had rented the room walked in and that's how Mario was born, or rather, that's how I met his Mom.

She had gone to the same university, Ohio Wesleyan, that I had. That's how she knew Wanda. However, she hadn't arrived at Ohio until I had graduated and so we had never laid eyes on one another before. She was a stacked blond virgin and would have been starting her junior year if she hadn't decided to come out West instead and find herself. So I said that since she was at loose ends, maybe she'd like to hang out with me for a while down in Southern California. She agreed and, as they say, as the pink rays of dawn started to crease the sky we were heading south for my base. The rest is history . . . sorta.

Anyway, getting back to recent events, the porno channel "technical difficulties" notwithstanding (God bless Pavlov), habit had worked its magic and I fell asleep.

MARIA

Mario was born in Mexico, where I learned to carry him in a rebozo, a long cotton shawl wrapped around my shoulder and tucked under him, making a snug tented hammock. Black-and-blond couples were very ususual, so people would line up to peek in at Mario, hoping he would be exotically striped, spotted, or something.

Mario first expressed unusual creativity with one tooth at three months, followed later with eight teeth at eight months, and sixteen teeth at sixteen months.

Baby Mario liked to be held constantly, so we brought him along to many art films and concerts which he seemed to find very interesting. I read to him frequently, varying my voice for the different characters of a story. When Mario was twenty-five months old and his little sister, Megan, was nine months old, we moved to Amsterdam. The Dutch children were delighted with them and began to teach them Dutch.

Mario enjoyed being photographed. I showed him a photo of the original sculpture and posed him as Rodin's "The Thinker."

When Melvin moved to Paris, the children came with me

to explore the world: Denmark, Stockholm, Belgium, Geneva, Spain, Morocco, Greece, Yugoslavia, Austria, and Italy. We traveled third-class on old-fashioned smoke-puffing trains that Mario particularly loved, and in steerage on ships among goats and chickens and peasants.

A child at heart, I got totally involved in glorious games with the children, climbing trees and playing horse, or hide-and-seek in the late afternoons when shadows helped the hidden. By candlelight in the evening we danced to *Swan Lake*, white towels flying behind us, held in outstretched hands as wings.

I taught the children to read and write by slowly sounding out words and I taught them basic math with counting games.

In 1962 we returned to San Francisco. Mario and Megan accompanied me to Documentary and Film Appreciation classes and learned to throw pots on the wheel in ceramics classes.

It was the glorious, creative-expression sixties, and they began to design and create outfits and string beads into necklaces. We went to "Be-ins" in Golden Gate Park and listened to the new bands. Mario made friends with Bill "K," of the Grateful Dead, who gave him drum lessons.

CHIP

"Show business is a business," Pops mumbled, "so if I had it to do over, I'd major in business. The golden rule is that he with the gold makes the rule." These were a couple of Melvin Van Movie quotables that I had basically tried to adhere to. I had majored in economics at Columbia and among other business jobs had worked for a year and a half as a budget analyst for Mayor Koch. Also, I had some corny idea about improving the planet, making the world a little better, so politics interested me as well. But after a while, it became clear that at my grass-roots-level position, in the mayor's office, it would be years before I could make a difference on a large scale. I had also worked briefly as a fiscal clerk in Mayor Moscones's office in San Francisco. At any rate, government did not seem to function as a cohesive unit but was rather made up of fragmented separate interest groups. Like some gigantic tug of war they would all pull like mad in different directions, with very little net movement of the rope. I had been working at OMB, the Office of Management and Budget, during Mayor Koch's reign. It was my job to help, shall we say, streamline the budget for the Department of Environmental Protection—what better place to improve the globe, right? But it soon became apparent that the items that should be cut from the budget would never be cut, because So-and-so #1 votes for So-and-so #2 and we can't piss him off. The reports I wrote and submitted with zeal had all been proposed by others preceding me and had never been carried out. Everyone seemed to know this but the token Ivy League, Brooks Brothers me.

I felt myself losing the desire to keep going mechanically through the day. I couldn't look into the face of a fifty-two-year-old workingman and say, Don't worry, we won't cut your job because treating raw sewage is important to the environment. I knew full well that the next day I might be ordered to do just that. Job cuts were more often "political" than "practical" and what I wrote was not going to make much difference. For someone who loves to work, who needs to help, the concept of settling into mediocrity, of ultimately being part of the problem, not part of the solution, is damned alarming. I realized I missed being around the arts, where even though a good 85 percent of the people were full of "we love ya, baby," one could still express oneself. I longed to make a difference in the world and I felt that Pops was correct when he said that exposure in the business and political arenas would help if I were to ever effect change rather than merely watch.

But what was the kid to do? Should I venture down to Wall Street and see if I could produce films from the business side? Maybe get connections, set up limited partnerships? While at Columbia, I had worked for a company on weekends that set up limited partnerships for film, complete with now defunct tax loopholes. But with only marginal success. Primarily because "real investors" are hard to separate from the "glamour grabbers" or "talkers" who just want to take some chick to dinner and say "Yeah, baby, I'm thinking about investing in Van Peebles's new movie." That same guy who made his financial nut in, say, pork bellies or software doesn't B.S. when it comes to buying or selling floppy disks. Why? Because there is no glamour factor in computer software. But he'd love to say he knows a star or that he's a producer. This "glamour factor" makes it very difficult to finance films independently—outside the majors. The trick is to separate the men from the boys as quickly as possible by making them put up or shut up financially, if not in full, then with a partial deposit of some sort. Dad has an uncanny ability to sniff out the phonies. I can't tell you how many self-professed potential investors I've brought before King Van Peebles, who gruffly pronounced 95 percent of them to be full of shit. And 95 percent of the time he proved to be correct. In general, however, I believe it's not healthy to tell people they're full of it. And this just is another area where Dad and I sometimes differ. Dad, a graduate of the Mike Tyson school of diplomacy, doesn't care. He will tell 'em to their faces that they are full of shit. I, on the other hand, only educate people I care about and/or people who can handle it. Look—if he's full of it and you hurt the dude's feelings, he's got a vested interest in seeing you fail. And this business is at least 50 percent crapshoot anyway. If he gets lucky and falls into the financial pot because yes, even full-of-bull people get lucky. Happens every day. Then you're still on good terms and maybe he comes back to you, and if not, at least he's not an enemy. Let sleeping dogs sleep, I say.

At any rate, after almost two years as a budget analyst, I realized it was cruel of me to go on denying the moviegoing public any longer. It was time to return to the silver screen.

NO IDENTITY CRISIS

Well, not actually return, because although I had done theatre and two movies of the week, I was never really on the
silver screen, except for a couple memorable minutes as
young Sweetback, and then there was a Dirty Harry, but my
part got cut out. Well, actually it wasn't a part. I was an
extra. I had to ride a bike with a bunch of other kids, so if
they had left the scene in I'm sure I would have been partially seen. I was the skinny Jackson Five clone with the big
afro. But like I said, no sense looking for it 'cause it got cut
out. Although I did include it in my résumé, not now of
course, but then. So as a kid I had done some plays, a couple
of TV movies and mostly extra work. Before the world of
academics and Mel Baby cut my budding acting career
short. Then it was off to boarding school, Columbia University, and the business world. Now I was a young man and
had to cough up some new résumé pictures. I had changed
somewhat since my Jackson Five days. I thought, first stop,
I'd go see Pops, see if he'd help me out. I rehearsed my
speech in my head. Would he freak out when I told him, "Yo,
Dad, I'm ready to leave my nice, secure, respectable job and
act, produce, direct, and write"? No, I'd say, "Hey, Dad, I
love you and respect you so damn much, see, that I want to
be just like you and. . . . " Na, he'd know that was overkill.
He'd say, "Good, then stay in business, idiot." Maybe I could
try the humble *shtick,* the ol' "I've been a good son, followed
your business advice and all, dear Dad" approach. Naw, too
direct. Hey, I'd been out of college two years, I could do what
I wanted anyway, but if I did it with his blessing or, better
yet, made it his idea, then Pops could call up some of his
powerful movie-mogul pals and like say "Put my kid in the
film, dig," make my big return to show business, which
wasn't much of a return, a lot faster. Okay, I knew this helping stuff was somewhat out of character for my Dad. Like I
said, he's a graduate of the do-it-yourself school of hard
knocks. But I hadn't asked him for a damn thing in years.
Yeah he paid for college and that funky motorcycle trip out
West, but that's all, so I figured I was overdue for some parental assistance. And if not, I'd damn sure do it anyway, so

what was to lose by asking—right? Better yet, I'd run the idea by Mom first. She knew I'd been interested in politics. But this low-level, civil-servant stuff was seriously stifling my creativity. Okay, I dialed up Mummy Dearest. "Hello, Mom, it's me," I said glumly.

"What's wrong, honey?" she said sweetly.

My mom always gets concerned when I'm down, probably 'cause I'm rarely depressed.

"Mom, I feel like I'm treading water career-wise. I want to quit my job and make films."

Big pause . . . very long pause. She was not answering. This was unusual for Mom. Then she spoke, choosing her words carefully. "Well, you know I want you to be happy, honey. Do what's best for you. How would you pay your rent?"

The subtext of that question was, Will you be hitting me up for a loan? To which I replied, very humbly, "Well, I have a little money saved up."

Pause . . . no response.

"Listen, Mom, Dad's advice about getting some business experience was fine, and I followed it, right?"

"Right."

"And you know I've always been interested in film and politics, right? Okay, I'm not making diddly of a difference politically. So I'm ready to give film a shot. If I screw up, I can always go back into business or politics. Hey, if Reagan did it—right? But if I am gonna give show biz a try it might as well be sooner than later. I've got no kids to feed or embarrass, I've done the 'supposed to's' like college, so better to starve now than later, right?"

"Well, if you say so, honey."

Damn! . . . I blew it! See, I had taken the lead in the conversation, allowing Mom off the hook and into the psychological safety zone of "Okay, if you say so, dear," i.e., of allowing me to commit myself without her helping me.

Pops could prove tricky. I made a mental note to play it cooler with him. I'd try to let him advise me to do what I ultimately was gonna do anyway, thus giving him a vested interest in seeing me succeed—i.e., help me if I should need it.

"Would you make meaningful films?" Mom asked hopefully.

"Yeah, Mom, I'd like to try, but I'll probably have to do a few losers before I get the power to shape a film myself. Besides what's meaningful is relative and different for everyone."

"Is your father gonna help?"

"Of course," I blurted. "I mean, he loves the idea. Who's gonna take over his business when he croaks if not me? What I mean is . . . the guy needs me. Who's gonna bring him into the mainstream? Who else is gonna keep him from going too far out? Who's ultimately gonna save our fat family?"

"It ain't me, babe," Mom laughed.

"I hear you," I chuckled. "Fat family" was our nickname for the Van Peebles clan. "Well, actually, I haven't like really told Pop yet . . . not that I need to . . . I'm sure he'll wanta help me get into show biz. He'd be a fool not to, right?"

I rated my pitch to my mom at about B +, so I figured it was time to test out my big plans for the future on my ol' lizard dad.

The oriental waiter appeared to be a nice shade of surrealistic green under the garish fluorescent lights. Dad frequents this joint every Thursday like clockwork, ordering up a juicy plate of Thursday's double-decker cholesterol special —oxtail, fried bananas, and steamed rice. Man, how this old brother stays so trim is beyond me, must be all that jogging or something. Anyway, we were at Dad's favorite Chinese restaurant on Seventh Avenue. Chinese Cubans. Can you believe that this Chinese guy speaks Spanish to us with an oriental accent? And we respond in kind. Wish Norman Rockwell could have seen this slice of Americana, or maybe he did and never got around to painting it. I speak Spanish like a Puerto Rican on account of my old girlfriend was a

Puerto Rican. I helped her enter the glossy world of model-ing. She helped me understand people like Raphael here, who was taking our order in his strange, atonal Spanish.

"Oh yeah, and one Tsingtao (a Chinese beer)," I said.

"*Dos vasos* (two glasses)," Dad added.

We always split the beer here.

"Well, son, you wanted to talk?" Dad said, giving me the blank lizard look and chomping down some bread. "Talk, I'm all ears."

Tonight I had decided to give Mel baby the early opportu-nity to get involved in my career, and I figured his favorite restaurant, with me treating, would serve as a favorable backdrop to the positive response I hoped to elicit.

I chuckled inwardly at his coming to the point directly and at my simultaneous realization that none of the prefab lead-ins I had amused myself by working up were gonna fly.

"What's so funny?" he said, smiling.

"Nothing, Dad," I said, surprised at my obvious transpar-ency. "It's just . . . you're so damn direct. Look, Pop, I'm tired of this job, man. I miss the arts. I know show business is business, but I've been doing the business and I feel like I'm missing the show." Silence. I continued, trying to read his poker face or at least get it all out before he derailed my train of thought. "Pop, I'm grateful for your advice and col-lege, man, and I intend to use my degree to produce one day, you know that, but listen, I want to quit my job and get back into the arts . . . and I'd like your advice. That's all." I meant to say *help,* but it came out *advice.* No, actually I meant to say advice and have him volunteer the help. I stopped and waited for his reaction. I hate when he takes these long, pensive, theatrical pauses. I rethought my spiel. It was okay, no fluff, no bull, pretty much to the point, hum-ble in that respect-you-Dad-son kinda way, not offensive or arrogant but strong, direct, earnest, and, yeah, what I basi-cally felt. So, okay, now I waited for the response. There it came. His mouth was opening slightly, but no, false alarm. He yelled out for Raphael to hurry up with the Chinese beer and stuffed another wad of bread into his mouth with his graceful, spiderlike fingers. Dad eats everything with his fingers—salad, rice—except soup. Never saw him do that . . . that would be a neat trick. Once he even bit his finger shoveling down a lettuce leaf.

Still no response from Mel baby.

Was this Negro asleep or what? Dad says I get too impatient: "You can't expect to learn French in one hour," "Rome wasn't built in a day," and all that wise crap an older guy can get away with telling an energetic young buck like myself. Okay, okay, cool. I tried to look serene, patient even. Just hurry the hell up before World War III breaks out and cancels the whole concept, damn man! I hate this pause stuff. Hurry up and say something, I thought, telepathically trying to encourage him. Pull a response out of his face.

"I'm thinking, son, okay?" he suddenly blurted out.

"Sure, Pop, take your time," I said insincerely. "I'm gonna take a quick nature break."

I walked toward the back of the joint and when I was out of sight, bolted downstairs to the funky sub-basement bathroom and took a wiz. Why are all Chinese bathrooms invariably painted that same pea-green color? I thought, trying to distract myself. And why do they have a tacky poster of a blond chick bending over a white Ferrari with her ass provocatively pointing at you over the urinal? What's that got to do with Chinese-Cuban food? So damn tacky, but there it is, your eyes keep drifting right back to her heart-shaped bottom, and you're looking sucker even though it's tacky, right? So, it works man, tacky but true, you're no more above it than the next putz. I laughed again at myself and my dueling sensibilities, cerebral vs. animal, finished up and took the stairs back up three at a time. Hope Dad's got an answer by now, must have. I rounded the corner. Oh, no, he's rapping to Raphael, damn. This could be another two days. Come on, Raphael, you're a great guy, but get your smiley self out of there, I thought as he cackled with Dad, throwing his head back and letting out a big one. Raphael, can't you see this is a matter of life and career? Man, go sauté a shrimp.

I sat down, and finally, after another couple rounds of

"No, you don't say?" and "Ain't it the truth?" in Chinese-sounding Spanish, Raphael bopped off jauntily to get the chow.

"Well, kid," Dad said between succulent chomps of oxtail that Rover wouldn't eat, "so ya want to be in show business." He chuckled. "You know when I paid for college, I would have supported you if you majored in bird watching. You know that, right?"

"Yeah, Pop, I know, I know, I."

"Your granddad tried to give me certain values, son, and I hope I've passed them on to you."

"You have, Dad . . . you definitely have."

"Good," he said, fighting with a piece of gristle. The gristle looked like it was gonna win the tug of war. It was holding on to the bone for dear life and, yes, but no, Van Peebles got it and most of the bone too . . . chomp! He leaned back, satisfied, and licked his fingers, a proud victor in the digestive war. Dad 10, oxtail 0.

"Son," he said, eyeballing the other customers and leaning forward confidently, "you see all these people? I bet each one of them is waiting for their big break. Raphael's probably been here for ten years, but that's just temporary in his mind till he gets that break. Cab drivers, waitresses, they all want to do movies. Now there's lots of ways to skin a cat, son. If the goal is to make films you can go through the writing door, the producing door, or the directing door. But if you choose to try the acting door—and I suspect that's what you mean—"

"Well, yeah, I mean, yeah essentially, or at least initially," I replied, growing concerned about the tone the conversation seemed to be taking.

"—Then unlike most of these folks, I recommend you get out and do it. Simply go act."

Great advice, Dad, I thought, I really needed that, like you need more oxtail. Go act. Right. What's that's shit supposed to mean?

"Could you elaborate a little on that statement, Dad?" I said coolly.

"Go act! Do a play, anything! Learn your craft."

"Well, I've already done some theatre and TV, as you know, when I was a kid, and actually I'd like to concentrate more on films now."

"Yeah, you and two million other people . . . act, son, write, direct, do whatever you can and I'll make you a promise, okay?"

"What's that?" I said dryly, smelling a setup.

"I'll come see you in anything you get," he promised earnestly. "And, son, remember my old motto, 'Early to bed, early to rise, work like hell, and advertise.' "

The wind was icy cold. The motherless New York hawk came whipping mercilessly down Seventh Avenue and slashed across our faces as we left the warmth of the restaurant. I had used my last money to pay for, you got it, Dad's oxtail. I still had some vague hope that Pop was gonna turn around and at the last moment, like in a Capra movie, say, "Hey, son, you've been a great kid. I'll give JR a call and fix up a flick for you first thing tomorrow." But as he waved good-bye and trudged off, his figure getting smaller and smaller in the snow, it became clear that the oxtail-eating-son-of-a-bitch just ate my Yellow Cab fare and wasn't about to help me. I stood there frozen, watching Dad's billowing coat disappear into the night.

RICHARD

The first time I laid eyes on Melvin Van Peebles was in a San Francisco movie house in 1971, in a film that was causing lines around the block—*Sweet Sweetback's Baadasssss Song*. He was on the big screen, I was in the audience. He was Sweetback, a street-wise hustler unjustly accused, who eats raw lizards, outbangs motorcycle gangs, and refuses to be nailed by the System. I was in the middle of researching a book on the world of inner-city hustlers.

At the time, Blacks in films were defined by White Hollywood as scaredy-cats, servants, or song-and-dancers, not hard-fisted, nimble-witted sex symbols. Melvin changed all that forever. After him came an era of "Blaxploitation" films like *The Mack* and *Superfly*, as producers discovered a Black audience hungry for recognizable heroes.

What shocked the industry more than *Sweetback*'s sex and violence were the credits at the end. Turns out Melvin not only starred in the movie but did everything else too, wrote, directed, edited, composed the music, produced, and probably punched the sprocket holes in the film. All this at a time when Blacks *behind* the camera were even rarer than dark leading men.

The first time I ever laid eyes on Mario Van Peebles was in the same theatre, same film. He played Sweetback as a boy. Young Mario was in bed with a very grown-up woman in a house of pleasure. As the twig is bent . . .

For trivia buffs, Mario's little sister, Megan, later a successful model, also appeared in *Sweetback*. Her trademark red hair haloing her face, she spoke the immortal line: "Wash your car, mister?"

The first time I met Melvin in the flesh was about five years later at a Halloween party given by Bob Silverstein, a mutual friend from the literary world. Bob had published some of our books. I remember Bob was dressed as a Chinese Mandarin and his then-wife as a dance-hall floozie and Melvin came cleverly disguised as himself. I had come in heavy "old man" makeup complete with white wig, false nose, and handlebar mustache. During my first two-hour conversation with Melvin, he had no idea what I looked like, nor did he give a shit. It was the beginning of a special friendship.

I've watched Mario from a distance over the years without retracing his father's footsteps following his path. When I first met Mario his show-business ambitions were on temporary hold until he graduated from Columbia. Melvin had insisted he prepare himself for the business of life where so many otherwise talented "show business" people make utter fools of themselves.

NO IDENTITY CRISIS

Mario's good looks and charm came naturally, but what he did with them took drive and ingenuity. In some, an obsession with one's own image would be narcissistic, but in Mario's case it was determined professionalism. He worked hard using himself as model and actor. Eventually, unlike most, he did not have to guess what the camera would see . . . he knew from hard-won experience.

In one of the early home-studio audition shots that Mario took of himself, he appears bare-chested as a tired boxer peering through the ropes after a victorious bout. The "ropes" were really cords stretched between two chairs, thickened by wrappings of toilet paper, he explained. The "sweat" was baby oil and water. I knew then that the kid had what it takes. While other young actor/models were whining about the costs of a good photographer, Mario had taken the do-it-yourself approach. I wonder where he picked that up?

CHIP

Okay, so there I was. See, Dad wasn't gonna help me get into films. Mom wanted me to be happy, but wasn't thrilled at my quitting my job. I had made a mental note that there could be some potential maternal loan money on the horizon if needed and if I begged. So Leslie, an Elite model who I was kinda going out with at the time, said I could model. Did she mean I could make a living at it? Or was she just saying like, maybe I could, or was it meant as some sort of a compliment? Who knows? Not knowing diddly about fashion, I was frankly not looking forward to hanging out with a bunch of superficial, egotistical airheads whose biggest fear was of someone getting between them and a mirror. My preconception, like most people's, was that all the male models were gonna be holding hands and snorting every drug in sight, while their female counterparts would be bitchy bimbos fighting over lipstick, magazine covers, and rich old farts. Leslie, although admittedly not a rocket scientist, seemed sweet, level-headed, and not at all self-involved. I figured she must be the exception to the rule. So okay, how to model? Go to a model agency, right? Throw on my boots, try to look taller than I really am, and act dumb.

But wait a minute, let me be honest. I was sorta looking forward to being around all those pretty women who must be sorta lonely, because, like I said, all the guys would be holding hands with each other. I envisioned myself serenely reading some French novel in the dressing room while demure, long-legged cover girls changed clothes all around me. They'd be so horny I'd have my pick of the pack. Plus, of course, there was the vision of making big money for practically nothing. After busting my buns at Columbia and number-crunching for the mayor, I was ready for pure, unadulterated, luxurious, inane, mindless, meaningless, lascivious, disco-dancing, decadent fun.

The big agencies at the time were Zoli, Elite, Wilhelmina, and Ford. Ford was all the blondes, and Zoli said, No, we don't need your ass—good thing my ego is not in my looks. I'd be an emotional roach by now. Wilhelmina said, Come back with more pictures, and lo and behold! Elite said yes.

I discovered, just like everything else, models who work get more work. Working models have composite cards, pictures of themselves, with magazine covers and model stuff on them, dig. You can tell they are covers because of the lettering over the photos that say, *Vogue, Elle,* or any number of exotic rag mags. The gag is, they leave this card with the photographer, the photographer looks it over, sees all the work, says this guy must be big-time cool, I'll book him. So, fine, I went out and bought myself a camera and, with a little guidance from my mother and an automatic timing device, shot my own self-portraits, bought some lettering from the local stationery store and made myself a couple of exotic, Eurotrash-looking magazine covers by slapping the lettering over the pictures. I didn't make it a *Time* magazine cover or anything, they could check of course, I'm not that crazy. I got a couple of hundred cards printed up that looked macho, suave, European, and, *Voilà,* I was a working model, or at least I looked like one.

Reality finally set in when I went on a casting call with a bunch of guys for a Calvin Klein ad that was going to run in *GQ.* I sat there happily, portfolio in hand until a lady came over and said nervously, "Excuse me, I don't think you're supposed to be here." Glancing around at the other models milling about, I said, "Didn't you ask for guys too?" She blushed and said, "Yes, but not Neg . . ah . . . Black guys." I was sure she was joking, because there were also a couple of Black girls and an Asian girl there. Until she pointed out that Calvin used a pretty ethnic girl on occasion, but never Black guys. It had never occurred to me, but in fact, come to think of it, I'd never seen a non-white male in a Calvin Klein ad. I left there not really angry, just sort of numb. I drifted across Fifty-ninth Street and into Central Park near the carousel. Often when I face a crisis in my life, I need to be alone, to listen to my inner voices, good and bad, and let 'em get it off their chests. This certainly was one of those times. I lay down on my back, the clouds drifting by as the battle of my various selves raged in my head.

KARMIC SELF
Mario, my son, do not be angered, they know not what they do.

BAD SELF
Well, maybe, I'd know not what I did too and while I was at it, I'd know not them a size 10½ foot in the ass!

KARMIC SELF
I'm disappointed in you, Mario. To react to anything in anger is to give it power in your life.

NAIVE SELF
I don't believe these guys! These are the 1980s. And those Calvin Klein ads are so advanced. I just don't think they could be . . .

BAD SELF

Racist? Man, you can't even say the word, ignorant fool.

NAIVE SELF

Listen, I know racism exists but I . . .

BAD SELF

. . . You don't know anything exists, my man! The only reason we're having this conversation is because suddenly it's happened to *you*. There's a big damn difference between hearing about racism and experiencing it isn't there, home boy? You've been up in those Ivy League schools intellectualizing with your elite, liberal friends and now the real world slapped you in the face.

NAIVE SELF

But are you then implying the real world is racist?

KARMIC SELF

Man sees what he thinks he sees. If you think along color lines, you will project that and soon your vision will be blinded by racism.

BAD SELF

You're calling me blind?! Man, that chick just told you to carry your dark ass outta there.

PASSIVE SELF

Please, fellas, listen, I don't think this conversation is going anywhere. Let's just not start trouble . . . I mean, there's lots of ways to pay the rent. Besides, modeling is for airheads, and it is not cool to be militant, this is the eighties. . . .

BAD SELF

Shut the fuck up, wimp! I say we do something!

NO IDENTITY CRISIS

NAIVE SELF
Kicking people won't get you in a Calvin Klein ad, and it won't get you in *GQ*.

KARMIC SELF
You've always been creative, do something constructive Mario, not destructive.

Yeah, so I kept modeling and started to rise toward the top of the "colored guy" heap. In the meantime I was shooting fashion editorials for magazines.

When I discovered that other photographers weren't thrilled that a model could also shoot pictures I created various pseudonyms, like Navoriam, which is Mario Van spelled backward, and Michelle V. Pigre, whose initials were MVP. I shot everyone—my sister Megan, my brother Max, my mom . . . they all ended up with modeling portfolios. And although I never worked for Calvin Klein—who needs underwear anyway?—*GQ* did end up hiring me to shoot myself for them. During this time, I also moonlighted as art director for a funky little magazine out of Baltimore where I made sure to use models of all colors.

Between modeling and photography, I had managed to pay for Script Interpretation and acting lessons at Stella Adler's. . . .

The normally half-empty house was packed and charged with a strange energy; something weird was happening out there. A ripple of excitement spread throughout the audience. Too late to figure it out . . . the spot swiveled, blasting me with a bolt of light. I felt the power surge up through my body. My favorite part of the play, the slide montage, began. The audience drawn in, feeding me . . . I took center stage, photos of the Old West dancing in counterpoint on the screens that flanked me.

I, in the lead, as Deadwood Dick, one of America's more notorious Black cowboys, began summing up my gunfighting career in a farewell soliloquy. As the faces of Deadwood's friends and foes stared from the screens, I felt the words build in my chest. It had been a bizarre audience, but I was on automatic pilot now . . . heading toward the climax of the play, a long dormant volcano about to erupt.

Suddenly a different ripple of excitement invaded the room. Some nut was actually climbing up on the stage! The guy came forward, reaching out to me as if trying to keep me from fading back into the pages of history. For a second that lasted forever he stood before me, wavering. Our usually verbose director/producer, Roger Furman, sat glued to his seat. Suddenly I realized the man was retarded. That's why the audience's reactions had been so different. They were mentally retarded!

Roger had packed the house with retarded folks, which was fine, but the son-of-a-bitch could have told us.

Without stepping out of character I took the young man's arm and guided him gently back to his seat. Then I struck the final pose of the legendary Deadwood Dick, and the audience went nuts as the curtain fell.

Later, backstage in the crowded dressing room the cast let loose, whooping and hollering and cracking on old-jive Roger, who probably got a deal filling up the house. "Yeah, ol' Roger usually talks more shit than a radio, but he sure was quiet when my man jumped up on stage tonight!" yelled the brother still dressed as the sheriff.

"Mario, some gangster-looking guy is asking for you," said the stage manager with big boobs and a suede skirt, poking her head through the curtain that served as a door. Our stage manager doubled as a squaw, which explained her sorry fringed outfit.

I picked up my check for the week, ten dollars and seventy-five cents carfare money. Nothing close to even the lowly salary I used to make as a budget analyst, but, hey, I was back in show biz. Back in the magic. And it felt damn good.

I stepped out of the dressing room and into the shadows of the backstage area, my eyes fighting to adjust to the darkness. I paused. No one was there. I turned to go back inside, when I heard a man's voice stage left.

"Not bad," it said.

NO IDENTITY CRISIS

Slouched in the shadows among the ropes and pulleys leaned a man in a dark fedora, none other than my pop, Melvin Van Movies . . . the brother of steel, the sepia Eliot Ness, the master of the dramatic pause, my oxtail-eating, cigar-chomping, free-advice-giving lizard dad. He came forward grinning.

I was always glad to see the man, but of all nights to come see the show, Pops had to turn up on the one where some joker gets up on the stage. True to his word since that supper at Chinese Cuban, where he devoured more money than I now made, both he and Mom had come to see me in every play, from little funky off-off-Broadway shows to Lincoln Center to Harlem to the Mabou Mines Theatre Group . . . from bad, good, futuristic, egoistical, avant-garde, reargarde, experimental, works-in-progress, you name it, they were there and I did them all. I played in every and any role I got. I wrote plays, read plays, directed, studied, and even, upon occasion, stage-managed. What about all that starring in films I was gonna do? I auditioned, auditioned, and auditioned and didn't get diddly. Sometimes I didn't even get auditions.

What about the rent and the ugly fact that even though I had quit my job as a budget analyst I hadn't quit eating— and eating as much as I do required money! I had long since run out of my measly savings from "life at the mayor's office" and although I didn't mind asking Pops to help me get that big "imaginary movie role," asking either of my parents for a loan at age twenty-one was out of the question. Well, not really out of the question. I mean it wouldn't have been if I had thought Dad would say yes. Also, I still owed my mom for that oak furniture I bought. Last year I preferred to think of it as a question of my being too proud to ask for a loan rather than the fact that they would probably both say "Beat it" or, even worse, explain why they were saying "Beat it."

But Lady Luck smiled down on me and handed me the best disco-dancing-decadent-money-for-nothing-chicks-for-free-total-bullshit-part-time job I'd ever dreamed of—modeling. People actually were willing to pay me to stand next to the likes of Iman, or Beverly Johnson in some ridiculous fly outfits I'd never buy or afford, and just to what? Just to take my picture! Damn, this was great, man. I'm a ham, I'd have done it for free but a hundred to two hundred bucks a friggin' hour?! Soon I was snapping pictures of other folks. People seem to freak out over my photography, but this all came naturally to me. As a kid I had always had an artistic eye. Building on the confidence I acquired from my portfolio scam, I just started using the camera to capture visions rather than a brush.

Actually, I suppose I secretly felt that cameras were like calculators. Calculators were for people who couldn't add and cameras for people who couldn't really draw. I can draw using a camera, it felt like cheating somehow. I felt real art had to emanate from one's hand, not a machine called a camera. But the more I delved into the colorful world of black and white, of diffused and reflected light, of angles, Dutch angles, and framing, the more addicted I became. I constantly expanded, got a great 85-millimeter portrait lens and became a still-photo-taking Kodachrome junkie, all of which served me well when I started directing.

Meanwhile back on the movie scene. Well, there was no movie scene as far as roles for me. So meanwhile, back on the theatre scene, I had been selected along with a scraggly group of starving students at Stella Adler's to do a strange version of the story of Mozart and Salieri, a piece based on the work of Alexander Pushkin, a Black Russian. It was directed by a bright, eccentric Russian from the Moscow Art Theatre, whose concept was to perform the piece in an art gallery using the huge graphic canvases as makeshift backdrops and do the play twice—once as a period piece and once as contemporary. I portrayed a lowly blind man in the first rendition and a self-proclaimed rock star in the second. Melanie Griffith played my seductive wife. Some of the other starving students in the piece were Judd Nelson, who infused the role of Mozart with a buoyant verve, and Stephen Bauer, who gave a cool, slinky rendition of what the director referred to in his thick Russian accent as "man in black." As to whether the play was a success or not is debatable. Mom, as usual, seemed to enjoy it, although its deeper meaning, if it had one, eluded her. Lizard Dad didn't have much to say about it either way and unlike the vocal audiences I was used to in Harlem, the intellectuals and pseudo-intellectuals who flocked nightly to see this piece were way too cool to react either way. Thus it was hard to get a reading. No, I wasn't any closer to acting in, directing, or writing for films, but I did meet a producer there who showed interest in reading one of the plays I had written. I sent the guy the script the next day. I actually had a copy handy in my bag at the time, but I didn't want to come off anxious, see? Two days later the guy called me back and—what do you know—he turned out to be both amiable and intelligent. I know he was intelligent 'cause he loved the script and wanted to produce it off-Broadway and introduce me to his partner! Hot damn! We set up a meeting for the following week.

RICHARD

Mario's painstaking experiments with light, angle, and image resulted in a portfolio that won him top gigs in advertising and fashion modeling. Often magazine art directors hiring him as a model would ask with admiration who the photographer was. They were amazed when he admitted he took his own pictures of himself.

Once I asked his mother, Maria, if she had ever suspected that baby Mario had the makings of a performer. "Oh, yes," she answered, beaming, "he was playing to crowds before he could even talk. Once when I was nursing him on a park bench, he discovered he could get people's reaction by exposing my breast. I had to stop him from doing that. He loved the attention it brought. Now Mario gets more attention than he wants just by walking down the street, and pretty girls compete to catch his eye."

For several years Mario knocked around between acting and modeling jobs, then he got a part on the daytime soap *One Life to Live* and was an immediate heartthrob with the female viewers. Although he received a considerable amount of fan mail, he wanted even more, so the producers would give him a bigger role. My live-in girlfriend at the time, Diane, loved to write letters and was in touch with hundreds of pen pals all over America. Unbeknownst to Mario, I asked Diane to start her buddies on a letter-writing campaign to the station. Melvin paid the postage, his gift to Mario's career.

Dozens of women from all over the country bombarded the show with love notes to Mario's character. Some sent Polaroids of themselves scantily clad. One even knitted a jockstrap with Mario's initials on it.

Mario may have impressed the station with his star quality, but being around Melvin, he had never developed a swelled head. In Melvin's Broadway show *Waltz of the Stork*, Mario was a background player, switching costumes a zillion times to give the illusion of a large cast. He helped with anything else he could—props, sets, promotion, and in between performances he and Melvin dressed up in goofy stork outfits with thousands of pink feathers and paraded around Times Square, drumming up business for the show.

One scene in that show called for a cow. I made a hollow model of a cow's head using plaster of paris, as I often do in my sculptures. Somehow I forgot that someone was going to have to wear the damn thing. It must have weighed sixty pounds. Mario played the front half, and he cursed me every night in moo talk.

CHIP

Family-tree-wise, my mother's parents were old-money WASPs, liberals who believed in higher education and civil rights. My granddad fled Germany when Hitler was coming to power, taught political science at both Harvard and Yale, and became a budget analyst for Harry Truman. His wife, my mother's mother, graduated from Columbia University and was one of the few White members of the NAACP. She sued the Virginia school system, saying her White children were being denied education because non-White kids were denied admission. The KKK burned a cross on her lawn and said, "We hope your daughters marry niggers." She replied politely, "Thank you, so do we."

My dad's dad was a hard-working, powerfully built Black man from Georgia with huge hands and a scar in one palm where some ill-advised attacker had stuck his knife. Unable to afford an education for himself, Grandpa had had to teach himself to read. He eventually became a small-business man in Chicago and managed to send my dad to college.

I was born in Mexico and raised in Europe until the age of seven. Traveling from Paris to Amsterdam to Morocco, I naturally learned to pick up languages and mimic accents.

My first inkling of the existence of discrimination happened when I was eight, although, as I have said, it didn't affect us, or rather, I was too young to realize that it did.

"We shall overcome! We shall overcome someday!" the crowd sang. It was midnight and I grasped my little sister Megan's hand tightly. This was the latest we'd ever been allowed to stay up. We were walking in a picket line in San Francisco outside a bank that practiced discrimination in its hiring policies.

"What's discrimination?" I asked my mother. Discrimination, she explained, was something we were all responsible to cleanse America of.

"That would be like making you go to bed every night and allowing Megan to stay up because she has red hair and you don't." I shot a glance at my now gloating, naturally red-headed sister and immediately let go her hand. "But I wouldn't do that," Mom continued, connecting our tiny hands together again, "because I try not to discriminate on the basis of color. This bank does when they hire people."

Discrimination must be a terrible thing, I thought, as I marched on. I tried to peer into the bank to see if any of those mean people were still in there working late. Somehow, I envisioned them all as redheads.

Maybe my do-unto-others-as-you-would-have-them-do-unto-you-save-the-world, sixties-minded mother and my maverick pull-yourself-up-by-your-bootstraps-you-can-do-it dad affected me more than I realize. At any rate, I feel that (1) helping people and not just getting ahead of others is honorable and that (2) personally, many things are possible if one sets one's mind to it.

ISABEL

I purchased a folding table in Harlem at Volunteers of America. I called a friend with a car and offered him lunch if he'd pick me and the table up and get us to my apartment. I could have taken a taxi, but I'd have to carry the table into the building myself. Besides, this fellow is vegetarian, so it was cheaper to feed him than get a taxi.

He was sitting at my dining-room table, crunching on a stick of celery, when he looked up and out of the blue said, "I need Melvin Van Peebles's telephone number. . . . "

This man is a little nerdy, always collecting business cards and telephone numbers, a real networking junkie, so I was ignoring him.

Again crunch, crunch, "Do you have Melvin Van Peebles's telephone number?"

I shot back something about not being the Social Register and his being a nerd and that I knew of Melvin Van Peebles and that I knew some of his work, but that we'd never met and I certainly didn't have his telephone number. I started into the living room to check out my newly acquired table. He followed. I suggested that we open it to be sure it was in working order. As he began to negotiate the clamps on the table, the telephone rang.

I said, "Hello," and a very pleasant male voice said, "Isabel Taylor-Helton?" I said, "Speaking." The voice spoke very slowly. "I have a clipping from *The New York Times,* June 18, 1980, about Black interior designers. Do you know about it?" It had been more than six years before, but of course I remembered it, and said so. The voice went on to wonder if I or any of the young people in the article would be interested in a project he was considering. We could meet and discuss it over coffee.

The folding table was opening but my friend was having a bit of difficulty and needed my help. He was gesturing to me. I was gesturing to him to keep quiet. He hadn't made a sound. I put my hand over the mouthpiece to tell him this could be interior-design work. Back to my caller, pencil in hand, I said in my most charming voice, "And who might I be speaking to?" He said,"My name is Melvin Van Peebles." I feigned the same cozy charm. "Melvin Van Peebles, how nice to meet you." At the same moment Mr. Nerd's eyes bulged as he matched my look of disbelief and amazement. Also at the same moment the table snapped shut on his finger, though he dared not yell.

Off the phone, I rescued my buppie-buddy from the table, packed his finger in ice, and sent him on his way, still freaked at the events of the afternoon. Me too. I had gotten the telephone number I had been asked for less than fifteen minutes before. I should have realized it was some kind of omen.

I had entered the interior-decorating profession to complement the talents of my late husband and had worked closely with him on every project. Working in the profession solo produced a lot of problems. So, in the two years since his death, I was still hesitating about returning to interior design. The reality was (a) I could use the money; (b) maybe I would get some direction; (c) I have a weakness for signs, and this strange coincidence was a kind of a "burning bush."

Ten days later Mr. Van Peebles and I met. I rang. He yelled, "Come in." Typically, Mr. Van Peebles was on the phone when I entered his apartment. He signaled me to have a cup of coffee without missing a beat in his conversation.

He was smaller than I expected—not shorter, smaller. Later I discovered this was a common reaction people had on finally meeting him. Strange, but these words come to mind: delicate, fragile.

While he was immersed in his phone call, I had the opportunity to study him. His mischievous smile could have been that of a used-car salesman or a friendly scoutmaster—it's the eyes that give credence, something safe and sincere. His eyes appear to read your thoughts, understanding or seeking to understand before you speak, half shut like those of a gypsy contemplating the message coming from a crystal ball. I've seen what appeared to be dollar signs in people's eyes, but this man has stop signs, as in Do Not Enter—poker player's eyes. He looked over and his hands, small with long, sculpted fingers—they evoked the delicate-and-fragile assumption in my mind most—offered me the sweetener, which I declined. Little did I know how wrong I was about those hands. They are famous for snatching folks up by their collars and cracking jaws. That his head, too, is small only adds a deceptive fragility to the Mr. Innocence look. After his phone call was over, we chatted about the work he wanted done.

I agreed to work on his apartment with him, a job that was completed to his liking. Cut to the chase (that's film talk), and here I am three years later, assistant to Melvin Van Peebles, deeply involved in the business of movie making, twenty-five pounds lighter, a lifetime younger, involved in challenging work, long hours, frantic pace, a phenomenal opportunity (on most days), a blessing straight from heaven.

Sure, "All's well that ends well," but, notwithstanding that, looking back, I didn't realize when we started *Identity Crisis* that I was a lamb headed for the slaughter.

> Nose to the grindstone
> Shoulders to the wheel
> Dazzle 'em with a grin
> and keep your eyes peeled for
> Opportunity . . . OPPORTUNITY !

. . . go the lyrics to an MVP song, not surprisingly entitled "Opportunity." The most interesting thing about "Opportunity" is the way individuals perceive what it is, or is not. I know MVP wrote it long before he met me, but I can't help feeling it's my song.

CHIP

I never really took my eye off my goal of doing movies. I did off-off-off-Broadway plays and musicals and, using some of the money I made from modeling, took acting classes with Stella Adler.

Periodically I would check in with my old man, a graduate of the sink-or-swim school of thought. Although he had refused to help me get into the film business, he was always there when I needed to talk. We'd while away the hours on his balcony watching the Manhattan sunset. He'd sit there with a stogie in the corner of his mouth, not at all surprised by what I was facing. He said, "Son, when I went to Hollywood to direct movies, they told me straight out, 'We don't need any elevator operators here.' The reason why I took the family to Europe was because I couldn't get anywhere in America. So, as you know, we ended up in Holland with me doing postgraduate work in astronomy. Then the French, basically, I believe, to embarrass the United States, let me make my first feature films. Sort of, 'Look, you racist Americans, your disenchanted Black director had to come here to make it.' "

My dad, in fact, was eventually a French delegate at the 1967 San Francisco Film Festival, where, much to the astonishment of all, his film *The Story of a Three Day Pass* was the critics' choice for Best Film. Later he went back to Columbia Pictures to direct a film called *Watermelon Man*.

Shortly after that he wrote, produced, directed, and starred in his own independent feature film, entitled *Sweet*

Sweetback's Baadasssss Song, a story about a pimp turned revolutionary. It became the top-grossing independent film for 1970 and started a wave of studio imitations which quickly deteriorated into what later were known as Black Exploitation Films.

During our talks, I asked him if the racism he faced had made him bitter. Had it scarred him? He replied that you had to view it in a global perspective. In Ireland, they were all White, but they persecuted each other over religious or territorial differences. In India, the Muslims and the Hindus look just alike, but they fight. The Chinese have a rivalry centuries old with their Yellow brothers the Japanese. In Haiti, Blacks repress each other viciously. The Pygmies chopped off the legs of the Watusi, and so on. To take any of this too personally would be to lose sight of the fact that this is a problem man has. It goes far beyond an American problem between Black and White, rich and poor, Indian vs. settler.

Racism had to be dealt with like any other hurdle. But to become bitter would poison the victim. Sure, if someone steps on your feet long enough, eventually you'll punch him out, and maybe that's what a repressor needs to wake up. Like the American Colonies' revolution against the British, breaking chains is not always easy or toll-free. What Pops had done with *Sweetback* had in effect awakened the industry. *Sweetback*'s message was loud and clear. It said, Hey, Hollywood, Blacks are tired of Mantan Moreland, of eye-rolling butlers, of being noble mammies and bucks that die in the sixth reel. I felt that, like any pioneer, being the first and breaking down the barriers that made it easier for my generation had taken its toll of him. He had been dubbed a militant, a potentially difficult genius not unlike Orson Welles. Had the tough, silent character Sweetback been played by a White actor, it would have been your average Clint Eastwood flick, but with a Black man in the lead, it was militant. I was determined to see my dad work again, unlike Orson Welles, to give something back to the man who helped break down the wall, and it was a dream of mine to play a part in that. Our eventually producing *Identity Crisis* would be a part of that dream come to fruition. For better or worse, we were destined to pick up the dice together, father and son, roll that sucker on the crap table, and yell out, Come on, lucky seven.

Shortly after one of my balcony bull sessions with my dad, I got another film. And there I was in the sunny Bahamas, acting in the art film *Jaws: The Revenge* and waiting for Bruce the shark to get his mechanical act together when I finally started the script then entitled, "To Die For." Like the other scripts I had written, I had kicked this particular idea around for a year or so. I'd jot down notes and futz with the structure, letting the scenario roll around in my head before getting down to the business of actually writing.

After several weeks of cracked-conch casinos and "ya, mon, no problem," it seemed I was faced with three primary options, time wise. Choice number one, work on my naturally enhanced tan, although departing the main island for secluded beaches of the outer islands was a no-no, as I was on call. Like I said, I could be summoned at a moment's notice if the shark was working and ready to nibble me.

Choice number two, casinos . . . well, yeah, but for some reason, like drink and drugs, the allure of casinos seems to have eluded me. I don't think it's a holier-than-thou sentiment; but rather something simpler. When it comes down to it, I guess I feel that pursuing a career in the arts is enough of a gamble without contributing to one's own propensity for self-sabotage. Why gamble or drink my hard-earned ducats away when I can make a movie and lose it on something I really enjoy, right? Okay, so casinos were basically out. Then there was choice number three.

Choice number three, sit on the floating *Jaws* camera barge and listen to fellow thespian Michael Caine spin out bittersweet tales of the English stage, British class struggle, and waiting in the unemployment line with the likes of Sean Connery and Roger Moore.

Choice number four, which I really didn't factor in, write the screenplay. Naturally, like anyone who loves a good story and is not subconsciously avoiding the start of a script, which top to bottom is a major task, I opted for listening to Mr. Caine whenever possible. When he wasn't available or feeling talkative, I'd bask in the Bahamian sunshine where I soon discovered that even though I was a "brother" and it took me a little longer, I burned just like everyone else. It was then, alone, sunburned, bedridden, smeared head to toe with cold cream, and with nothing left to shield me from facing the music that I finally picked up my pen and began writing "To Die For," which would later become *Identity Crisis.*

Sometimes, when I was a kid, Dad would drag me along to his various production and script meetings; more often than not they were boring. I'd sit in a corner listening quietly until afterward, when he'd ask me for my analysis of the meeting. Then he'd explain who the various players were and their hidden agendas. After a while certain patterns began to emerge and I found myself asking to tag along and follow up on the results. I must have been about fifteen when I started doing a little ghostwriting for Pop. I remember at one point in the discussion of a play I had written, Dad offered his expert analysis.

"Piece of shit," he said.

"You mean it needs work?" I asked hopefully.

"No, son, it's a piece of shit; too linear."

"Bull! It just needs polish!" I retorted.

I learned two things from that brief encounter. One, Don't take Dad's criticism too personally, and two, after several attempts at reworking my play, You can't polish a turd. The old man's beef about it being too linear, too predictable, was pretty accurate. I had started from the beginning and ended at the end, editing in my head as I went. I cast aside ideas that didn't seem to work before giving them a chance to breathe. Pop encouraged me to open the floodgates of my imagination, letting the dinosaurs, mammals, and reptiles all come thundering out en masse and then try to thread them into a story. The result, hopefully, a less predictable script. With "To Die For" I took this to an extreme, indulging myself during my "note taking" phase. My only criterion being, the situation or character had to make me laugh. Since I was writing this script on spec—personal freebie, not a gig—I figured I should at least amuse myself. At worst it would be cerebral masturbation and at best a thriller.

After letting the beasts of my imagination roam freely, I go into my "killus el babyus" phase—that's Latin for "kill the kid" or initial editing phase. I pour through all my notes, pretending I can decide which elements, if any, I can use and if so, in what sequence (don't burn your bridges and don't throw out your notes!). This eventually leads to a rough plot outline. Throughout these initial phases, I like to think that I retain some level of objectivity, like a conscientious parent not labeling his toddler a premed or prelaw just yet, but rather allowing the script to reveal its own identity. "Let it talk to you, boy," Dad would say. Easier said than done; but thinking of it as an "action adventure," or "comedy" prematurely can obscure your ability to find the crux of its appeal. I had initially thought of *Identity Crisis*, the then entitled "To Die For," as a whodunit with humorous characters, but with the emphasis on intense situations. This became an ongoing point of contention with Dad, who, when he read the script, perceived it as a flat-out nutty comedy, à la *Ghostbusters* meets *Married to the Mob*, rather than *48 Hours* meets *Diva*.

Anyway, back to the script's floor plan. By this time a couple of weeks had passed. The Bahamian sun was still shining, although after my burn experience it seemed to take on a sinister quality. The casinos were still happily taking tourists' money, Michael Caine had won the Oscar as Best Supporting Actor for *Hannah and Her Sisters*, and, I had finished the script outline. Also, during this time, I had met an energetic young lady who seemed enthralled with the fact that I acted and wrote. She enthusiastically insisted on helping me with the typing of the script, saying she was a Libra and needed the spiritual stimulation of being close to the creative process. I guess my creative process wasn't all that stimulating, because after a few nights with her sitting there dressed to the nines while I slouched around and wrote, three things became apparent. One, yes, I really did intend to stay in this tired hotel and scribble on my notepad. Two, I probably wasn't going to bop over to the local disco and hang out with her friends. Three, Miss Thing couldn't type a lick. She mumbled something about my being a boring, inflexible, Capricorn shithead, and split. So much for the creative flame and all that.

Okay, so now I had the rough story outline. How was I gonna tell this bad boy ("bad boy" in this case meaning "jive")? And when? I knew that Yves's effeminate spirit had inhabited home-boy Chilly D.'s body. But at what point did I reveal this to the audience? The ever sinister Narish was behind Yves's untimely demise. Again, did I inform our audience up front or let them discover it along with our heroes, Chilly and Sebastian, to heighten the suspense? In Sherlock Holmes, the audience shares Dr. Watson's point of view, reading the clues when he does but always remaining a few steps behind the Baker Street master Holmes himself. Although one could pose arguments as to what degree Sir Arthur Conan Doyle's work relied on the use of "mystery," most would agree it was a central element. However, if the crux of a script's appeal lies in its comedy and/or characters, a convoluted plot that requires our strict attention quickly becomes tedious. We as an audience would much rather sit back and watch our heroes bumble through a relatively simple plot that acts as a backdrop to their antics. After arguing back and forth with Pop over the jeopardy element, i.e., how tough I could make the script without dropping the comic elements, I agreed that this script's appeal lay in its comedy.

Although the plot got somewhat complicated at times, I consciously tried to keep those juicy plot twists and character reversals to a minimum. Early on the audience is shown the villains, the heroes, and the hurdles they must overcome to triumph. The fun is watching them do it. Later Stephen Cannell, the writer/producer of *Sonny Spoon*, would put it succinctly when he said, "Your plot is basically a stage for Chilly D. to dance on."

NO IDENTITY CRISIS

In general, once I have made some decisions as to what I reveal and when, I take on the time-consuming and often tedious task of hammering out a scene-by-scene breakdown using my story outline as a general guide. Usually about this time I'm feeling a touch self-righteous about having finished the plot outline. Self-righteousness leads to indulgence, which leads to guilt, which leads me back into working with a vengeance to punish myself for slacking off. Eventually I'll get tired, feel noble, left out of the fun, alone, denied, hard-working and then self-righteous again; and thus the cycle repeats itself. The trick is to sustain the hard-working phase while keeping the indulgent break periods to a minimum. Sometimes, if I feel myself slipping into an indulgent phase, I'll call up the old man. Melvin Van Peebles seems to have similar work, denial, rest cycle, perhaps a distant cousin of the Protestant work ethic, that pull-yourself-up-by-your-bootstraps mentality. Although I always suspected Dad might have more discipline than me, then again, it could just be a front. However, I must add to all this hard-work-martyr talk one admission: We both love our work. We feel lucky to work and our work has everything to do with life. You can't act, direct, or write about life without experiencing it. Right? So if I've stopped to smell the proverbial daisies and Dad asks, "Hey, son, whatcha doing?" I can legitimately say, "Pop, I'm working, working hard, babe." Art imitates life, they say, and as I think someone, maybe Woody Allen, once said, "Life imitates TV."

So, now I was in my self-indulgent rest period. Nothing like a healthy round of procrastination. I called all the people I should have called, then all the people I hadn't called, then all the people I might as well call while I had the phone book open. I went swimming, dancing (at the risk of sounding like a racial stereotype, man, I do love to dance), and the nice thing about partying in the Bahamas is you get to rehear all that music you dug two years ago, but mixed to the reggae beat. Oh no! Who did I meet on the dance floor? None other than Miss Diva Libra, can't type a lick. I teased her about her Libra love for the creative process. She didn't seem amused. But that didn't bother me. I was on a roll now. I love to tease; it's a family tradition. Feeling good, Jack! Got the outline done, working on a film, not Kurosawa, but a film nonetheless, and, hey, the checks were clearing. And so, why not tease the chick some more? I cracked on her Patty Duke hairstyle, her round, wide-screen, you-can-play-checkers-on-me Bahamian rear end, and her seventies retro disco dress. Now she's waggin' her head, nostrils flaring, eyes ablaze. Oh yeah, here it comes! Come on, baby, say it! Let it fly, girl! She was ranking on my bummy beat-up jeans, my counterfeit Bahamian accent, which I was so proud of in *Jaws*, my American macho attitude, and was just going to crack on my high-top home-boy sneakers when the DJ threw on an old James Brown forty-five and Sex Machine blasted forth, calling me! I grabbed her hand and pulled her onto the dance floor.

"But no one's dancin', mon," she pleaded.

"We are, Libra! It stimulates the creative process!" I yelled.

I laughed, she laughed, we had a great time, and I never saw her again. But I think of her whenever I try to type . . . 'cause I can't type a lick.

A writer buddy of mine and I have a running difference in philosophies. If scripts are like children, he gives birth to delicate virgin daughters which at present he has no power to protect, intricate, artsy scripts that require specific actors and precise direction or they're hopelessly mismanaged.

I, on the other hand, feel that as a beginning filmmaker, I'll have marginal power at best to oversee the script, especially if I sell it. So at present I prefer to have a healthy, ass-kicking son, a script that doesn't require the perfect sunset but relies more on what is actually on the page.

Of course this could all change and change back again in an instant. But at this point I felt a perky, doable, hopefully minimally screw-upable script was the way to go.

In addition, I felt that as a young man I'd be better off doing a script that a young man would do well as opposed to talking about something that could come off pretentious or that I personally might execute better ten years from now.

"To Die For" would just be an entertaining mystery, no big attempt at deeper significance. If the studio cut a scene or two, the plot would be simple enough to survive. The numerous cameos could be played in any number of ways and still work like empty slots in an accordion file I could fill as seemed fit. If a producer insisted his plump secretary have a part, the movie could contain it without going under. Whereas with a script like *The Kiss of the Spider Woman* or *Sophie's Choice*, the wrong casting could prove fatal. In short, I had to prepare myself to face the slings and arrows of outrageous interference new writers must endure. I wasn't Clint Eastwood or Woody Allen. A studio would be much more inclined to leave them alone. I had no delusion of grandeur.

I felt that at this juncture in my career I was at a point where my acting in the film would probably be perceived as an asset. So I wrote a part I could play. However, I would be willing to step down if the producer desired. But if chosen, I knew there would be at least one actor on the set who wasn't going to pull a star trip, show up late, or high . . . ME.

Plenty of action but easy on the special effects, or I'd be venturing into the *Star Wars/E.T.* territory, which to do correctly requires humongous budgets. Big budget means less likely to get done and less control for the little guy, especially when the little guy is me, myself, and I. In short, I wanted to write a fun movie, a movie that could be done. Nevertheless, although I was willing to lose several battles in order to win the war of getting the picture done, I felt it needed to move. That was essential.

Once my dad had said as a writer you figure out what you want to say and then how to hide saying it. I wanted some part of character evolution in terms of people reaching some plateau of mutual understanding. The spirit of Yves, the disenchanted, aging designer queen, gets trapped inside the body of a janitor rapper, playboy, thief. Yves's yuppified son who cannot even accept his father in his original form is then forced to deal with his dad as a Black street kid or lose the company he hopes to inherit. Yves and Chilly D., stereotypical opposites, become the better for their physical union in one form and evolve into more whole, hopefully more understanding human beings. In the process the son comes to understand both Chilly D., the street kid whom he would never have dealt with otherwise, and his father.

Speaking of fathers, Mom and I had agreed that since I had taken her to a cushy film shoot in Australia, this time around, with *Jaws* I'd invite the old man and my brother, Max. Dad, who has several Wall Street businesses going and my brother, Max, who works on Wall Street, both managed to get some time off. Now, one must understand that up until Clint (Make My Day) Eastwood's *Heartbreak Ridge*, I was basically the king of B-movies done mostly at scale with often minimalist accommodations. On *Last Resort*, my "open accommodations" literally doubled as one of the sets and I often woke up to the distinctive sound of a wild boar gnawing my one pair of hightop leather home-boy sneakers.

Pop once remarked that there seemed to be four phases in an actor's life. Mario who? Get me Mario, baby. Get me a young Mario. Mario who? (Again.) Post *Heartbreak Ridge*, I felt my name had been temporarily changed to "Mario baby." Suddenly, I was being invited to do big-budget B-movies and fly first class. Being of sound body and frugal mind and having the ever present suspicion that this "Mario baby" phase might not be an indefinite one, I usually exchange my first-class ticket for two coaches and invite a member of my family along. Perhaps I invite them for the sake of sheer surprise, perhaps out of, Look, folks, I'm finally making it, get some while it's hot, perhaps because family has that wonderful ability to keep me real. My siblings tend to be my toughest critics. My sister once said of my performance in a play, my acting was okay but that I had gotten upstaged by my own ears, which stick out and get backlit giving me a sort of luminescent Dumbo effect. And then sometimes it seems that time gallops along so fast that you'd better just go ahead and spend some of it with people you love while you still can. No one ever seems to go to the grave saying, "I wish I'd spent more time at the office."

I remember when my granddad passed away. My dad said, "Well, guess we better put the old man in to bake and shake." It was my granddad's wish to be cremated. Some folks would undoubtedly be taken aback at my dad's sense of humor about Granddad's passing into the great beyond. But while the man was alive, we spent time loving, laughing, and playing cards and whooping it up. Do it when you're alive. We made a big deal about Granddad while he was alive, not when he was dead. Love me while I'm still alive and kicking seems to be the unspoken family outlook of the Van Peebles clan.

It was another crystal-clear day in the Bahamas, except that the choppy, turquoise water was still too rough to submerge the mechanical shark in. If Bruce the shark was not going to cooperate, then Mario the actor was not really needed.

I marched over to Joseph Sargent, our gutsy Italian director on *Jaws: The Revenge*. Josepi, as I called him, knew what I was thinking because we went through this routine on almost a daily basis.

"Eh, Josepi?" I said, waving my hand, "I thought you were gonna talk to the guy upstairs about calming the water."

"Mariuch, my friend," he said, squinting at me, "I know you've grown up in this cockamamie business and you and I both know that the damn shark probably ain't gonna get in the water today either. But if by some small chance it does and you're not back . . ."

"*Si*, señor Josepi," I said, finishing his sentence, "we're all in deep shit."

"You check in, right?" he asked, wanting reassurance.

"Of course, every twenty minutes like usual," I replied, grinning and heading back to the hotel.

Joe trusted me and having worn the director's hat before, I had empathy for his dilemma and would not let him down.

I hauled ass back to my hotel in Nassau Beach as I was

expecting Dad and Max. I was staying in the ultra-deluxe James Bond Suite. Apparently Roger Moore had stayed there; thus its name. I opened the door to find my lizard dad looking very Bogart with his Panama hat cocked backed on his head and his foot propped jauntily on his one bag. My cool brother, Max, was already on the balcony sporting shades and counting the nubile nymphets lounging by the pool comparing suntan lines.

"How ya doin', kid?" Dad grinned, giving me a hug.

"*Ça va, petit con?*" said Max, playfully slapping me up-side my square head. Translated, that means, Everything OK, dummy? Max, my half brother, was born in Paris. Hence the French. Max is the elegant one in the family, with a penchant for Pierre Cardin suits and expensive hand-crafted wing-tipped shoes. My dad, ever the paradox of style, sports forties pleated and pegged trousers finished off with what he refers to as his "I hit the numbers" black-and-white pointy-toed patent-leather shoes, two pairs for thirty-eight dollars on Hollywood Boulevard. While I have an odd, eclectic sort of summer-meets-beat-up-Levi's chic.

"*C'est bien!* How's my favorite brother?" I asked, counter-ing with a punch to his bean. "And ze only brother," he replied, embracing me warmly. Back in New York, Max and I are the hopeless duo, sometimes hitting the hip night spots predicting that tonight these wild-and-crazy dudes are going to meet some fun and foxy ladies. Inevitably, the wild-and-fun ladies seem to avoid us and we come home tired, laugh-ing, and alone. See, I'm okay once I meet them and get to talking—it's just meeting them that's a drag. Especially if the young lady thinks you're coming on to her and she shoots you that, "yeah, sure," look New York women handle so deftly. Perhaps I'm rejection phobic. Perhaps Max is as well. So usually I just dance, play it cool, and meet whomever I meet or more likely don't meet. But puffing a cigarette and doing his best Jean-Paul Belmondo, Max usually mutters something in French. (Max gets very talkative when he's nervous.) Now the girl says who's he. I introduce him as my cool French brother, Max.

NO IDENTITY CRISIS

Dad, on the other hand, has what he calls the "ugly rap." "I ain't good-looking like you *GQ* boys, I got the Chicago approach," he says. On one memorable occasion, Max and I were admiring some young ladies and Dad marched right up to them and said, "My chicken-shit sons over there think you're fine. Now are you gonna give them some play or not?" That totally blew Max and me out of the water. This guy will embarrass you to death. Man! Max, fresh from N.Y.C. and ready for another round of rejection, was anxious to hit the local Bahamian clubs (*sans* Papa). We were both trying to persuade Daddy Van Peebles the local club scene at best would be mundane and perhaps he should stay his butt home and like read, sleep. Anything. No dice, MVP was on to us. "What's any young lady gonna want with you sorry suckers when she could have a dance with the original? You see, dance, my boys, is the vertical manifestation of horizontal desires. Now just watch your dear old dad, boys, and learn. Learn! Learn!"

The next day was a Saturday, I was stretched out on the beach, notepad in hand. . . . Hard to write on the beach, I thought, as a curvy young lady in a fluorescent bikini plopped down beside me. Radio blasting. Too many distractions on the beach, I thought. However, if I stay in, I'll feel sorry for myself alone, half listening to all the giggling, splashing, ho-ha going on outside. And then of course I won't be able to write, feeling sorry for myself. In college, I did my best writing late at night. It gave me that nice false sense of self-righteousness without feeling that I was missing all the action. There I was, nobly writing into the wee hours while all lesser beings slept, which just meant I slept all day while the lesser beings who did their work on time were in class. During my senior year at Columbia, when I had several papers due, I was almost entirely nocturnal. Part of the problem is I'm not naturally a book person. I'd rather experience it than read about it. Ever think about the great philosophers or scientists? Take Mendel, for example, noted for his genetic experiments with peas. But who wants to be cooped up with a bunch of peas when there's a beach outside with a bouncy girl in a fluorescent bikini beside you who's now lacquering her body in coconut oil, while chomping on green bubble gum to the reggae beat? I mean, hey.

"Hold it, ain't you somebody?" the girl said suddenly in a thick Brooklyn accent, staring at me blankly.

"Me?" I said, startled. Does this girl know I'm writing about her? Did she see my notepad? "Oh, I do X-rated movies," I said jokingly. No reaction. She continued to stare at me. Probably Italian, about twenty-two, beauty-school or stenotype variety. No doubt bridge-and-tunnel crowd (as Manhattanites refer to those who pour into the discos on weekends via the bridges and tunnels).

"Hey, Roxanne, don't he look like somebody?" she suddenly bellowed out. Real class, this girl. Subtle as a sledgehammer. Half the beach turned around as her frosted-tips counterpart came over, also munching green bubble gum. She scanned me like someone eyeing a suspect bag of potatoes.

"Naw, not to me he don't. Hey, you from the Island?" she snapped as she splashed on some of her friend's tanning oil.

"Island of Manhattan," I said.

"Funny, he looks like Tony, he freakin' looks like Tony. Don't he, Gina?! You know, Tony?" she asked, shamelessly adjusting the bottom of her bikini.

This girl talks too much. Roxanne from Brooklyn. Deaf mute, I scribbled on my pad. Lacquered in oil like a female body builder or oil wrestler. Better yet, mud *wrestler.* I added that to my notes and put the pad down lest these two glistening nymphets get suspicious.

"Hi, son, how's the writing going?" said Dad, suddenly appearing out of nowhere. He's always appearing out of nowhere, this dad.

"Fine, Dad." Damn, I just put my pad down. Right, he thinks I'm procrastinating, which I am in a way but not entirely. Yeah, bet he says something embarrassing. Here it comes, the old cigar is being plucked from his lips. Dad only removes his cigar when he wants to be understood.

"You gonna introduce me to your friends, son?" he said, grinning that I-caught-you grin.

Oh yeah, right, my "friends"—the implication being I'm

out cruising girls and not writing. Or that these girls are my type . . . then here comes brother Max, circling like a hawk, hot on the scent of fresh coconut oil. What a nose this kid has. French. I bet he says something in French to impress the bimbettes.

"Alors, tu dragues pour nous deux, Mario."

See, French. I knew it. Max grinned, imitating Dad. The French having had its desired effect, the girls were puzzled, although that's not saying much, but after all, how many Black Parisian guys do you meet on the beach every day? So now it was incumbent upon me to introduce these two clowns to the ladies. Quickly, in French, I told Max to kiss my butt, and he smiled sweetly as I introduced him to Roxanne and Shameless Bikini. Oh well, guess I'm busted. Man, they know I'm procrastinating. Might as well roll with the punches or they'll be on my case all day.

Anyway, back to the script. Roxanne became Roxy, the sexy, deaf, mud-wrestling Amazon. I gave her dreadlocks also inspired by the Bahamas. Actually the writing was progressing at a decent clip. I was up to the section where Chilly D., the rapping janitor, is stashing Yves Malmaison gowns in his goody bag for distribution to his assortment of lady friends. Chilly is growing into one of those motormouth characters that has a line for everything, not unlike the character I played on *Sonny Spoon*, except Chilly is more of the urban-funk variety. Once my sister Megan had on one of her stop-traffic miniskirts, and she said some brother swooped by in a pink Eldorado and yelled out, "Look at those candy hips!" It's times like this when I put my little gray-cell computer on recall and whip out lines that capture an image like "candy hips." Let's see. Chilly removes a green gown from a rack of dresses and says:

CHILLY
Green, green would look mean on my sexy candy-hipped Sharleen!

. . .

Yeah, okay, it's not Shakespeare, but for brother Chilly D., it'll do just fine.

It was Sunday. The previous night cool bro Max and I had finally escaped to a club without Pops. Determined to show Max a good time, I felt it was my duty as a big brother to get poor Max to at least dance with a girl. What a selfless gesture, eh? So I started dancing. She was talking to her friend. Not bad, friend was okay too, short, but okay. She smiled at me? Maybe, maybe not, I hate to misread signals, could prove embarrassing. Like I said, humiliation ain't my bag. I glanced around coolly, no one else there but me, so okay, I guess she had smiled at me. A sorta half smile, but, hey, that's better than a stick in the eye. Cool, I smiled back, she smiled again. I danced, she swayed slightly . . . and yes . . . she was gonna almost . . . yes she was dancing with me. Something odd about this girl, but too late, 'cause, yes, here came Max, circling, circling, swoop, he was dancing with the friend. Great relief. Now we could go home and at least say the sorry Van Peebles duo did actually dance with someone other than themselves. Dance number 1 led to dance number 2 and then, Max was talking to the friend and it seemed they'd like to go have doughnuts with us.

"Max, is this true? She said that or you said that?"

"Okay, I suggested the doughnuts, but she said okay . . . so, let's go, huh?"

"You got money, I paid to get in this joint. You got doughnut money?" I asked.

"I'll pay for her, you pay for ze oser one."

For better or worse, we ended up at the Bahamian version of Twin Donuts at two in the morning with these two girls. Like I said, something about these girls was slightly askew. Anyway, we strolled into the doughnut palace. All was casual and then Max and I froze. Under the garish fluorescent lights, for the first time, we really got a good look. These girls were scary, exorcist scary. The one I was talking to had jagged teeth and deep-set, disturbing eyes. No wonder she had only half smiled. She was hiding those choppers. I swear, man, she looked normal in the club. The one Max was talking to had slightly better skin than the elephant man, but her physical appearance wasn't what I really found unnerving. She grinned and kinda snorted with her friend as if in cahoots on some darker plan. Excellent nightmare material, those two. . . . It's at times like that that I come down with a sudden attack of guilt for not writing. I paid my respects politely, so as not to offend or incur wrath, gladly paid for the damn doughnuts, and split. Max was not far behind. In the safety of the elevator, I whispered, "Max, look outside. Did Helter and Skelter follow us?"

"Shit, you look, man," he retorted.

"Did you see her eyes burning? Scary. Max, your taste at best is foul."

"Bullshit, man, you picked 'em!"

"I did it for you, man, I could easily have stayed home and written. I sacrificed creativity for you, bro," I explained. "Hey, imagine if we got upstairs and they were waiting for us! Grinning and gnashing their teeth in unison."

"Don't say that, man, shit," he whispered, suddenly getting serious.

"Yo, listen up," I said. "I'm gonna do a horror flick one day and call it, *Max's Women*, or better yet, *The Last Dance*."

"You picked 'em," he muttered, reassuring himself.

"Ingrate . . . we should have brought them home and sicked them on Pops, huh?" (We slapped five.)

"That's cold." He chuckled in that French way he does.

Max had been bitching that if you slept beside Dad and didn't fall asleep first, you were shit outa luck, 'cause Dad's snoring would keep you awake. Pop, of course, dismissed this theory, insisting that he didn't snore. When we came in that night, having narrowly escaped Helter and her friend, Skelter, we found Mel baby curled up comfortably with a towel wrapped like a turban draped over his eyes and snoring like a rhino. Naturally, we whipped out the cassette player and recorded him doing a couple of bars of "snooze you lose." Max and I usually regress to a comfortable state of adolescence when we're together, so this sort of behavior becomes normal.

. . .

Later that same night, after tucking in, I must have been
asleep for an hour when I suddenly woke up. Something was
wrong. Dad was still snoring, looking like a towel head, and
it seemed heredity had got the best of brother Max and now
he was keeping harmony with Dad. The moon was full and
wide awake, its rays dancing off the black water. Everything
was quiet except for the strange, atonal song of sleep that
Dad and Max were drowning out. Then it hit me. That girl's
eyes . . . those haunting, deep-set, glaring eyes. My karma-
continuous mother believes that whatever you criticize in
this life or cannot accept will come back to you. Did I say
anything to this chick to offend her? Okay, I called her Helter Skelter, but that was a joke between Max and me. It's
not like I said, "Yo, baby, you got some scary, exorcist eyes
and I'm taking my ass home!" I was cool, right? I paid for
the doughnuts, even if I had lost my appetite. So why is she
haunting me? Hey, I'm going to sleep, man. Tomorrow's
Monday, I've got to get up early and do battle with the mechanical shark. That's it, Mario, think about the shark and
his dead-looking muppetlike eyes, nothing scary there.
All through the night the image of that girl's eyes kept
floating up to the surface of my consciousness. I sat up,
annoyed at my inability to sleep. The clock said 3:00
A.M. Damn! I glanced over at Dad. He had rolled over in his
sleep and now the towel was wrapped tightly around his
head turban style. He muttered something in his sleep,
opened one bleary eye, glanced at me, smiled, and fell back
asleep. I lay there staring at the moon staring back at me
like a single blank white eye. Suddenly I knew it! I dived
for the notepad that I kept near for moments like this,
scribbled down some notes furiously, rolled over, and fell
fast asleep.

My notes usually don't seem as profound in the morning
when I reread them almost as if for the first time. I could
barely read my writing on this particular morning, but I had
a feeling the villain of "To Die For" had been born. The
notes said, "Punjab wears a turban wrapped tightly around
his skull and is marked by one evil, milky white eye as if his

inner turmoil had boiled up through the very window to his soul and scarred him for life."

Toward the end of the *Jaws* shoot, just as I was finishing up the rough draft of "To Die For" . . . Whammo! I got a call from NBC saying that they wanted to do an hour action adventure series especially written for me. Yeah, *sure*. I was, as any somewhat level-headed fellow would be, a bit skeptical. Actually an understatement—I thought they were outright pulling my chain. Not that I understood the vast intricacies or philosophy of network programming. My only real exposure to TV at the time was *L.A. Law*. They had agreed that if I did two episodes (which later grew to six and proved to be a very positive experience), I'd be free to go off and do features, which was my main career focus. Other than that I had done *The Cosby Show*, a couple of movies of the week, and a PBS special on the playwright Eugene O'Neill that I was actually proud of.

Then enter my dad. I called him up and told him about my latest script. I had written a couple of others, some he liked, others he wasn't so crazy about. It was a little late when I called, but fueled by my own excitement, I roughly outlined the plot for Pops.

He said, "Yeah, yeah," in his you-woke-me-up voice and mumbled something about sending him a copy. Next morning I did. I had no idea he would end up directing it. But then I probably wouldn't have called the director at 2:00 in the morning either.

BLOCK

The next day, late August of '87, thirty years since Maria, Mario's mother, came through Wanda's door (I wonder whatever happened to Wanda, anyway) the script arrived, prepaid. *Prepaid?!*

Barely two days later, not even the blink of an eye in

script-reading time, the long-distance operator asked if I would accept a collect call. I knew it wasn't Max. He was only sixty-two blocks down the road, on Wall Street, and Megan in S.F. would sleep late on Saturday.

"Operator, go ahead."

"Hi, Dad."

"Hi, son, where are you, anyway?"

He was still in Los Angeles. NBC had wanted to talk to him again, as long as he was out there he had taken a couple of plush modeling jobs, and his agent had lined up a string of acting auditions for him.

"So what's up with NBC these days?" I asked, trying to sound neutral so as not to get his hopes up or dash his dreams.

"What do you think, Dad?"

On one hand it sounded like they were stringing him along, but if so, on the other hand, what could their ulterior motive be?

"Well, I'll have to give it some thought," I stalled, not wanting to jeopardize my role as the infallible wise one. Up to then, I had had an incredible string of luck reading the tea leaves and I was batting one hundred with Mario.

"I don't mean NBC, Dad, I mean the script."

Mario not being a novice, I didn't feel I had to coddle him. He had written several scripts, and one, called "Blazes" about an arsonist, had been optioned and almost made. Almost. Close, but no horseshoe. I told him what I thought, which was that the draft was cluttered but when cleaned up and focused it had potential of being a really good comedy. Mario bristled at my calling his masterpiece a comedy. He saw it more as a detective story *cum* adventure.

"Okay," I said, back-peddling and giving him the benefit of my doubt. "Maybe a caper with humor." But Mario wasn't appeased. He saw it as a serious rough, tough killer thriller. We don't discuss our writing with one another until it is in rough first-draft form. So we come upon it cold, like any other reader. But I had overheard Mario and Max giggling over part of the story when we were down in the Bahamas during the making of *Jaws* 4. Maybe that influenced me to look at it as a comedy, but I didn't think so.

"Jesus, Mario, how serious can it be if you've got a gay French dress designer's spirit popping in and out of a Black rapper's body?"

"Dad, you were the one who always said just write it the way you see it and that mixing-up genre was okay." (The kid was a tenacious son-of-a-bitch, probably got it from his mom.)

"I don't give a shit what I said, there's a difference between scrambling genre and misleading advertising. A horse ain't a camel just because you say so. You can't pull a label out of thin air just because it suits you and make it fit."

There was silence on the phone. I wasn't sure what I had on the other end—a respectful son or an artiste convinced.

"Look, what the fuck do I know," I relented, "maybe you're right. Prune it some and we'll take another look when you get back. . . . "

BERNARD

Melvin and I go back over twenty years, and it has been the most exciting, turbulent, delightful, hair-raising, worry-you-nutball, crazy experience I have ever had and I wouldn't trade a minute of it. Melvin and I met on a dance drama that he was doing for the Harkness Foundation, where he was conceiving what would actually be a play within a dance. He needed somebody who could get into his way of thinking to design some costumes for his presentation for the characters, and I was recommended. We had a slight conference, as he always does. Melvin pays you your worth. Now Melvin is not one to be generous. But he is not one to be stingy. Melvin just knows the value of a buck and you gotta deliver for that buck. Now, once he makes a deal with you, it is sealed. It is sealed and it is whatever you want to call it in

stone. It's in marble. He goes for it. So he says how much
money. I said, "Boom." He said, "I need these many
sketches by this time." I said, "Just fine. Should I pick out
the characters?" He said, "Go for yourself. Give me the presentation that's goin' to show the various characters I conceived." So I went. I did the sketches. I brought 'em back.
He handed me my money. He was pleased with what I had
done. The only thing was the dancers, as sometimes happens—certain artists do not realize that the boss is the boss!
—were trying to give him some kind of back talk, which as
far as I was concerned was flak . . . because you have to go
along with what is being conceived so that the man can find
out what he is doing. Editing and that other stuff comes
later. So when I found out that they were trying to give him
a hard time . . . I know all of the dancers. I took them aside
and cussed them out off the East Side of Detroit, Michigan,
where I am from and said, "Coons, do you know that you
have a job? Do you know how many dancers are working
now? Do you know what you were doing before you got this
job? Did Mr. Balanchine or Jerome Robbins want you in
their next production? Shut the fuck up and do what you're
told." Obviously somebody told him. After that, he and I
became fast friends. And he never forgot it either. "Boom"
years later, 1971 if I am not mistaken, he called me honey
out of the blue, and we did *Aint Supposed to Die a Natural
Death* on Broadway.

I think it was the very first time any designer had ever
gotten credit on the marquee. I think this was even before
Cecil Beaton had the court the next time around. Oh, baby,
right in the middle. I mean . . . it was like launching your
career and making you important. And after that, people all
saw me differently. Actually, I must say, now that I look
back on it, I did a hell of a job. But the hell of a job I did was
such that people did not know that these were not clothes
that I had just snatched off people in the street . . . like I
didn't go either to Harlem or the South Side of Chicago or
the East Side of Detroit and just take these people's clothes.
Each one of those things was a designed garment that was

specially built for each character in each scene. But I did get a fan letter from Hal Prince, and I thought that was fabulous. I kinda hid it, but I got it somewhere so every now and then I can look at it, 'cause he thought I had done a splendid job. Melvin and I can work so well together because we know the shit that we're getting into.

We did *Don't Play Us Cheap*. We did *Waltz of the Stork*. And now, *Identity Crisis*. I didn't do *Champeeen* because I was out in the woods of Holly, and I think I was making the film *Bingo Long and the Traveling All Stars*. I did *Star Jockey* and *King of Ragtime*. I did *Claudine* too, with Diahann Carroll and James Earl Jones, which was quite successful. In *Bingo Long* there was Billy Dee Williams, James Earl Jones, Richard Pryor. It was a ball. All old friends. See, sometimes you get a chance to work with your old friends, you can even be more creative because they're already used to your nuttiness. They know that somewhere down the line it will come out, even though Billy Dee might not have wanted to wear that pale, cream-colored-yellow suit, but he knew once I put it on him, he'd be gorgeous. It's that kind of thing. So Melvin and I usually do a lot of things together. Melvin will definitely try to serendipity your butt. And you have to tell him, "Melvin, some of this stuff has to shoot several days and it might get wet." If you can convince him that everything you are doing is exactly what he wants anyway, you can get it. And whenever you have an idea, if he has a minute, you can take him aside so you can discuss it privately and he can present it as his idea like most bosses, but then he always goes and gives you the credit and laughs. Our energies are very good together because we know each other. And while everybody else at times seems to get upset or distressed at him—distressed!—I get tickled, because I'm used to it. And some days we cuss each other out just to get our energies flowing and everybody thinks we're having an argument. Which is really an inside joke for us.

Melvin and Mario are as alike as father and son can possibly be without being clones. Now Mario has had that other kind of Hollywood exposure, and Melvin has had the road that he had to come up. But they're both strong personalities. And people kept asking me, "What did you do with the two of them?" I said, "Didn't you ever notice, I talk to each one of them on a different side of the room. Then I go to the middle and I talk to me, which I am known to talk to myself, come up with a compromise, and then when they both hear it, it seems exactly like they want it and as long as it works in the film, you don't get any flak." So . . . one day, Mario was talking to me and his father came up and I turned to Mario and I said, "You know, I started to call your father a slave-driving, low-life, evil, don't-give-me-any-time-or-energy bum, but I know he would have liked it." You know he could laugh out loud, 'cause he knew . . . I knew he was with me, and that's how we work. And for me, it's always exciting because there's not been a project that we haven't worked on that wasn't already a new challenge. And I always get well paid and I always get good billings and quite apart from other producers . . . I can't mention any names because it would be devastating because I might get blackballed. But I did a film where I couldn't figure out what the man wanted and every day he changed his mind.

Now when I worked with Sidney Poitier on *Hanky Panky,* Sidney was fabulous. Once he established that this is what you can do, and we knew we were going to do it and deliver it on time and we were gonna roll, he was a dream.

There was no conflict between Mario as a writer/star and Melvin as director/producer . . . not one bit. Of course, you have to remember that Melvin has a strong hand and ultimately the final decision. When he says no, there is no appeal. And Mario had the sense and the admiration for Melvin as the artist even before his father. He knows that Melvin sees things in his brain and you have to wait until he is finished to find out what he is seeing. So you just go along with it and you get the product. Also the script itself was so full of interesting things that whatever Melvin didn't do, there was still enough there for it to work out just fine. And they both have that high energy. If you can keep up with the two of them, then you're fine. Because you will get a call from either or both of them with some ideas about tomorrow.

Melvin is known to fire you quicker than a cat can lick his

ass or if you get too far down, he gets the street in him, and
he'll kick your butt. I saw him do it. Of course, I was tickled
because I had warned the guilty party. What had happened
was that this young man . . . he was talented but he came
from the so-called "theatre." You know, in quotes and some
of the most exciting theatre that I have ever seen has been
done by somebody who just didn't know the rules or didn't
give a shit about 'em and went ahead on and did something
exciting. Nobody could even figure out what to call *Aint
Supposed to Die a Natural Death,* but everybody knew it
was brilliant. And that was all that counted. Well, this cat
was supposed to be directing, and he kept jumping in Melvin's chair. And I kept trying to tell him, "Don't sell no wolf
ticket to no gorilla." Melvin is from the South Side of Chicago. There is a point that happens in all that sophistication
from being in Europe all those years and traveling and all
and Wall Street and everything like that that it becomes
completely obliterated and the roots come out. I'm trying to
tell the man, "Cool it. Just shut up. PLEASE don't do it."
The next thing I know across the theatre, it was over five or
six rows, I just saw Melvin fly. So, of course, the first thing I
do was duck. Then as I ducked, I knew it wasn't for me
'cause I knew I hadn't done nothin'. He was on this man like
white on rice, tooth and nail. It took about thirty seconds
and all was quiet on the front. So now I gotta run up the
aisle, not let anyone see me, so I can laugh like I want to.

What ticked Melvin off was that this particular person
kept taking the production past where it was written, looking for some kind of validity or somethin'. You know how
they find all those wonderful words that don't mean shit but
it means that you been to college and you sat and tore things
apart and after you tore things apart, you couldn't put it back
together. And I think what he did was come up with "Melvin, you don't know what you're talking about, and why in
the hell are you going on like this and I'm going to do it my
way or else."

Once we were in Chicago, and we were doing a production
of *Don't Play Us Cheap,* and Norman Kean, who was co-

producing it with Melvin, decided that Melvin would be box office. Of course, he is. And that Melvin should be in the play. Melvin said, "Well, if I'm going in the play, Bernard, you're getting your butt back on the stage too. I'm carrying somebody down with me."

I told Melvin the one and only time that I had been quite right. I said, "Melvin, you're on a wagon. Now you know I've danced all my life, and I'm not trying to be a prima donna, but if you're going to jump off the wagon while the wagon is in motion moving backward onto the deck of the stage, you oughta rehearse a couple of times. I know you're busy with the rest of the play"—'cause he was also directing it—"Melvin, just rehearse it couple of times." "Oh, it's all right, B. I'll get it," he said.

The first performance I think was a Tuesday and he did do the jump beautifully. And the wagon was moving backward. Melvin jumped—it must have been nine feet. But somebody had spilled water, and he landed right in it. And the next thing we knew, Melvin was lying down on the stage, asshole over appetite. Both of us laughed over it during the intermission.

Once we were in Santa Fe or Albuquerque or somewhere or other in the West. Anyhow, it was one of those places. Melvin had decided that the only way to control the actors was to put them in a controlled environment and he had us so far out in the sticks that all you saw was red dust and red dirt and each other. Yes, each other. Most of us spent the whole time either fightin', laughin', or cryin'. Because you know how you see each other so much that it becomes a cohesive presentation so by the time you get through with it, you can't stand the sight of each other. There was one of the ladies who was so angry with Melvin that she was goin' to take the crutch of Mabel King, who had hurt her leg and was on crutches. She snatched the crutch from Mabel. Now, you know, Mabel is a big woman, gigantic . . . gorgeous, big woman. I don't know how Mabel held herself up. She snatched the crutch and got ready to hit Melvin upside the head with the crutch and Melvin just punched her square in the chops. Do you know that she calmed down just like that, the same day. And the next day she sang and acted like an angel. Sang better than other times. If ever I had ever heard her sing in her life. And I said, "Now maybe it's true, every now and then some women need a little beating for inspiration." I wouldn't try it. He just *bosh*. It was just one little light hit. It wasn't even like he was a woman beater. But it was like . . . you know how somebody will slap you to bring you back to your senses? That was it. Like, Thanks, I needed that. And the next day saaaaaaaang.

When I first met Mario, he must have been what . . . early teens or subteens . . . twelve or thirteen. It never occurred to me that he would grow up to be a movie star or TV star. Not because I didn't think he had talent. We never even got that far because he was just in awe of the whole thing. Because, you see, all of these people surrounding Melvin . . . Melvin has a tendency to surround himself with a cornucopia of everything and everybody. People will be there from superintellects to supersophisticated to superinsane. I'm afraid I've been in the last one . . . eccentrics, geniuses, also-rans. As long as the pot is cooking and it's a smorgasbord, Melvin is happy. So Mario was this wonderful little boy who had spent a lot of years in Paris speaking French, the language that we were speaking. I mean, we knew English but we don't necessarily speak English. As you can tell, I speak somethin' else. So he was like . . . like he was on the set of a film . . . like a kid in a candy store. 'Cause he was just looking around at all of it. And of course he was fascinated by me because of the way I act and the way I come in all draped up or dressed up. You can never tell what I'm going to have on or do next or say next. I don't even know. So, it was like he was absorbing so much of his father and all of these different people.

The costume room, that was part of Mario's hangout. He was also backstage when we did *Don't Play Us Cheap*. And then I had, you know, the conk wigs and in *Aint Supposed to Die* we had a DA for the lady who was playing the lesbian, and we had the rags for the bag lady, and the crushed velvet suits and leather. I mean there was stuff everywhere and so for a kid who was fascinated by all of this junk, it's like putting him in a toy store and sayin' "Go for yourself." And he was very respectful of everything. He never destroyed anything at all. But just the whole idea of telling Avon Long, "Can I put on that leather cape with that pearl?" You know, watch him develop that. Because when I saw Mario quite a bit later, after Melvin told me he was an actor, the adjustment for me had to be very quick. Because once there was this skinny little boy and now in the door walks this man with biceps and triceps and pecs and lats and . . . and I'm looking up . . . Mario? You know, it's like the transition. But I was glad to see him as an adult. I knew he could act 'cause I had seen that. Then I found out he could write. I told Melvin, "You ain't the only star in the family!"

TOBIE

Mario and I have come a long ways together. From Mario starring in low budget feature films like *Exterminator II* and *Rappin* to major studio pictures like Warner Bros.' *Heartbreak Ridge* with Clint Eastwood and Universal's *Jaws: The Revenge* with Michael Caine.

Mario was introduced to me by a casting director at ABC television who recognized his exceptional talent. At the time Mario was making the transition from model to actor.

Mario impressed me immediately. He seemed able to handle any kind of role. He could sing, dance, do comedy or drama, play good guys or bad guys, all with the same ease. Although he was very attractive, Mario never let his good looks stand in the way of creating a character. In fact, character roles seemed more important to him. He enjoyed overcoming obstacles that would prevent a director or producer from seeing that he could fit a certain role.

I had never before met an actor that so thoroughly prepared for every audition or part. I remember one film in particular where the casting director was looking specifically for a karate champion from the streets of New York. The casting director felt Mario looked too sophisticated and he was not a black belt. That certainly did not stop Mario from going after the role. He prepared a video of himself doing a scene from the screenplay as the character. No stone was ever left unturned or strategy unplotted that stood in his way.

As my relationship with Mario grew, he told me he wanted me to meet his dad. Of course I had lots of trepidation. Fearing Melvin's overinvolvement in Mario's career decisions or undermining my opinion in certain issues made me nervous. I knew Melvin was a pioneer filmmaker and a powerhouse writer, producer, and director, but I was not prepared to understand the closeness of Mario's relationship to his dad.

My fears were unwarranted. Although Melvin was astute and talented in show business, he was willing to let Mario explore his career on his own. Instead of feeling threatened by Melvin's presence, I felt supported and guided by it. We would together discuss the pros and cons of different issues in Mario's career. I began to understand why Mario felt so close to Melvin. Melvin taught Mario that show business was a business and he better get out there and learn it for himself. As Melvin and I got to know each other our mutual respect grew and I enjoyed exchanging ideas and working with Melvin. Often Melvin and I will conspire to make a point. Of course Mario always knows it. Melvin takes many opportunities to let me know that the job I do for Mario is valued and appreciated. Of course that makes me feel great. Slowly I feel I have become not only Mario's personal manager but part of the family.

Before *Heartbreak Ridge* was released I arranged for some private screenings in Hollywood for some key casting people I thought would have an impact on Mario's career. One of those people was Joel Thurm. His position at the time was V.P. of talent at NBC. After seeing the film Joel called and said he would like to arrange a meeting between Mario and Brandon Tartikoff, the head of the network.

CHIP

When my energetic little Jewish New York manager, Tobie, pointed out that there was to date no single Black guy starring in his own one-hour action show, I realized how even more full of bull these cats must be. She said to her knowledge it had been tried twice before, but never went beyond a couple of episodes. She reasoned that maybe White America could laugh with or at Blacks in a safe "comedic" half-hour show, the kind of thing where you could peek in at their world in a voyeuristic fashion and never have the Black world interfere with their world. I don't know, perhaps some young guy, my color, running around on the tube like the brother of steel, saving, fighting, and interacting with men and women of all colors might be still too threatening. Tobie had raised some salient points that were hard to ignore.

Having to think along color lines is such a damn drag, maybe because certain patterns become painfully clear, as good old Tobie was pointing out. Okay, no leading Black guys in an action show. They have to be paired with a White counterpart who usually accidentally on purpose kicks most of the butt. But why? Because there are very few Black executives in TV. There are also very few Black cameramen, soundmen, casting directors at all, for that matter. The more you look, the more you see it. How do they rate a show, a TV show? With a little box called a Nielsen Box? Guess what? You got it, those boxes are placed in proportionately very few Black homes, even though, unfortunately, poor old Black folks, who should be reading books, watch more TV than the average White. They thus watch more ads and believe most of the crap TV sells the public—e.g., Buy this car and you'll be somebody. Wear this fur coat and you'll look *Dynasty* rich.

When I was a kid, I used to identify with Bogart and think, gee, isn't Lauren Bacall beautiful . . . isn't Marilyn Monroe sexy, isn't James Dean cool! Except later on in life someone like Tobie taps you on the shoulder and the realization hits you that if Mario Van Peebles had been alive back then he'd be lucky to play a butler. Kissing Lauren Bacall would definitely be a big-time no-no. Watching White people in movies and now on TV, Blacks have become brainwashed to the point that they believe Black is ugly and White is right. Too often American Blacks seem to even think of themselves as more attractive when they look closer to White!

I was modeling and Black folks seemed to embrace me. A pretty, young, dark-skinned girl came up to me and whispered, "I love seeing you in all those fancy magazines."

"Why?" I asked, embarrassed a little at the compliment.

" 'Cause," she replied sweetly, "you're just as cute as all them *GQ* White boys."

I was taken aback a little and she sensed my reaction.

"I'm sorry," she apologized. "I just meant it's nice for us to have someone to look at, too. And you are just as fine as those White guys. You're almost White, but you're still Black. Like Vanessa Williams or Lena Horne."

Ain't that a bitch?! I'm good-looking 'cause I'm almost White?! Black people, our people, Red people, Yellow people, any people are in serious fucking trouble when we think like that. I'm not saying that most Blacks think that way, but enough do to make it pretty alarming. Well, there it is, plain as day.

So when I said NBC for some reason was pulling my leg about being an action hero in some one-hour TV series, I was skeptical, polite, and frankly, looking forward to what I hoped would be a nice, tasty Hollywood "we've got something in mind for you" power lunch. I like to eat. I love to do lunch (which is often all these lunches ever come to). Here comes Mario, off to NBC with his appetite.

I met with two nice NBC execs, one being Joel Thurm, head of casting, the other, Brandon Tartikoff. Bad news, they didn't order me any lunch, but instead kept on plugging the series idea. I was sorta half listening to them, half listening to my stomach grumble and they were going on about how they liked me in *L.A. Law*, which turns out was also on their network. Obviously, I was not well-informed about TV, but they loved my ability to improvise in *Heartbreak Ridge*. I write, I direct, I'm sort of a "jack of all—" My ears pricked up waiting for them to drop the other shoe, or other half of that phrase which is, "and master of none," but politely, they never did. This Brandon guy seemed pretty down to earth and downright excited by this whole concept of me as an offbeat private detective. He waved his hands, talked about colors, neon and wet streets, an urban hip look. Later they introduced me to another executive named Perry Simon. Smiley and energetic, this guy actually brought in a couple of people who looked a hell of a lot like writers to jot down some of my ideas. What's going on here, Mario? I thought. Called up Dad later that night. He didn't seem to have a reading on it either, so play it by ear, I guess. Another day, another meeting. This time accompanied by lunch (the cafeteria variety, but who's complaining).

Meanwhile, I was starting to enjoy pretending that these guys were actually writing down some of my ideas like this was for real. The show was tentatively entitled *Sonny Spoon*, a stupid name, but, hey, you did remember it.

"So does Sonny carry a gun?" they asked me, jotting down notes madly as if the character were alive.

"He carries only a sense of humor," I replied, thinking of my lovely, nonviolent, sixties-minded mom and how she'd like it when I could report back "Mom, I told those big network executives, no gun, so of course, they'll never do the project." As if it would have gotten off the ground in the first place. Hey, I decided, why not throw in a couple more goodies, like my dad should play my dad on TV? That's great, now I can tell Dad I didn't forget him and Mom about the no-gun deal. I had a personal fear of being straitjacketed into a role, so I said, "Yeah, yeah, and I play, I mean, Sonny plays lots of characters, see, yeah, that's the ticket."

These guys were actually writing this stuff down. I felt like someone in the black-and-white success montage of a Frank Capra movie. Yeah, I was Jimmy Stewart telling those big suits what a positive image this could be . . . that's the ticket now, everyone's smiling, patting me on the back,

escorting me out. Lots of "Well, that was innovative". . . .
"Food for thought". . . . "Way to go". . . . and "We'll be in
touch." Naturally, I knew I'd never hear from them again.
They seemed nice enough, but we'll be in touch. In Hollywood that means, Have a nice life. . . . I had enjoyed playing Jimmy Stewart and basically we all seemed to have fun.
. . . I started out into the California sunshine and called Dad
back in cold New York so we could laugh about it together.

BLOCK

The NBC project sounded like another one of those break-
your-heart deals that comes along once in a while. It's called
break-your-heart because it seems too good to be true (and it
usually is), but an opportunity too important not to pursue
(it can string you out for weeks, months, years), but unlikely
to come true except in one of those show-biz fantasies where
the lead breaks his/her or its leg and the diligent, talented
greenhorn understudy goes on and mesmerizes the audience
and a new star is born.

Well, not quite that way, but close. Mario had caught the
eye of Brandon Tartikoff, who just happened to be the head
of NBC, and here they were talking about building an hour
TV detective series around him and his talents. His own
series! An actor's dream, right? However, with one thing or
another, that had been over a year ago. Still, astronomical
odds against you or not, the pot of gold was too tantalizing
not to give it every shot and the umpteenth trip to Los Angeles to yet another meeting.

"Well, I think they're thinking about talking about talking
contract . . . maybe."

"Congratulations, you're all set," I chuckled

"Well, not quite," Mario laughed back. "After that they
have to find exactly the right producer for the pilot." (Before
a series is given a final okay, the network shoots a prototype

episode or pilot and studies it before committing to going ahead with the series. *I told you it was a long shot.* Only a few hundred of the thousands of ideas tossed around even make it to script and of these hundred scripts only ten or so even make it to pilot and maybe three of the ten pilots go on to become a series and they say about one out of three get renewed. I told you it was a long shot.)

CHRIS

When I first met Mario I developed an immediate dislike for him. Not because he was better-looking or taller than me or anything like that. No. Maybe my reticence was due to the way the guy ran around the set of *One Life to Live* wearing this incessant grin, a shit-eating grin, if you will. Yes! Yes! Home boy sported a just-pumped-the-neighbor's-cat grin as he greeted *everybody* from the maintenance crew to the producers.

From his attitude you'd have thought he was a special guest star or something. Perhaps he was a politician running for reelection? Quite naturally I wondered what the hell was up with this dude? *Who* was he? And *why* was he so, you know, Mr. Personality? I mean, damn, he even greeted me with a smile and handshake as if I mattered or something. Yeah, I thought, I left Indiana for New York to watch out for those actors. I mean, he's just under-five like me, right? So why is he acting like such a, I don't know, such a *star*? Well, little did I know that during the next six years Square Head, as I came to call him, would become my closest and most trusted friend.

Despite our early clashes in personality, we soon struck an alliance whereby we would work out together, or pump up our muscles for the numerous beefcake scenes we would have as football players on the ABC soap. As fate would have it, Mario was soon upgraded on the show from an under-five

NO IDENTITY CRISIS

(a player with five or fewer lines of dialogue), to a day player. In a move which was proven to be characteristic of his personality, he soon pulled me up with him, and his dressing room became my dressing room. I was liberated from the bull pen, where all the extras and under-fives changed, to a rental dressing room, and I would beat Mario to work, have my feet up on the vanity table, and be eating my breakfast when he walked in the door.

So that's how it went for about four months on *One Life to Live*. I had a small role as quarterback Jeff Cole, and Mario was the loud, bellicose troublemaker Doc Gilmore. Jeff Cole would have his usual five lines or so about getting sacked too often or something like that, while Doc Gilmore went on to romance some character portrayed by Phylicia Rashad. In no time Mario went on to have roles in films like *The Cotton Club, Exterminator II*, and *Rappin*, while yours truly continued to have mostly small roles in soaps. In retrospect, maybe I could have used a personality transplant, because Mr. Personality was leaving me in the dust.

Sometime in the fall of 1984, Square Head and I were working out in my apartment, when he came up with a brainstorm that proved convenient for us both. It turned out that while he had been in Los Angeles filming *Exterminator II*, Mario stumbled into a nice old apartment building in the heart of Hollywood. He said he was staying there during the filming and explained to me how cheap the rent was, and how convenient the location. Keeping our apartment in New York, we became roommates in Los Angeles.

L.A. was a trip! I couldn't believe how warm it was in the dead of winter, and compared to New York the place was like a ghost town. Hot damn!

And everything was so cheap! The building dated from sometime in the early 1920s and was well maintained. Compared to New York standards the apartment was huge, although it was just a studio. It had a separate kitchen with its own entrance from the building's main hallway. Well, with a little ingenuity, Square Head had converted a studio apartment into two apartments. Mario's room was the kitchen, while I slept in the front room. The two rooms were separated by a curtain we'd constructed by combining layers of old draperies. Mario had spray-painted the partition with psychedelic-fluorescent paint, and enhanced the whole place with vegetation, shrubs, and vines. The kitchen reeked of lemon incense, and was soon dubbed the Love Hut, not only for its look but also for the harem of stray females traipsing in and out at all hours of the night.

Sometime during the Love Hut's heyday, Mario and I were at a local grocery store in Hollywood when I stopped dead in my tracks and said, "Wait a minute!" "What's wrong, man?" Mario wanted to know. "You push the cart," I replied. "Why?" Mario asked. " 'Cause they're going to think I'm the Bitch!" Well, that was all the encouragement Mario needed. He began chasing me through the store doing a character that would make Liberace seem macho. "Oh, Chrith, Chrith," he called, as I ran with embarrassment. Needless to say, I've never found myself in a grocery store with Square Head since.

I'm no Jack Kennedy, but unlike Dan Quayle, I know my stuff. And I was more than qualified for any bones old Square Head was willing to throw me. And he'd thrown me a few good ones over the years. Let me tell you about *Heartbreak Ridge*.

Sometime in the spring of 1986, I was back in New York, working out in my apartment, when the phone rang. Since I was in the middle of my workout, I let my answering machine do its job while I heard the following: "Beep . . . Chris, it's Mario, Mario. I'm here in L.A. and I've got some great news. I just found out I got that role in the new Clint Eastwood movie. . . . " Well, somewhere around that time I managed to become pinned under about 250 pounds of weight. As I struggled to get the weight off my chest the message continued: "Check it out, man. I want you to come out to L.A. and meet the legend. . . . " By this time a simple chest exercise had become a fight for my life as I listened on. "Yeah, man, come on out and meet Clint!" Don't ask me how, but at that point the weight had made its way to the floor, and I made my way to the phone!

Heartbreak Ridge was to be filmed on location at Camp

Pendleton and around the San Clemente area. Mario had gotten me a job as his stand-in and had given up his first-class suite in exchange for a double-occupancy room so that I'd have a place to stay. Clint Eastwood is an actor I've admired for as long as I can remember. And of all the famous people I've met and worked with, he is one of the few I can say I admire more after having worked with him. I can remember him taking Mario and me to work out after work. The first time I worked out with Clint we weren't sure what to expect. I mean, Clint's twice our age, right? Well, we were doing bench presses with a pretty good weight and Mario and I had both done some pretty good sets, but Clint was matching us rep for rep! As the weight got heavier Mario and I would look at each other and think silently to ourselves, Yeah, this is his last one! Well, we stood behind Clint and he slowly raised his arms, then suddenly snatched the weight from the rack and started pushing the weight we had just struggled with as if it were a warmup! Mario and I just looked at each other with our mouths open and slowly and simultaneously mouthed the word *damn!*

CHIP

I never did hear from NBC again—that is, until almost half a year later, when I was back in New York having one of those rare domestic attacks in which I actually try to do the dishes.

Ring! Ring! went the phone, trying to distract me and testing my personal resolve to be a neater guy.

"Yeah," I said, hand all soapy.

"Is this Mario?" a friendly, relaxed man's voice asked.

"Yes, it is," I said, hoping to figure out what this was about before my domestic mood faded.

"This is Steve," he said, friendly and still relaxed as hell.

"Okay," I replied drawing a complete blank.

"Stephen Cannell. Brandon called me about co-producing *Sonny Spoon*. I don't typically do fifty-fifty ventures with a network, but I saw *Heartbreak Ridge* and I'm a fan."

By the way, I had later found out, again from my *nudgy* little lady manager, Tobie, that the guy I had the NBC meeting with was Brandon Tartikoff, the head of programming for NBC, which at the time was the number one network in the world and that *Sonny Spoon* was his own idea.

Later when I spoke to Mr. Tartikoff again, he asked me what I thought of the show's name, *Sonny Spoon*. I asked if that name was his idea. He said yes. So I flat-out gave him a piece of my mind and said, "Gee, I think it's a great name. Easy to remember, hard to forget."

So back to this Mr. Cannell fella on the phone. He seemed nice enough, but I had sort of placed the whole *Sonny Spoon* joke on a coal on the back burner and was trying to grasp what the bottom line was here, wondering if this pleasant prankster could be legit or was just Chris or somebody playing a gag.

If by some slim chance this guy was legit, I didn't want to piss him off, so the conversation washed back and forth. Finally, in one elegant display of my vast ignorance, TV-wise, I flat-out asked, "Excuse me, but what shows have you done?" There was a slight pause at the other end.

"Well," he replied, seemingly not offended in the least, "a little show called *The Rockford Files, The A-Team, Hunter, Wiseguy, 21 Jump Street, Ten Speed and Brown Shoe, Baa Baa Black Sheep, Riptide.* . . . "

"*Rockford* is one of my pop's favorite shows," I blurted out, getting genuinely excited. "Rockford seemed to be the embodiment of the everyday Joe trying to make a buck and not get ground up in the gears." I explained that I thought that James Garner infused the role with a certain tongue-in-cheek cynical charm that gave it an intelligence, as if to say to some hostile heavy, Look, I really don't want to punch you in the mouth, 'cause I hurt my hand opening some tuna fish earlier today, so like, please just give me the money you owe me and I'll go back to my trailer.

NO IDENTITY CRISIS

Cannell and I laughed, shouted, and agreed that we'd meet for an hour sometime early next week in L.A. to discuss doing this pilot idea for *Sonny Spoon*. So chances of getting stuck on some series even if this were legit and this idea became a pilot were beyond slim. I chuckled to myself, picked up the pen, forgot about the dishes, and continued working on my second draft of "To Die For." At this point, as usual, I had given out copies of a very overwritten first draft to a couple of folks to get some general feedback. I try to hand it out to a cross-cultural section of friends—a couple of writers, a couple of not so literate *amigos* (real people), and even a couple of folks predisposed to not like it, me, or any damn thing else. The latter group is just as important as the former. They take a certain pride in pointing out the plot holes and inconsistencies before the official critics get their shot and thus help keep my illusions of grandeur from evolving into anything more than illusions. This latter group reacted unusually well to the first draft of "To Die For," the long version, with bold comments of praise like, "mildly humorous at best," "inane," "wacky," "totally unbelievable characters," "the script has no idea what it is or where it's going and I'm not sure I care," "barely salvageable." The middle group of *amigos,* not-in-the-business real people, said "Fun, I dug it. Love the characters, I know them all!! But why did what's his name speak—French, was it—or no, Spanish? Was that supposed to be Yves's son or something?" This middle group is really the core group of movie-ticket buyers. The rest of us who enjoy feeling we have our fingers on the pulse of what America is willing to shell out seven bucks to go see are mostly listening to our echo. To quote William Goldman, *Adventures in the Screen Trade,* "No one knows anything." My couple of writer buddies whom I occasionally exchange scripts with (i.e., I'll show you mine if you show me yours), are usually inclined to be more constructive and, I like to think, fairly honest. Perhaps, having gone the distance of completing a script oneself makes one a little more forgiving, or perhaps they hope I'll be more diplomatic if not kinder when I critique theirs. At any rate, my writer friends reacted very favorably to the wacky, over-loaded first draft of *Identity Crisis*, so now I felt I knew where most of the bones lay and was starting on my hope-fully tightened second draft. Pop had always cautioned me not just about taking people's opinions verbatim, but their suggestions as to how to rectify what they saw as the prob-lems. Oh yeah, I sent a first draft to Pops, who loved the damn script! Ain't that a killer? What's more, he's even mak-ing noise about forming a production company together and producing the mother ourselves! So, no way am I gonna let this supposed *Sonny Spoon* pilot idea interfere with what could be our *own* feature. One must have one's priorities in order, I thought, as I delved back into the second draft.

The second draft was busting out at a vicious pace. No one was bugging me; *Jaws* had more than covered my modest overhead which I deliberately kept low on my places in New York and L.A. The young lady I had been living with had moved out and had been gone for almost half a year now. Although I still missed her sweetness, creatively, I seemed to be on a roll. She wasn't picking on me, I wasn't picking on her, and I had come to suspect the awful truth: that I only criticized the poor child because I loved her so damn much, although that's not much consolation to her. Theoretically, if I didn't care, or rather, cared more objectively, I could be much cooler. If you be you, I be me, then whatever will be will be. Apparently I hadn't mastered that level of objective love, as my mother would put it, although I'm still attempt-ing to, I suppose. So at this point we weren't being "we" and all that rechanneled energy seemed to be flowing right through the old cerebral computer and out onto the page. Even Mom was out of town. I love Mom dearly, but I'm a slob, she's a Virgo neatnik, and she's not all that damn Zen-like and objective herself when it comes to my neatness or "naughty habits," as she refers to them. So right now I'm a young, happily unemployed, voluntarily semitemporarily single slob. With cash in the bank, life is good.

Thursday, I indulged in an extra-hot portion of New York local Upper East Side Indian cuisine. I took along my notepad, of course, and scribbled like a madman. Friday, I broke off my relationship with my notepad long enough to hit both Nell's and MK's, the hot nightclubs that particular week. I even bopped over to 1018 and partied with the serious homeboy, rock-hard, young, street hip-hop crowd. As I said, I love to dance, and those kids can wear you out big time. They keep you fresh, and if you're gonna write about them, like I was in *Identity Crisis*, then you serve yourself well by hanging out a little, keeping abreast of what's up—or maybe that was just my excuse to go dance. Besides, at MK's and Nell's, everyone's so damn chic no one wants to sweat up their outfit, dig, but these people let loose. In fact, there seems to be a vague correlation between money and dance. Like Mexican food. The more Mexican food costs, the worse it tastes. The more money folks have, the harder it is for them to keep a beat.

Saturday, Van Peebles challenged me to a game of pool. An offer not to refuse if one was to save face. Seven times out of ten he kicked my ass, with brother Max not far behind. But lately I had been on a winning streak. On the way to his place I strolled through Central Park and thought about possibilities of us doing this film ourselves. A horse ambled by pulling a carriage and jarred my memory back to when I had first come to New York and Pops had taken me to ride in one of those buggies. At the time, New York seemed vast, dirty, foreign, and yet intrinsically exciting. It was a city of characters, of racial clichés all hurtling along in some strobe-lit subway like a deafening underground disco for the desensitized. The hard-core Hasidics, the Freakin' Puerto Ricans, the Beboppin' Brothers, the Madison Avenue types, colors, cabs, and canyons of glass and concrete all dazzled me and still do. They inspired me, intrigued, amazed me. I wrote about them in *Identity Crisis*, unaware that I would soon be called upon to portray almost two of these characters a week in a silly TV series destined to be in direct conflict time-wise with the making of *Identity Crisis*.

Pops kicked my ass in pool with some jive Christmas-comes-once-a-year behind the back corner pocket luck shot, and brother Max played looser, and again I lost. So much for my winning streak. Max was elated. He danced his way victoriously around the pool table, spinning his pool cue like a refugee from *The Color of Money*. I casually mentioned to Pops that I'd be heading out to Los Angeles to take a meeting with this Stephen Cannell guy about that series stuff again, and we both chuckled at what was sure to be an endless series of meetings about meetings to have other meetings.

Sunday I flew out to Los Angeles, and Tuesday I met the man. His name was on the building, making it easier for me to locate it. I had kept a place in L.A. for a couple of years, primarily for work reasons, but had never really explored the area and thus never underestimated my ability to get lost going in and out of its several cities.

Cannell, a tall, sturdy-looking guy with a goatee, shook my hand, and we trudged off down Hollywood Boulevard for our one-hour power lunch. Six hours later, I left his office. This guy was sharp, alive, unpretentious, and best of all seemed to enjoy the hell out of his work. We rapped about everything from *Heartbreak Ridge* and working with my favorite ex-mayor, Clint Eastwood, to films, camera movement, the advantage of natural light sources, north-south directing, working with one's dad, how to parlay a talent like Cannell did with writing, into an enterprise. The dichotomy of artist versus businessman in both of us, TV series, deficit financing, children and how to raise them, how to exist in Hollywood and stay married for over twenty years, which Cannell and his lovely wife Marsha have done, and last but not least, this plot idea for *Sonny Spoon*. What did I think about the name *Sonny Spoon*, he asked casually. I told him, not much until I realized Brandon Tartikoff had thought of it personally, at which point, of course, I realized what a great name it was. He laughed and said, "I understand, great name that *Sonny Spoon*."

More important, what did I think about the script that NBC had worked up for the pilot? I felt I could talk to the guy straight. I said I thought it was important to keep the protagonist from being too cool, too slick, let him be an occasional screw-up, let him get beat up a tad, not unlike an urban Rockford. As we talked, Sonny's Bugs Bunnyesque I-won't-shoot-you-but-I'll-put-on-a-disguise-and-outwit-you philosophy began to emerge. I showed him *Juliet,* a black-and-white, half-hour short that I had directed, produced, and written. (Man, producing will make you go gray quicker than anything else.) In *Juliet,* I played five characters, some of which eventually turned up on *Sonny Spoon.*

BLOCK

August came and went. In between, Mario arrived from Los Angeles with a new draft of the script, deepening the conflict. We later agreed the revision was a step in the right direction and an improvement. But whereas to me it seemed funnier and funnier, he believed it was more mysterious and deadlier than ever. He had even come up with a title—"To Die For."

"It's a little misleading, son, the title is all wrong," I protested. "This is closer to Ghostbusters Meets the Three Stooges than Massacre on Elm Street Meets the Maltese Falcon."

"Outside of that, Dad, what do you think?"

"I think it's good, moving toward better."

"Do you think we could do it ourselves? Dad, I showed it to a friend of mine who works at one of the studios and he thinks if we were careful it could be kept on the edge of low-budget film."

"Big deal. Don't forget out there in Hollywood anything under seven million dollars is considered low budget. And *we* . . . you did say *we,* right?"

"Yes, sir, I mean, we, us, put this package together and control it ourselves."

"Son, the only way you control something in this life is to control the money behind it. The Golden Rule is, He who has the gold makes the rules. How much are you willing to put up?"

"How much you want, sir?"

"If we're doing it through a studio, it won't be much. If we are willing to put up 80 percent of our net worth each, and that would only be seed money, then we'll talk about playing ball. That's a lot of money to lose, especially on something that could go belly-up because the title is misleading." I knew it was a cheap shot but I'd do it all over again. "Besides, I've got this itch to write a novel again. I've been mulling it over for a couple of years. And I've just managed my Wall Street affairs so it's not time-intensive and I don't have to handle the minute-to-minute."

"We could start shooting it in the spring."

"Oh yeah, how about the busy, uneasy question of finding the rest of the money?"

"How about a bunch of your Wall Street friends?"

How about kissing my ass, I thought, but instead I decided to cut him off at the pass more diplomatically. "You have an option on your services with NBC."

"Only two more months to go. Their option runs out in December. Dad, you oughta be directing. Nobody does it better. And people are waiting for you to make a comeback. Between the two of us we almost represent a complete film package!"

For an instant I thought maybe we could pull it off—then I did some quick calculations in my head and realized that there was no way. A package is a compilation of the major artistic elements of a movie. And, yes—we did have a head start because, it could be argued that together we represented a viable, if not boffo film package. The script was good, moving toward great. Mario was a well-thought-of new actor with star potential. I was more of an enigma: successful director/producer, but without a film credit in more than ten years and, if the distaste for my rough-and-ready entrepreneurship were not viewed in the historical context from which it sprang, i.e., the-first-minority-oughta-to-be-grateful-just-to-be-in-the-game, a strident personality.

NO IDENTITY CRISIS

Just putting a package together can in itself require a great deal of time and money—nothing, however, in proportion to the actual making of the film. Packaging, as it is usually dubbed, is a favorite vehicle of dilettante millionaires and half-assed film companies for dabbling in the movie industry. After the creative package is put together it is then shopped to a big player, a major or new major studio for financial backing. Sometimes it is offered directly to a distributor. No two deals are the same. The formulas are endless.

Packages, like proposals for TV series, far outnumber the number of films actually made. Often after half a year, or even a decade of accumulating the perfect pieces of a package, an entrepreneur will abandon a project if there are no takers at a studio. The conventional wisdom is that they oughta know if an idea is commercial. That's a belief that has always eluded me, since if the studios know unerringly what will, or won't sell, why do they make so many flops year after year? Stands to reason if they knew so much they would only churn out hits. If a guy comes to me and claims he can fly like a bird, I don't argue with him, I open the window. If he goes off the ledge and splats all over the sidewalk below, well, you gotta figure he was full of shit. If he flies out the window, climbs into the sky and does a loop-de-loop or two, and then glides back into the room, I tip my hat.

As far as I can see, looking back over films you have a large number of movies splattered up and down the street. So much for the myth somebody has the secret to success. Obviously, the public's taste is pretty much up for grabs.

Like I said, I did a rapid calculation. It came up no way. Since an essential part of this package was for Mario to play the lead, it was impossible to peddle the project until his option had expired in late December. The script itself was far from being presentable to a studio. Selling the package was no sure thing. On the other hand, why should I be the bad guy and rain on his parade? So I settled for the coward's road and said, "Well, if you have it all finished, I'm talking final draft, mind you, by the end of September, first of October, who knows what can happen."

"Sure thing, Dad," Mario said, taking the bait. I knew that deadline was almost impossible to meet, but he didn't.

Anyway, August came and went and Mario sent me bits and pieces before he took off on an acting assignment. The story was being tightened, improving it substantially (funnier than ever, it seemed to me, but I held my peace).

September found me starting to get fidgety. On Wall Street, Ted Hayes, a longtime associate and friend, the junior partner of my new firm, VP & Hayes Municipal Securities, was managing the business so efficiently that I had more and more free time on my hands.

Then, out of the blue, I found the right home for my novel. At the first meeting I had fallen in love with both the editor and the publisher. We had concluded negotiations, but I hadn't received the signed contract or my advance against royalties.

Inquiries elicited the check's-in-the-mail bullshit, that it was all only a matter of due process and that I would be receiving the goods any day. However, loving someone and trusting them are not the same thing, so I held off starting the story.

I knew I was going to write the book eventually, but I was reluctant to start on it without the check in the bank. Why? you ask. Well, two reasons. First, negotiation and creation, for me at least, require two different disciplines, and I find the latter very demanding. You are at a disadvantage when you undertake the two simultaneously. Secondly, if you begin the project you are going to become a fierce protective parent, willing to do anything so that your child, book, baby, film, play, or painting sees the light of day, so much so you are extremely vulnerable to making a bad deal to ensure that the child you're creating can live.

Alas, I had already fallen in love with my "new baby," the book, and so many ideas for it were rushing at me that I was having a great deal of trouble battling the temptation to not drop my pants and leap into bed. Mailman or no mailman.

Just in the nick of time the phone rang and I got some breathing space. It was a TV station in Washington, or, more accurately, the secretary of a TV executive who was a friend

84

of mine at a station in D.C., asking if I could speak with Ms. Robinson. Ms. Robinson, the TV exec, was a majestic, dark-brown lady with a deep, warm laugh that perfectly matched her cordial personality.

"I haven't heard from you in a coon's age," I said when she came on the line. "No pun intended."

She cracked up and I heard that wonderful laugh.

"What's up?"

She congratulated me on the Emmy I had won that spring. She hated to bother me and said that she would understand if I refused, but could I do her a favor.

To make a long story short, I ended up acting in a TV special being shot in Canada. There I was in the middle of an ice-cold lagoon after midnight, sitting on the behind of a swan-shaped boat that had sprung a bad leak, playing "Stardust" on a frozen saxophone, as the guardian angel for two affection-starved kids . . . show biz . . .

Incidentally, I just missed Mario, who flew into Toronto the day after I left, to play a depraved, child-abusing dope dealer.

The last couple of weeks in October and the first week of November were the most serene days of my adult life. Down on Wall Street, the ramifications of the Gramm-Rudman Act, a new tax law, was having a damaging effect on the municipal-bond business, including our fledgling company, but we were holding our own. Max, my younger son, had had a whiff of success and had suddenly decided to rejoin the human race from which he had slouched away in adolescent disdain (for disdain read fear of not measuring up) and started back to college. And my daughter, who a year earlier had been relocated to San Francisco by her company, was doing well, at work and socially (at least a man answered her phone in the middle of the night). All in all, the empty-nest syndrome suited me fine. Adding to my good fortunes, this widow lady, Isabel Taylor-Helton, whom I had hired as a consultant when I was fixing up my apartment, had metamorphosed into that rarest of creatures, a species I long ago assumed was extinct, a competent assistant who wasn't trying to either break into show business or marry me. Isabel turned out to be perfect; eager, meticulous, agreeably good-humored, and a little pompous (which added dignity to the various proceedings).

When I had returned from near death by freezing in Toronto, I had found the book contract and check waiting for me. I started to work immediately. My muse was on a roll. I sat at the keyboard hour after hour chuckling to myself over some brilliant observation I had just made. My cup was truly running over, as they say. I had even wangled a free AIDS test and the results had come back negative.

The only cloud on the horizon was Mario's script. In less than two weeks his option would expire at NBC and he would be trying to talk me into making the rounds of the studios with "our package." I pushed away the prospect of the smart-assed faces and endless meetings that that would mean. (Besides, Mario hadn't made the final draft deadline I had given him, had he? . . . So my hands were clean, at least technically.)

Back to the novel on the computer screen. All my writing career I had had to work under some frightful deadline, but this time it was going to be different. This time my muse and I were going to meander through the meadows and forests of my mind and get to know one another. Sort of a delayed honeymoon. Instead of being shackled to a galley oar, we would leisurely explore the universe. The novel was going to be called *Dirty Pictures* and was based on a group of Central Park joggers who find a dead body by the boathouse one morning; and intertwined would be essays on the machinations of the female sex.

Where was I? I scanned the computer screen.

. . . He was the guy who absconded with . . .

. . . I caught her giving . . .

"The phone's ringing." (Where the hell did that come from?)

"The phone's ringing. The phone . . . "

Finally I realized that it wasn't onscreen—it was my faithful colored assistant, Ms. Helton, yelling at me from two rooms away.

"You're the secretary," I shouted. (She hated being called

a secretary and I knew it, but I hated being interrupted.) "You've got a phone on your desk too—use it."

Pause.

"It's for you," Ms. Helton screamed.

"Who the fuck is it?"

"Long distance, collect."

"Mario?"

"Yes."

(Who else?) I snatched up my phone. "What's up, son, and what the hell is all that racket in the background?"

"It's traffic, Dad. I'm in a phone booth on the corner of Hollywood and La Brea." Mario hadn't sounded so excited since the time he got a minibike for Christmas. "Dad, you won't believe what happened." He must have finished the script.

"Try me." My mind raced for excuses. First, he's late. Second, I was really rolling on the novel. What could it be?

"They found a producer."

"What?!"

"You remember my option at NBC? Well they've found a producer and they've picked it up! We're going to start shooting the pilot immediately, and if NBC likes it, the show might go on as a midseason replacement. I know it's a long shot. . . . "

"Well, not as long a shot as it was yesterday. Congratulations."

"I know you're working on your new novel, but will you come out and meet with the producer and his guys and tell me what you think? I'll pay for the ticket."

"I'm on my way."

Over the years, without ever talking about it, Mario and I have fallen into a method for taking meetings and assessing situations. A sort of good-cop, bad-cop routine. Back when he was a kid and I would drag him to meetings with me.

I was in the extremely difficult position of an upstart Black guy trying to negotiate an ironclad fair shake in a notoriously sleazy game. As far as I'm concerned, "Trust me,

Mel" is only an invitation to drop your pants or pick up your dress. Sometimes perhaps I'm a wee bit curt, but as far as I'm concerned, manners are only condoms to isolate the disease during the fucking you are sure to get. Believing in someone is okay, I suppose, if you have some other recourse to justice which, needless to say, at the time I didn't. It was strictly money-talking, bullshit-walking, cash-and-carry deals with me. I secretly looked forward to the day that Mario would become a tough guy too and take some of the weight off me. But as he grew older, instead of his emulating me, my rough ways came to be an embarrassment to him.

One day, while he was in prep school, as we were leaving a meeting he chided me. "Dad, do you have to be so gruff?"

"What's the matter, your tuition not paid?" I said.

"No, sir, it's paid."

"Then shut the fuck up."

Mario stood his ground. "He seemed like a nice man, why did you have to holler at him?" Mario was a spunky kid from day one, gentle but spunky.

"Well, read this contract. Come on, study it." I shoved some papers under his nose and showed him where that "nice man" was trying to cheat us out of 12 percent.

Mario was tough as nails under his polite exterior and our goals were always the same, but whereas I snarled, he remained subdued in his approach. So in deference to his genteel temperament, our modus operandi evolved into the good-cop, bad-cop routine.

The nature-versus-nurture question fascinates me. Was Mario laid back because, no matter what, he was just that way, or was it because he could, with his looks, education, and a father reputed to bite a head off at the drop of a hat, afford to be? Which came first—the temperament or the opportunity?

There are a couple of major dilemmas in raising children in the upper-middle-class world, especially if you yourself have come up through the ranks. It's soothing to think if life has gone well for you that you are only getting what you deserve through your charisma, or that the Lord, the zodiac, destiny, or whatever has preordained your rise to the top. But if you believe, like me, that Lady Luck had a hand in your success—I keep feeling that it could have me getting tossed in the clink instead of my cousin—then you are faced with one of those dilemmas I was talking about.

First, if you believe chance played a part in your good luck, what do you do with your offspring? Toss them to the fickle finger of fate, or act as a quiet shield, a buffer without portfolio, against the slings and arrows of outrageous failure? And if you do choose door number two and act as a shield and supplier of synthetic luck, how do you manage not to end up with a self-assured, pompous asshole of a kid out of touch with the nitty-gritty realities, someone you wouldn't want to spend an evening with, let alone have for a friend. Well, nobody said it would be easy.

Moving on to major dilemma number two, what is the correct balance for instilling compassion for the underdog in your kids without saddling them with a crippling guilt for personal success, if they should be so fortunate?

Anyway, Mario could have saved himself my carfare. The producer Stephen Cannell turned out to be a great guy. Not only smart and energetic, but tall, dark, and handsome too. (This is not an idle observation. Unattractive producers often tend to be hostile to good looks and brains in the same body.)

CHIP

In a matter of weeks, Cannell had cleverly reworked and infused a new life into the the original NBC scripts, turning them into one pilot, and next thing we knew, we were shooting the damn pilot. Dad was stunned. Hey, I was stunned! TV? Me, the kid? Dad had flown out to meet Cannell, and the two had hit it off right away. But neither of us could have predicted that Cannell would wind up acting in *Iden-*

tity Crisis or that I would direct them both, my boss and my dad, in a scene I had written or that I'd be directed by Cannell in *Sonny Spoon,* which he wrote, or that I'd end up directing for him on *Spoon* and other TV shows, that Dad would in fact end up playing my dad on *Sonny Spoon,* and we would all be changing hats constantly. Cannell, like Dad, was secure enough to be not only the chief, but also the Indian. On the second day of shooting the pilot, I gave Pops a call back in New York. I had a five-minute break from the set and something told me to call the old man. Had I finished the second draft of *Identity Crisis* yet? Pop asked dryly.

"Yeah . . . er . . . well, almost," I stammered.

"Good," he said, "nothing like striking while the iron is hot."

"Listen, Dad," I said, wondering if I had missed something. Too late. He had already hung up in that abrupt way he does. Neither of us seems to have much grace when it comes to terminating a phone conversation.

"Mario, man, you're wanted on the set," my buddy Chris said. I had gotten him a job as my Man Friday on *Sonny Spoon.*

"Yeah, I'm flying in," I replied, running to the tailor shop where we were shooting a scene from the pilot. Something was disturbing me, I guess. There's a world of difference between writing a script just because you want to, as I had done with *Identity Crisis,* and cutting and reshaping and meeting other people's specifications and deadlines as I was now having to do on the second draft. Was that bugging me? Shouldn't be. I've written on deadlines for years. Was it the feeling of losing the script, my baby, and giving it up? No, that's what I wrote it for, right? Was it Dad's tone of voice? The pilot, that could be it. Did I really want to be on TV? Would it leave an indelible mark on my career like *Kojak* did to Telly Savalas? What about the movie? Bull, man, very few pilots ever get picked up, and even so, they have to air it first to decide if they even want to pick it up. That would give us ample time to do *Identity Crisis.* I felt better, having reassured myself that there would be no time conflict, no other dilemma. Suddenly an AD told me in hushed tones that the Big Boss was on the phone and wanted to speak to me. As real and down to earth as Cannell was, the whole set seemed to get quiet when the word passed that he wanted to speak to me. Ears would prick up waiting for news from up top.

"Hello, boss," I said, trying not to act like I was worried. Had I screwed up? Did my acting suck? Maybe I wasn't funny . . . probably the gay scene. Did I overplay the gay dude and NBC refused to let it pass? Shit, or the Puerto Rican—would Spanish people be insulted? Hey, why worry, I didn't ask to do this pilot in the first place.

"Hi, pal," Cannell said in his usual reassuring, friendly tone. "I've got good news and bad news."

Just then Stu Segal, the no-nonsense line producer for *Spoon*, walked by. I shifted uneasily as he signaled, letting me know we needed to get back to work. Typical. Stu doesn't care whom you're talking to, boss or not, we ain't going overtime.

"The good news," Cannell said, "is NBC is exercising its option, we got picked up. . . . " Pause.

"But it's only the third day of shooting," I said. "How can they tell if . . . "

"They like what they're seeing in the dailies," he interrupted. "We're on a roll! The bad news is—and I only say this because I've been this road before and I know how tough it's gonna be on all of us, especially the guy on the front line—*you* . . . they want more shows *now*. Hey, by the way, besides his other talents, your old man is an actor too, right?"

"Yeah, he's great . . . how come?"

"Just asking. Now, here's the game plan. We're not gonna break production, we'll just keep the cameras rolling. I thought I'd tell you so you could announce it to the troops. So, you ready, pal?"

"Of course," I said, "I just can't believe it, that's great, I mean damn, so fast, I can't believe it's real."

"Oh, you will . . . believe me, you will." He chuckled

knowingly, the exact way my lizard dad does when the old geezer thinks he knows something you don't.

Still a little dazed by it all, I made the announcement to the crew, who whooped and hollered. They were union, good ol' boys who had seen it all before, but this was an exceptionally fast pickup.

Little did I know that after endless weeks and months of sixteen-hour days back to back, these guys would become like family to me. Chris slapped me five, beaming, and said, "Shit, man, Square Head has a series, damn! That's great, bro. Hey, wait a minute, what about the movie?"

I walked over to Stu Segal. At the time I also had no idea that down the road I would start directing *Sonny Spoon*. Stu would turn out to be a hell of an ally and a graduate of the same "run and gun" shoot-it-yourself school of street film I was, but like I said, that was later. At present, he seemed to occasionally take a certain pleasure in bluntly delivering not so pleasant news. Now would turn out to be one of those times.

"Congratulations," he said, seeming to sense I had something on my mind.

"Stu," I said, trying to formulate the right words, "what exactly does this pick-up mean time-wise? When and how long will our first big break be, because I wrote this film, and . . . "

"Well," he said, interrupting in his happily borderline abrasive tone, "the first break is a little thing called 'hiatus.' "

I know what the damn thing is called, I thought to myself, get to the point, man.

"The reason I call it little," he went on, "is that with this schedule, it probably won't be longer than a nine-ten week break at max, but that is several months away. Until then, it's only weekends off or just Sundays if you do publicity on Saturday, which I'm sure you will. . . . " Then, leaning forward for effect, with a big grin, he said happily, "You, my friend, ain't going nowhere. Welcome to TV!"

Stu started away and then turned back. "Oh yeah, that

suggestion about your dad playing your dad on the show? Well, the Powers That Be love it. Do you think your dad would come out and be in the episode after this one?"

BLOCK

The day before New Year's, there I was hunched over the keyboard of my computer plugging away on the novel, happier than ever, when the phone rang.

It was Mario and another oily rag on the pile. "Hi, Dad," he said. "Who is one of the sweetest, smartest kids a parent ever had?"

"Why, you, dearest kid," I said. "What's up?" (Whenever Mario played around about being a model child, he had good news.)

"They loved the pilot."

"You've finished already?"

"No, but after three days of shooting, they liked what they saw so much that they have ordered six more episodes."

"My God, son, that's great. You're on your way."

"Yeah, by the way did you know Mom was in New York?"

"Maria? Oh really, that's nice."

"She doesn't have any plans for New Year's dinner."

"So."

"Well, Dad . . ."

" 'Well, Dad' my ass, maybe I got my own plans."

"Ah, c'mon, Dad, you can fix it. You could bring her along."

Pause.

"Jesus . . . c'mon, Dad, please."

I could hear my mother's voice saying some platitude about thou loving this or that. I could feel myself weakening, so I quickly laid down my nonnegotiable conditions. "No yogurt, UFO, or soybean discussions, none of that shit, is that understood?"

"Sure, Dad, she'll behave."

"Okay," I agreed, "you got a deal."

"Would you call and invite her yourself? That would really be nice."

"Anything else?" What the hell, why not? In for a penny, in for a pound. "All right. I'll call her."

"Am I still a lovely, wonderful son?"

"Don't push it, kid. . . ."

". . . A dear, darling boy?"

"Yeah, yeah."

"Good, 'cause Mr. Cannell and the head of casting told me to ask you if you would agree to be in an episode of *Sonny Spoon*."

"Doing what?"

"Playing my dad."

"You got a deal."

My date was a nice woman and even wrapped a belated present for Maria. I cooked dinner and the four of us—Max, the two ladies, and myself—had a happy, uneventful meal.

When I went to L.A. after New Year's to do my stint, they only had two more episodes to shoot and the production was in full swing. The show had been well received, with special accolades going to Mario in the title role of Sonny Spoon, and everything was coming up peaches and cream.

On the set (going to it and coming from it included) Mario was treated like a king, waited on hand and foot. But the amenities an actor receives are only half of the story. Especially in episodic TV, the pampered kings and queens work like dogs to keep abreast of the schedule. The hand-and-foot service is more necessity than benevolence. While the directors change each episode and the writers can stockpile stories, the star is chained to the juggernaut of each and every episode, learning lines, getting into character, and focusing on the story line, plenty for a platoon let alone one person. No time is left for spotting stray lint, or fetching your own lunch.

Mario was exhausted when I arrived. I could sense the circles lurking under his eyes, beneath his makeup, but never having had a serious brush with his own mortality, Mario didn't even know that he was tired and was his usual ebullient self.

"The boy is going to wear himself out," I told the producer. "He can't go on being in every scene. He doesn't even get time to piss."

"All the money is on him right now, that's for sure," Cannell agreed, "but we'll be able to establish a better pace by next season if we get renewed. You should be proud of him, he's coming through like a trouper, he's a hard worker, one of the nicest young men I've ever met."

Be that as it may, applause notwithstanding, I thought Mario was killing himself, and the first moment I was alone with him I told him so.

I remember it well, 2:07 on Saturday afternoon, we were on the pleasant little balcony of a pleasant little condo with a pleasant, smog-softened blue sky and the pastel high-rise panorama of Los Angeles as a backdrop.

"Son, I think you're killing yourself," I said.

"I'm okay," he said, "but I could use a rest."

"You never get a minute to yourself," I nagged.

Was this me, the original workaholic old nine-days-a week-twice-as-hard-on-Saturday-and-Sunday Mel? I couldn't believe what my lips were saying. Nothing like seeing your own kid struggling to bring out the mother in you.

"Well, I did get some time to myself at Christmas."

"Well, that's a relief. What did you do?" I leered. "Sleep, I hope."

"I finished the script, Dad."

I had noticed that he was hiding something behind his back but I hadn't focused on the fact.

"Here," Mario said, handing me his script. "Shooting stops on *Sonny Spoon* the eleventh of March and I'll be available."

My soul sank. The script! It wasn't as if I had forgotten it. It was just that it had been assigned to the never-never land of some distant future.

"And if the show gets renewed, when would you have to come back to L.A.?"

"Well, we don't know if we are even gonna get picked up. That's too much to count on right now . . . but if we do get picked up, we wouldn't have to be back until near the end of the summer."

Mario pulled over two canvas chairs and I sat down and started to read.

I was so absorbed in the revised script that I hadn't been aware of his scrutiny. However, as soon as I finished the last page, Mario pounced on me.

"Well, Dad, what do you think?"

For a moment there . . . on the pleasant balcony, with a pleasant Los Angeles panorama as backdrop and my pleasant son, I considered doing the project all over again.

Maybe I should explain here my arrogant theory on how to come to a conclusion.

First and foremost you must quick as a wink take your personal opinion (which always tries to poke its nose in too early, not to mention trying to stuff the ballot box) and set it aside, totally blanking it out. If you even take a tiny peek at your personal opinion before you have thought a situation through you lose your objectivity, difficult enough to maintain under the best of circumstances. The good news is that the rest is easy. You make two lists, a plus and a minus one, and assign the facts to one column or the other and then you add 'em up to see if you've got more pro or con. Often the totals are pretty close but never even. Usually when people complain about difficulty in coming to the right decision, what they really mean is they are having trouble reconciling their natural/intuitive/one-with-the-universe, aka preconceived choice, with the pro/con column. "Difficult decision" usually means that in the face of the facts, one is having trouble finding a nice, solid, reasonable, rational, and plausible excuse to do what one wants to do.

The whole exchange, with Mario asking, "What do you think?" and my answering him, happened in the twinkling of an eye, but it's more cumbersome in the telling than it was in the doing.

This is what I did:

Mentally, I made two lists. On the pro side I came up with:

(1)   The project had big commercial potential. The script had turned out to be terrific. Plus, small *a* under one, Mario, who would be perfect in the lead was becoming a big star and a box-office draw in his own right. Also, small *b* under one, there was me, return of a filmmaking legend and that would be good for selling a couple of tickets.

(2)   I would be making a film again, something I enjoy immensely and I would be getting the chance to pass along my craft to Mario before it was too late. By too late I didn't mean I was contemplating any near future demise. What I mean is, I just wanted to get my two cents in before he accepted as gospel the filmmaking procedures with which he was becoming surrounded. This sticking my two cents in, I later discovered, was not a moment too soon. Mario is a very fast learner. The problem with first-come-first-confiscated fast learning is that other perspectives are lost in the shuffle. The pragmatic "Does it work?" is the rule of the day, never "Is there another way?" Once a method is acquired . . . well, let's just say there seems to be a human tendency to buttress one's method as being the only rational way, with phrases like "common sense," and "Everybody does it this way."

On the con side, I came up with:

(1)   There was not enough time to woo the money out of a studio. Such courtships last months, even years.

(2)   I wasn't free. *Dirty Pictures*. I had taken on the novel and agreed to a delivery date, and a deal is a deal.

(3)   I didn't feel that Mario and I saw eye to eye on the movie. He thought he had a mystery and I saw it as a comedy.

Anyway, back to that blink-of-an-eye decision. My plus/minus calculations had come up 3 to 2 against trying to give it a go.

I told him I didn't think it was a go.

Well, actually, not so bluntly, not in so many words. Thinking I saw an easy way out, I took negative number three and threw it in his face.

"Look, son, I think the film would be great, but as a comedy-adventure caper sort of thing. As a murder mystery it's soggy—not to mention the title you've given it. 'To Die For' really sucks. It's totally misleading for this film, in fact . . ."

"You could be right, Dad," Mario cut in just as I was building up a good ranting and raving head of steam, "you're the director, you should do it as you see it."

Now this was hard to handle.

"Well," I said, swelling out my chest, taking a serious puff on my producer cigar, and refusing his genial surrender, "it's important that the writer and the director agree. What would we do about the title?"

Mario said he had tossed around some others and didn't really have an opinion. Well, ignoble as it may have been, the truth is, here I was, heels dug in, defending my refusal to participate, hoping that his other titles wouldn't work. Unfortunately for me, the very next one he proposed was perfect.

"How about *Identity Crisis?*"

"Great," I blurted. (I was glad to see there was a shred of decency and fair play left in me.) But that did leave me in a bind trying to reason why and why not to do it.

I explained my dilemma to Mario. He, of course, wanted me to agree on the spot, and started to marshal the arguments: "Your public needs you. . . ." "You may not realize it but you're an important figure, I need you. . . ." "I need you. . . ." In other words, whatever he thought it would take.

I said I wanted some time to delve more deeply into the remaining factors and assess their importance to me.

The following day was Super Bowl Sunday, and I had a date to watch the game in New York at Dave Picker's place. Mario drove me to the airport and only once lost the struggle with himself to give me thinking space.

"Dad, it would really be great if . . ." he started.

"I'll let you know soon, son, promise," I cut him off.

RICHARD

Mario's and Melvin's careers have an interesting counterpoint, culminating in *Identity Crisis*. Melvin, of course, was the original fast-talkin'-slippin'-and slidin' dude, the prototype of Chilly D. (is that short for Chili-Dog?). And there's an "in" joke about it in the movie. When the character of the designer's son and Chilly Dee are running from the bad guys in the company boardroom, a television is on—showing a much younger Melvin running for his life in *Sweetback*. Mario glances at the screen and throws away the line "I just love those Black movies." In *Identity Crisis*, of course, Melvin is no longer running from the cops—he *is* the cops.

He's always been an authority figure to Mario, who often calls him "sir" and always treats him with respect. But one time, on an episode of *Sonny Spoon*, Mario got to impersonate a tough blood-and-guts army general. Only Mario put a little twist on the intonations and chomped on a cigar butt so that insiders would recognize the takeoff of his old man.

Melvin had his rough edge, and it ain't pretty. He will put himself out for friends or family to the nth degree. But the minute he feels crossed, bullshitted, or fucked over, a steel door clanks down and then, beware! Once a film distributor tried to hold out a large sum of money he owed Melvin. Melvin reasoned with him by dangling him from a thirteenth-story window.

Another time I was watching Melvin direct *Champeeen*, one of his plays, and there were a couple of people onstage who were singers as well as actors and somewhat prima-donna-ish, and he wanted to have a scene in which someone is singing and someone else is carrying on a conversation and a fight starts while the song is being sung. So he told the woman to start singing and the other people to do their thing and start the action. The woman stopped and said, "I cannot sing with all this going on around me. And Melvin answered, "No, that's what I want them to do. That's what they are supposed to do. You just keep singing no matter what goes on around you." So they started again. That was the point of the scene. It was supposed to be a rowdy party. So she started singing again, and the people did their action, which included a guy getting mad, yelling at his girlfriend, and dragging her across the stage. The woman stopped and said, "Mr. Van Peebles, I simply cannot sing a song with all these distractions." And Melvin said—I remember his words very softly delivered—"I know that my directions may seem bizarre to you, but I can assure you that I know what the fuck I'm doing."

Mario, born into a gentler age, with some of the sand traps and swamps already cleared for him, sometimes cannot understand Melvin's tough attitude. Melvin, for his part, thinks Mario is somewhat sheltered. Though he has worked long and hard for his success, Mario has found that doors opened a lot more easily to him than to his father in his years as a pioneer.

"It's like in the early days of the West," Melvin once told me pointedly. "The sheriff has to go in with six-guns blazing so decent folks can come in and live. After they've built their schools and churches, the old lawman with his "peace-makers" make them nervous. They'd rather not see him around, but he did what was necessary to make it possible for them to be there.

I've worked on many projects with Melvin—and I've watched him work on everything from options trading on the floor of the Stock Exchange, to making film deals, to directing his own musicals, to building ornate archways in his home (one room inspired by the trim of an old jukebox). His method of working is a revelation, from which I have gained many valuable lessons.

Melvin has no tolerance for idle analysis. Most of us are trained in school to find flaws in artistic works without knowing how to correct them. Melvin will not put up with such abstract critiques. If you want to point out a problem in his work, be prepared to solve it better than he has, or you'll wish you never brought it up. He will instantly recognize and accept a real improvement without arguing or ego —but his motto is "Fix it or shut up." It's one of those useful things I've learned from Melvin; and it sure as hell saves a lot of time on a project.

Another basic lesson from the Maestro is the proper sequence of activity. "It's all timing," he says, "like in cooking. You don't fry the eggs before the bacon. Each element has to be ready when it's needed—and not before."

Once when I was involved in a movie project, I was telling Melvin about the wonderful cameraman I wanted to use, and a location I wanted, and an actor I thought I could get.

"You're picking out the curtains before you've dug the foundation for the house," he snapped. "First concentrate on the structure of your *deal*. That comes before anything else in making movies."

Melvin is usually thought of as a writer and director, but he is also very much a visual artist. One day Melvin called me up and said, "We have to make three commuters from scratch, and they have to look real, and they have to be lightweight and . . ."

"Melvin," I answered, "what are you getting me into this time?"

"Commuters," he said, "can you make commuters?"

I told him I knew nothing about computers. He took the cigar stub out of his mouth and started enunciating like a motherfucker into the telephone. Now I knew I was in serious shit.

"I said *commuters,* as in people who travel to work together in vehicles," he said. "We've got to build a couple. Look." Melvin laid it out. "I've got this friend in New Jersey who drives his car into New York every day, but they charge you an arm and a leg on the expressway if there's a single driver in the car. You're supposed to carry four riders in a car pool to get past the toll booth cheap. So I told him I could get him three dummy commuters—mannequins—that would be lifelike enough to get past the toll-takers. Now, since you're always bragging that you are also a sculptor, I think you ought to prove how good you are."

Next thing I knew, we'd converted Melvin's apartment into a temporary sculpture studio. Regular mannequins are too heavy and costly, so I went out and found Styrofoam parts—heads, hands, legs. We got into it. I changed the faces, modeled new noses and cheekbones on them, painted them, experimented with wigs and mustaches. Melvin got completely involved along with me, crossing the ladies' legs, arguing over how they should be dressed, raiding his own closet for ties, jackets, trousers.

It became a happily insane collaboration, during which the two Dr. Frankensteins—neither of whom would ever be caught dead commuting in a car pool—were creating an elderly advertising exec, a hard-boiled businessman, and a semi-attractive yuppie lady. They started to take on personalities. We argued over what they would or would not wear. Melvin even contributed his long-abused cigar stub to the businessman.

After several weeks, our commuters were finished. They sat silently by the window in Melvin's living room, changing moods and appearances with the shifting sunlight. He really hated the day when we shipped them off to the friend in New Jersey who had, after all, commissioned them.

When the friend received them, he decided they were too good to sit in his car as decoys to fool the toll-collector (besides, his attorney had advised him against it). Instead he gave them a place of honor in one of his rooms in his house as permanent art pieces. There they sit to this day.

Before they left for their new home in New Jersey, Melvin photographed me sitting next to them in the natural light of his living-room window. I liked that shot so much I used it as my Christmas card that year. Some of my friends said they had a hard time picking me out.

PACKAGING?

BLOCK

I had expected the flight back to New York for the Super Bowl game to be fraught with tension: what to do about *Identity Crisis*. Instead, when I boarded the plane that morning and settled in, I found myself feeling really peaceful. I was puzzled. "What the hell am I so happy about?" I asked me. Slowly the mist cleared. I stumbled out of the forest, and there, way up on the top of the hill, glistening emerald bright, was the Castle of Truth. I made my way up the golden path, crossed the drawbridge, knocked at the portal, entered, and discovered that what I had dreaded about the thought of doing a film was not the filmmaking process itself, with its chaos and endless hours of arduous work. It was the part about crawling from one studio door to another, wilted script in trembling hand, on my knees, begging for the money and endless meetings and patronizing lectures. Beyond that there was the pain of losing, to studio overhead, $300,000 of every million raised, plus giving some person the right to second-guess your every move—and on top of that, not own the copyright.

Eureka! It was all clear. In the back of my mind I had already figured out that since the time frame made studio funding impossible, I was free to do it my way. But Akerue! (eureka spelled backward) I would be short an insurmountable sum. Now that I realized it was only a question of money, I desperately wanted to do the film. I could feel the old adrenaline racing. We would make a terrific movie.

I almost called Mario as soon as I landed at Kennedy to give him the big news. Then reality set in. What big news? What was I going to say? "Okay, son, I'll do it . . . you got a deal. We'll make a movie." Implicit in that "I'll do it" was a commitment not only to direct, but to produce it too, on short notice to come up with the wherewithal to finance plus a topnotch technical team.

And, oh yes, how was I going to write the novel *Dirty Pictures* and produce and direct the film simultaneously? The questions swirled around in my head. How could I put together a team of feature-film caliber, scout locations (the script required a zillion), build sets, and hire actors in less than six months, let alone the two months we really had? And oh yeah, again, where, incidentally, would I get all that money?

On second thought, it seemed a good idea not to call Mario. Yet, on the other hand, I felt strangely lighthearted as I headed to the Super Bowl party.

Dave Picker, a large, six-foot-plus, open-faced man, was the most thoughtful of hosts. TVs had been set up in several rooms for game watching, and the guests were the movers and shakers of the entertainment industry.

Before I finished my first beer, the Washington Redskins were behind 10–0. The first time Elway, the Denver Broncos' quarterback, got his hands on the ball, he threw a touchdown to one of his rookies. Washington couldn't do diddly when their time came. The second time Denver got the ball, they marched down to field-goal range and kicked one in for 3 more points and the score stood 10–zip. Then, adding insult to injury, the Redskins almost fumbled the kickoff after the field goal.

I got up from the thirty-inch screen in the living room and moved to the twenty-four-inch screen in the library.

It didn't help. The Washington Redskins were getting the shit kicked out of them on that TV too. In fact, in the time it had taken me to negotiate the guests at the entrance to the library, Doug Williams, the colored guy, Washington's starting quarterback, had slipped and reinjured an old wound and had been pulled out of the game. The announcers were beginning to predict a rout.

I slumped down in my chair thinking about slings and

arrows and impossibilities. The game was a metaphor for the realities I was used to in life, the questions that always arise each time a Black breaks a barrier. Is he really doing it? Can they really read? Do you really think they are equal? Be serious. Impossible, a Black starting quarterback in the Super Bowl.

But then the Redskins backup quarterback couldn't get anything going and here comes ol' Black Doug Williams with his leg in a brace, humping back into the game. Even the staunchest Redskins fans looking at the insurmountable score knew that winning was impossible. There was Denver leading 10–zip at the end of the first quarter and there were the Redskins saddled with a crippled Negro quarterback. It seemed all over for Washington.

Contingency conversations were beginning. People were hoping the Redskins would at least not get blown out but would go down with dignity. And right there, in a turn-around that would make a Disney scriptwriter blush, the Redskins brought the Denver Broncos to a dead stop. Their crippled quarterback exploded on the offensive, scoring 35 points, and the Black guy with the brace on his wounded knee led his team to the biggest-scoring Super Bowl quarter in history, 35 points!!

Yeah, God damn it, count 'em—five touchdowns. At half time, Washington was 25 points ahead and the score was 35–10.

I hurried into the kitchen, where I had spotted a couple of dark faces preparing the food.

"Well," was all I had to say.

"Damn right," they grinned back. We gave each other five. I wandered back out to the dining room, smiling. A lawyer I knew joined me at the buffet. He and I had met at a party I attended with both my sons just before Mario had gone to L.A.

He congratulated me on my boys being such fine young men and told me he was sure my younger son, Max, was going to be a great success on Wall Street. Then he asked what Mario was doing. He had heard that his pilot was good and that the series had been picked up.

Suddenly, I heard myself blurt out that it had gone well and that during the hiatus, sometime around the end of spring, we were going to make a feature film.

"Congratulations," he said, raising his glass to me, "what studio will you be working for?"

"No studio."

"Who's doing it for you?"

"Nobody."

"What's that supposed . . ."

"Well, not exactly nobody . . . each other. We're going to do it ourselves," I said, placing the last oily rag on the pile.

"That's impossible. You can't put up your own money. The odds are too high against you."

"We're going to do it ourselves," I repeated. And I knew it was true.

"That's a major undertaking," he said.

What would have happened if I had talked to my lawyer friend before the end of the first half? Would I have been so bold as to dig me and Mario into a hole without the Redskin Black quarterback saving the day? Like everyone else, I like to boast and preen, but just like everybody else, I hate to eat my words (and I have long known that the higher the monkey climbs the pole, the more he shows his ass). Normally I prefer to reserve bragging for deeds done. Maybe I could retract my boast, or at least water it down to the conditional . . . *too late*. My lawyer friend had told two other friends heading toward the buffet.

"Melvin and his son are doing a feature."

A blur of smiling faces bore down and zoomed in on me with, "Congratulations!!"

Oh shit. A warning went off in my head—echoes from the past. I heard a ghetto-dipped voice admonishing, "Don't never go writing no check with your mouth, young 'un, that your ass can't cash."

"So, are you and Mario really going to do a movie?" one of the smiling faces said. "A real feature all by yourselves?"

"That's right," I replied, and I meant it too. My moment of weakness had come and gone, and I had swung back to your basic Jack Armstrong, lion-tamer, conqueror of Mount Everest mode. Hadn't I just seen a miracle on TV? Why couldn't another be just around the corner for Mario and me?

"That's right," I repeated, tossing a symbolic match on the metaphorical pile of oily rags. I grinned at the concerned expressions in the semicircle of friendly faces. As the oily rags burst into flames, I sauntered off to the nearest phone and called Mario, collect, to tell him it was a go. *Identity Crisis* was born, and the Redskins scored another in the second half and went on to win 42–10.

A few days later, I got a call from the secretary of my friendly Super Bowl lawyer to set up an appointment for us to meet.

Frankly, I was perplexed. Super Bowl buddy was one of the most respected and successful lawyers in the entertainment business who already had, as they say, "a bevy of talented showbiz luminaries" as clients, and was, besides, much too sterling a character to try to lure me away from my own lawyer.

The secretary showed me into his eclectically, expensively furnished office. He was a thin, almost emaciated man with a nervous tic and a photograph of his wife and kids prominently displayed on his desk. He was fiftyish and a dead ringer for what I suppose Jesus would have looked like if Jesus had shaved and avoided the crucifixion for a couple more decades.

He offered me a seat and began to talk. It turned out the meeting was about old-fashioned Norman Rockwell heartwarming altruism. He was worried about me. There it was, as simple as Mom's apple pie! The exception to the rule in the dog-eat-dog industry. Caring! He told me he hadn't been able to sleep since our half-time conversation. I said I was sorry to hear that. He said small independent films were a big risk.

"Who said anything about small?" I said, and elaborated that we intended to make your basic, garden-variety, middle-of-the-road-adventure-comedy film. "Big production value action, stereo, the whole shebang."

He whistled and said that he didn't know my financial state, but did I realize that it would take a lot of money? I allowed as how I knew that, but that I wasn't putting up all my own money, I had another investor. He said he was glad to hear that, and that it was fast work, and could he be so indiscreet as to ask who. I told him, "Mario," and he almost fainted.

"Your son!" he shouted, pointing to the picture of his kids. "How will you feel if you fail before your son?"

"Okay," I replied and added that I had never claimed to be infallible.

"I would never risk that," he said. There was a distinct chill in the room as we parted—the kind you probably might feel when you left someone who thought you were going to die of AIDS.

I knew he was feeling sorry for me and Mario and the risk we were taking. For my part, I felt sorry for him not being able to take that risk . . . on himself and his son.

Well, anyway, I told myself, at least he wasn't my lawyer.

But then a couple of evenings later, I was having dinner at Rosa's, a wonderful Mexican restaurant on Forty-eighth Street, with Marsha, my lawyer, and her husband, Larry. Marsh looks like an angel—big eyes, great grin—but beneath her deceptive exterior lies a mind like a computer and an iron will. We have been friends since our first deal.

I was feeling as rosy as the restaurant walls. I love dining with Marsh and Larry, who are a rarity among couples. They never try to involve you in their fights. In fact, down through the years, I had never seen them fight nor have I ever detected any hostility in them toward one another.

Larry raised his frozen double margarita and I raised mine. Marsha, who was only having a single, raised hers too.

"Happy birthday," Larry toasted me, although it was the end of January and I was born in August. But the evening was the occasion of my slightly delayed annual birthday party.

"What's new?" Larry asked.

It's an unspoken rule that we don't talk shop at social get-togethers for at least twenty seconds. So I took a couple of sips of my drink before I told them about *Identity Crisis.*

"That's risky business," said Larry, who is in the business too.

"I suppose so," I said.

Marsha groaned and glared. Short of an articulated professional opinion, that meant she was against it.

Larry chuckled and said, "Save your breath, honey."

We reviewed the various and sundry legal requirements over dinner, swordfish for both Marsha and Larry and marinated pork chops for me.

I discussed my intention with several more friends in the business, and of course, being friends, they all told me not to do it. So I hit upon the perfect solution. I stopped discussing my intentions with friends in the business.

MARSHA

The lawyer for the production entity of an independent theatrical feature film is involved at every level of the production starting with the acquisition of rights and formation of the production entity all the way through to registering the film for copyright with the U.S. Copyright Office and negotiating and reviewing the various distribution agreements. Being the lawyer for an independent feature film is a rare specialty.

The legal aspects of producing an independent theatrical feature film are difficult at best, but, as usual, Melvin was adding a new twist on that scenario. The financing for an independent theatrical feature film is usually an arduous and painstaking ordeal. The most common procedure is to "presell" various distribution rights to a film, e.g., domestic, theatrical, foreign theatrical and television, home video rights and the like. These fully executed distribution contracts are then taken to a bank which has experience handling these transactions. After rigorous review by the bank's attorneys and after a number of additional documents have been furnished, the bank "discounts the paper"—the full value of the monies payable in the distribution contracts to the production entity upon delivery of the film—and remits a loan to the production entity to produce the film. When a film is delivered, the relevant provisions of the various distribution contracts come into effect and the bank is repaid the amount of the loan plus agreed upon interest. Another method is to make a deal with a United States distributor at the onset. There are a number of variations on this theme. Not so for the Van Peebleses.

I first learned of the "film" from Melvin at a deceptively casual Friday night dinner at Rosa's—a wonderful midtown New York City Mexican restaurant which is a favorite among theatre professionals. While the guacamole and chips were being consumed, Melvin mentioned that he was currently in preproduction for the "film" and that principal photography was going to commence in a couple of weeks. The main course had not yet been served when I realized that I was already weeks behind in the legal work. My raised eyebrow and a very steely look did nothing to deter Melvin. He was ready for my reaction. He said, "No problem, babe." My response: "Who are you calling babe?" We proceeded from there. I ran down the kinds and types of signed documents Melvin would need before he switched on the cameras. He gave his special "no problem" shrug.

Melvin had decided to produce the picture without approaching distributors—domestic or foreign—or record companies or any other industry sources that are a customary component of the financing of independent theatrical feature films. Melvin felt this would ensure two things: (1) that they would get started almost immediately so that principal photography would be completed before Mario had to return to star in the *Sonny Spoon* television series; and (2) they would maintain creative control from start to finish of the film. Despite what you may have seen on television, this is not the way a theatrical feature film usually begins. Once

again, Melvin was doing it his way. He assured me his partner and son, Mario, was in total agreement. And also as
usual, Melvin was telling the truth.

Melvin and I met in 1976. Melvin was co-producing a Chicago revival of his musical *Don't Play Us Cheap* and I was
the "kid" lawyer in the office assigned to the project. I have
been Melvin's lawyer ever since. Mario and I met in 1981,
when he was a chorus boy in Melvin's urban musical *Waltz
of the Stork*. Even before I met Mario, I knew of him from
Melvin. Mario was leitmotif: Mario at Columbia, Mario as a
model, Mario in soap operas, in films, as a television series
star. Or just "My son Mario." On those rare occasions that
Mario was present at meetings with Melvin he was polite,
reserved, intelligent, pleasant, and somewhat removed.
Whatever area of the entertainment industry he was currently involved in, he seemed preoccupied with that area.
From time to time he would ask questions but did not encourage any in return. Can a handsome Columbia University economics major find happiness in show business? Yes.
Can he write, co-produce, and star in a film directed by his
father? Yes, and he has done just that.

There was a lot to do and not a lot of time. While Mario
polished the script, Melvin handled the negotiation of the
deals. He started with the unions and went on to cast members, crew, and other personnel, negotiating directly. In the
meantime, a New York corporation called Block & Chip,
Inc. was formed to produce the film. No one has ever had to
ask the derivation of this name.

BLOCK

Captain's Log 2/8/88
Anyway, it was time to stop screwing around, clear my
head, and come up with a battle plan. When I decided to
make *Sweetback* (what seemed like a couple of lifetimes
ago) and I was trying to pull my mind together, I drove out

to the Mojave Desert and abused myself, as they say. But the Mojave was on the other side of the continent; besides, it was the dead of winter in New York, and being a bit older, I decided against wasting any of my vital juices growing hair on my palms. Anyway, the next best thing I could find to do with my hands was play a few games of solitaire. Actually, I love solitaire. I know three varieties, two of which I rarely win. Not being in a masochistic (hair-shirt) mood, I played my preferred kind, the third, the one where you start with seven ascending piles. Seven-pile solitaire is my favorite, not because I win 40 to 50 percent of the time, but because to me it seemed to imitate life, i.e., the more options you manage to keep open, the more you increase your flexibility and the better you do.

My immediate options, money-raising-wise, seemed to be pretty few. So I decided my first move should be something dramatic. Therefore, killing two birds with one stone, I mortgaged an apartment, Dead Bird One: It committed me, or more accurately overcommitted me psychologically to carrying through the project. Just the expense and the pain in the ass of taking out a mortgage vetoed any second thoughts I might have about turning back. Dead Bird Two: It supplied a hefty chunk of start-up capital to get the ball rolling.

In the first of a series of lucky (and often crucial) breaks associated with the making of *Identity Crisis*, the apartment I was mortgaging was featured in *The New York Times* as an ideal home, raising substantially its value, which in turn increased the amount I was able to borrow on it.

While I was haggling with the banks for elbow room *cum* cash, I began the filmmaking process. Preproduction is generally considered one of the most crucial phases of the feature-film-making process. I personally feel the "packaging" stage (which I maintain it would be more accurate to call *pre*preproduction) is even more crucial. Where that ever nebulous beast "the essence" of the film begins to crystallize is equally as important as and a hundred times more elusive than any plain ol' preproduction.

Waxing sorta poetic, if filmmaking is a journey, then

"packaging," *pre*preproduction, is the choosing of the destination and figuring out the route part, and preproduction is the preparing for the trip part, and then the rest, the principal photography, the editing part, etc., is about getting there. By the time you reach the preproduction stage the road has been chosen. Of course, a great deal of work remains to still be done before the voyage has begun. Points must be set and a zillion technical creative ends must be finagled until they meet.

I had never made a feature on the East Coast and I didn't know where the bones were buried, but I had an ace up my sleeve, I knew someone who did—Jim Hinton.

Jim is without a doubt one of the best director of photography in the world. The D.P. is the fellow who has the ultimate responsibility for the pictorial quality. However, since he is Black his career has been very rocky despite his excellence. Jim was not only a D.P. but an all-around filmmaker in his own right, having produced and directed a large number of documentaries. He had worked for me on several occasions and we had been fast friends and sort of uncles to each other's kids since the first time I hired him almost twenty years ago. Crews usually marveled at how smoothly we functioned together (we seemed such an ill-suited pair). On the surface we appeared to be totally opposite. But our styles represented occupational deformities rather than any real underlying disparity.

JIM

I knew a lot of people who said they knew Melvin, but they all seemed reluctant to introduce me. The truth is they were just bragging, like people do. Most did not know him at all and the rest only barely. I met him when *Penthouse* magazine gave me a photographic assignment to shoot him when he had *Aint Supposed to Die a Natural Death* on Broadway.

I photographed him in his black leather trench coat under the marquee, beautiful shots. I still have them.

I did not make small talk with him at the time because it was an assignment. When I saw him next it was in the street. I approached him and said, "Hey, I want to have a conversation with you." He looked me in the eye and said, "What about?" I told him that I had done the photographs of him for *Penthouse,* that I was also a filmmaker, and that I wanted to do some work with him and would like to show him my work. He said, "Well, when can you come over?" I said, "At your convenience." He told me to come the next day. I brought films to show him and he said that he thought he might be doing some work soon. I said, "Fine," and went home.

Three weeks later, I got a long-distance phone call from him and he told me he was in Santa Fe, New Mexico, producing and directing a film and asked, "How long will it take you to get out here?" I told him it would take a week. Then he said they were using the Mitchell camera and asked me if I was familiar with it. I said that I was not familiar with it but that I would get checked out on it. I went down and joined up as second cameraman.

The first time that I met Melvin he impressed me as a tough, very intelligent man, an interesting combination of street and intellectual. I more or less consider myself to be the same.

I'm self-taught, cinematically speaking. I went to school at Howard University as a political science major. I discovered that I didn't belong in that department. I was hanging out in the Art Department all the time. Back when I went to Howard they didn't even have a darkroom on campus.

I learned filmmaking through the apprenticeship system. In my career I've done everything from hard news to features, every kind of filmmaking there is with the exception of pornography and surveillance.

I apprenticed with some Chicago filmmakers as an assistant, in '63, '64, and '65. It introduced me to the media. And then I moved to New York where I became successful as a still photographer. Then I got the opportunity to be a cameraman for a producer named Bill Anderson. My first real assignment was to film the antiwar Pentagon demonstrations.

The producer put together a sixty-minute piece and I discovered that even though there were twelve cameramen, I had shot more than 60 percent of the footage that was used. I discovered then that I was a cinemaphotographic natural. And I realized that I could become a successful filmmaker.

After that I did *Can This Be America,* a sixty-minute program on Black politics in Newark with Amiri Baraka, formerly known as Leroi Jones. I did an educational labor film, called *Movin' On Up,* for the A. Philip Randolph Institute, which was headed by former Secretary of Labor Ernest Green. I got a chance to be a cameraman and director of photography for Al Freeman, Jr., when he did *The Slaves.* Since I had a limited technical background at the time, I started but then replaced myself with someone else.

I've been in about twenty countries.

Don't Play Us Cheap, the movie I went down to New Mexico to work on with Melvin, was an interesting picture, especially because of some of the ladies who worked in it— Esther Rolle, Rhetta Hughes, and Mabel King. That film wound up being the catalyzing force for all those great actresses and that's one of Melvin's great accomplishments. He was the first one out the door as a directorial and producer activist in film circles. And I credit him with having opened Hollywood up to Black people. When he went to do *Watermelon Man,* he told studio heads he didn't see anybody that looked like him and they immediately took steps to change that. I credit him with that and also *Sweet Sweetback* has also had a tremendous impact. I did a feature film called *Ganga and Hess* as director of photography and won the Critics' Choice award at the Cannes Film Festival.

When my telephone stopped ringing . . . after I did *Ganga and Hess,* I became a producer in order to put myself to work. That's sorta Melvin's strategy too. If they won't hire you . . . you work for yourself.

Greased Lightning was written, cast, and partially directed by Melvin. And it was on track to be an excellent film, but the producer, Hanna Weinstein, got into a creative struggle with Melvin, and since one of her daughters was a vice president at Warners, whose film it was, she was able to ultimately remove him from the production. But his stamp on the production is indelible because, as I said before, he wrote. It was also Richard Pryor's first starring role. Melvin picked him, and I sanctioned it. That was Pam Grier's first dramatic, non-sexual role, a big breathrough for her, and a breakthrough for Richard.

Hanna Weinstein was a strong personality and so was Melvin. Hanna was elderly, and she tended to be maternalistic. Melvin would absolutely not permit or pander to maternalism or paternalism. I was caught in the middle and it was difficult. I tried to heal the wounds, but I didn't succeed. I didn't have the power, and Pryor was being very laid-back. He knew that this was his big chance and didn't want to be perceived as making waves. True, it was his big shot, his first role as a lead and a star, but it was Melvin who gave it to him, and I know personally he had to fight to get Richard the role. I don't know if they are friends today. I've never heard Melvin mention Richard since that production, and I've never heard of Richard inviting Melvin to direct any pictures for him, but I do know for a fact that it was Melvin who got him his shot. And I was privileged to sanction it. Hanna Weinstein and Warner Bros. were very concerned with whether Richard could deliver. And they asked us both separately whether we thought he could deliver and wouldn't be a problem for the production. So I credit Melvin with getting him his shot . . . his major shot.

My first allegiance was to Melvin, and I would have quit the film when he left, but he ordered me to stay on the production, to look after and ensure the job security of the ethnic and racial minorities and women we had hired. So that's what I did.

I did the day-to-day of the producer. The only thing I did

not do was make the deals for the principal actors. As associate producer everything else, I dealt with the unions, etc.

Greased Lightning gave me credibility. It let me know my skills were equal to the skills of the Hollywood people.

My boys spent the summer in Athens, Georgia, when we were doing the production. They were very young, eight and five at the time, and called Melvin "Uncle Melvin," which they still do today. He's watched them grow up.

Over the years, I've watched his two oldest, Mario and Megan, grow up. In fact, Megan worked for me that summer in Georgia. I am very proud of Mario because he has assimilated very rapidly what Melvin had to offer and teach. He has incorporated Melvin's mountain of experience into his own persona. And in addition to that, Mario is very, very intelligent, like his father. He assimilates knowledge, facts, and details rapidly. The name of the Van Peebles production company, Block & Chip, is appropriate because I see so much of Melvin in Mario. Mario was raised mostly by his mother until he was fourteen. But Melvin felt Mario wasn't applying himself the way he should. So he brought him to New York and got him on the case and made him buckle down and do what he was supposed to do and helped him through his delicate teenage years into manhood, as a father should do. I feel that Mario is a man's man, rather than a ladies' man because he had the strong hand of his father at that critical time.

BLOCK

Jim's manner was precise, almost ponderous. He was the quintessential director of photography who had had to read too many light meters, I suppose. I, on the other hand, having had to make too many writing deadlines, was Mr. Catch-as-Catch-Can. Notwithstanding our superficial differences in style, since I was meticulous and Jim was flexible, we overlapped in the middle of the stick and always got along just fine.

It turned out Jim aspired to be "more" than just a director of photography, so I made him a co-producer, a title he shared with Mario. It was a marriage of pure genius, if I do say so myself. Plus, Jim loved to explain and Mario wanted to learn.

Jim understood filmmaking from beginning to end and could rapidly fathom the assessment of priorities that dictated the choices I made. Whereas, on the surface, on the first layer, Mario and I seemed to be in sync, I knew that underneath, in the second layer, he seethed with impatience to do things his way. This always tickled me because I knew that even deeper down, in a third layer, my way, was his way, *or would be*, give or take a quirk or two, as soon as he understood and mastered all the elements that went into each decision I made. Mario knew a lot, but there was a lot he didn't know; unfortunately, he had no clue as to which was which, and in the best of times having to cope with the demure arrogance of the unaware can be a pain in the ass. Plus, I figured, on the other side notwithstanding, blood being thicker than water, etc., even Mario's love and admiration might wear a bit thin with sixteen-hour days and my making what would seem like arbitrary decisions wearing on him. By making Jim and Mario a team I felt I had defused a potentially volatile situation. Yes, a stroke of pure genius, if you ask me.

Along with his future Boswell duties, we were still in *pre*-preproduction, mind you. I assigned Jim the task of scouting out the technical components of the movie: the labs, the equipment, the office personnel, and the crew for my approval. Then, when Mario arrived after his TV series stopped shooting, I would assign him parallel duties on the creative side: rounding up the cast and developing the film's look.

We—the tiny *pre*preproduction troika of Jim Hinton, Preston Holmes (our production manager), and yours truly— were sitting around one evening toward the end of phase one feeling rather satisfied with ourselves because up until then everything had gone smoothly, all things considered, of course. All things considered meaning a few minor glitches that I don't remember and a couple of major ones that I do. First, the time we lost checking out some newfangled video equipment that was going-to-revolutionize-the-industry. It didn't.

Second, our discovery that we were a little short on days. As a rule of thumb you like to allocate one day of preproduction for each day of principal photography (the actual shooting of the movie). We had planned to shoot the movie in eight five-day weeks, a brisk but reasonable schedule. In the normal course of events, we would have allocated another eight weeks to prepare for the filming, sixteen weeks in all. Unfortunately, no specific date for the recommencement of the shooting of *Sonny Spoon* had been given, and Mario's hiatus from filming his series could be as short as fifteen weeks. That obviously would leave us a week short for the preproduction and shooting of *Identity Crisis* (not even counting throwing in a contingency week to be on the safe side).

I decided to cut the preproduction time by two weeks. Six weeks prep, eight weeks shoot, with an extra contingency week thrown in just in case, fifteen weeks in all, right on the money. It was going to be a tight squeeze to get everything ready, but we had juggled and finagled the pieces until they fit, finally. That's what we were sitting around feeling so pleased with ourselves about.

Then disaster struck via the telephone.

It was Mario, so Isabel, who was taking notes at our little party, passed the phone to me.

It seemed the series was going so well that NBC had decided to shorten his hiatus and get a jump on the fall competition and call them back even sooner than originally planned.

My jaw must have fallen, because after we finished talking and I raised my head, there was a circle of worried faces staring at me.

"What's up?" Jim said.

"We just lost another month," I explained. "Mario's got to be back earlier."

Stunned, pregnant pause.

"What's that mean?" Isabel asked innocently.

Preston fiddled with the spreadsheet in his P.C. "It means we're in trouble."

"What are you gonna do?" Jim said, his voice full of worry. "We're already short on time. We've cut down the days all we can already."

"I'm gonna do just what Scarlett O'Hara said," I replied.

"You mean Scarlett O'Hara, like in *Gone With the Wind*?" Isabel said, all puzzled.

"Yep, I'll think about it tomorrow. See ya." And on that note, we called it a day.

I know there are things like the *I Ching,* astrology, numerology, etc. I'm not a practitioner, but still sometimes all that hocus-pocus does seem feasible, in the light of various events, if you know what I mean.

There I was, sitting on the side of the bed, pondering, pondering, going over and over the shooting schedule in my head . . . eight five-day weeks, forty days . . . forty days . . . thirty-six days of actual shooting and four days of travel . . . eight five-day weeks, forty days, eight weeks of shooting . . . eight weeks . . .

Over and over . . . eleven days on locations up in Rhode Island, thirteen down in Baltimore, and then twelve back in New York City for atmosphere . . . thirty-six days of shooting, plus four for travel, forty days . . . forty days equals eight weeks. Although the entire film supposedly took place in Manhattan, the noise, multitudes, and congestion often made shooting in the Big Apple unfeasible. So a common industry ploy is to film all but the most identifiable locations in calmer towns.

What's all this got to do with the *I Ching*, Ouija boards, and seances? you might ask. Well, that's what I'm coming to.

I lay down, but I couldn't sleep, so I turned to my old

standby, the TV, but I misdialed the remote and I got the news report instead of my usual raunchy channel. A reporter was saying the Williamsburg Bridge had just been found to be structurally unsound and would be closed indefinitely. BONG! FLASH! (traditional). LEAPIN' LIZARDS! (comic strip). FAR OUT! (passé). NEAT! (preppie). YO! (urban ethnic). Something went off in my head, *an idea,* I had an idea. The bad news was I couldn't quite come up with what the idea was. The good news was that I was trying so hard to coax it out that I made myself drowsy and fell asleep.

By the next morning, my brainstorm had sorted itself out.

When we were assembled around the library table, Preston with his coffee and P.C., Jim with his coffee, worried look, and four extra sugars, and Isabel with her extra-light and notebook. I rose majestically to my feet, hooked my left thumb into my left suspender, and informed them that I had gone over the schedule carefully and that I was pleased to announce that I had managed to cut another five weeks from the timetable.

"How are you going to do that?"

"Two weeks' less preproduction and two weeks' less principal photography."

"Two weeks' less preproduction," Preston moaned, "means we'd only have four weeks, we'll never be ready and . . ." Preston moaned.

"Two weeks' less photography! That's impossible," Jim said, throwing in his two cents. "Six weeks' shooting—we'll never make it. Six times five is thirty days . . . and don't forget you have to subtract four of those for travel, that only leaves twenty-six days. That's not enough time . . . no way!"

"Gentlemen, gentlemen, please, hear me out," I said. (I still can't remember what role in what movie I borrowed that from.) "Look, Preston, I know four weeks' preproduction is gonna be a bit sticky but we'll get done what we can and if we don't get it finished, we'll just have to do the rest as we go along."

"Maybe Preston can pull it together," Jim grumbled, "but

there is no way we're gonna shoot this film in twenty-six days unless you cut out at least a third of the script."

"We're going to have the same amount of days for principal photography as before. We're not going to change a thing shootingwise."

"C'mon, cut the shit, Melvin, what's the magic?"

"You should listen to the news. The Williamsburg Bridge is falling down. *Silence*. Don't you get it?" I knew they didn't, I knew I was being obtuse, but it was my big moment and I couldn't help milking it.

"No! Shit no, man, I don't get it," Jim grumbled. "Six weeks ain't eight weeks. Five times eight is forty minus four traveling days is thirty-six and six times five is thirty minus four traveling days is . . ."

". . . We're not going to do any traveling," I interrupted. "With the Williamsburg Bridge closed, the Lower East Side of Manhattan will almost be a ghost town, at least as manageable as Rhode Island or Baltimore. We're going to stay right here. That will save us the four traveling days. Next we'll shoot six-day weeks instead of five-day weeks . . . six times six is thirty-six, so we're back to our thirty-six days' principal photography."

"Six-day weeks! That's gonna cost a lot of overtime," Preston observed.

"Yeah, not to mention the crew will be more tired than shit," Jim warned.

"We'll make some of that back in what the moves would have cost us in transportation and per diem."

"Oh God. Boy, you sure come up with some shit," Jim chuckled, "always some shit. I suppose it could work though."

Isabel, the neophyte whose pretty head had been swiveling back and forth among the three of us experts, said, "That makes four."

"Four what?"

"Four weeks. You said you had found a way of saving a fifth week."

"Oh, the other week . . . er . . . that other week was the

contingency week we were saving in case something went wrong," I explained.

"Yeh, so how about the contingency in case we get delayed and can't make it up?"

"How about the contingency?"

"Well . . . er . . . uh . . . there isn't one."

Jim rolled his eyes to heaven. I don't think he meant it as giving his blessing to my plan, *but I preferred to take it that way*. So we charged full speed ahead into preproduction.

DESERT DAYS—MARIO'S GRADUATION TRIP

Me and my old Suzuki.

Mario and the Mojave.

Edwin Griffin (maiden name), my mom, on her first trip North, visiting New York at age sixteen.

Me as a lieutenant, navigator, Air Force, 1954.

Me as a painter/dad, Maria *(on canvas)*, Mario *(on pillow)*, Mexico City.

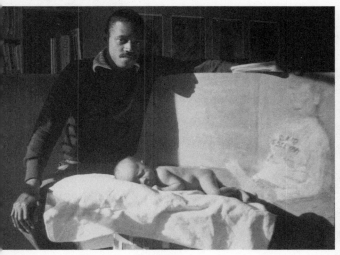

Mario, Megan, and a palace guard, Copenhagen, Denmark.

Mario, Megan, and "The Leaning Tower of Pisa," Italy.

Me as a French journalist. Paris, 1964.

Middle of the Atlantic Ocean. Me, Megan, Maria, and Mario, bound for Europe.

Me reincarnated as a French delegate to the San Francisco Film Festival
(reunited with Mario and Megan on the steps of the Mark Hopkins Hotel),
1967.

he cover of my fourth novel (never
ranslated into English), published in
rance, 1966.

Mario's rendition *(clockwise)*, of himself,
Megan, Max, and me, during the shooting of
Watermelon Man. Los Angeles, 1969.

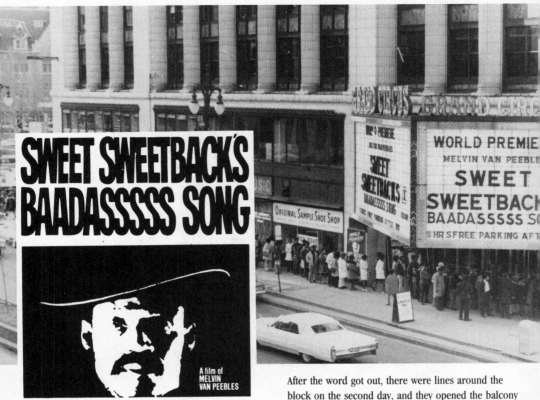

SWEET SWEETBACK'S BAADASSSSS SONG

A film of
MELVIN
VAN PEEBLES

**YOU BLED MY MOMMA
YOU BLED MY POPPA
BUT YOU <u>WONT</u> BLEED ME**

MELVIN VAN PEEBLES and JERRY GROSS present SWEET SWEETBACK'S BAADASSSSS SONG
a CINEMATION INDUSTRIES Release · COLOR

RATED
BY AN
ALL WHITE JURY

After the word got out, there were lines around the block on the second day, and they opened the balcony for the first time in fifteen years, April 1, 1971. Detroit, Michigan.

A typical up-in-your-face ad I designed for the movie.

The finale of *Aint Supposed to Die a Natural Death,* my first Broadway musical. It received nine Tony nominations and was voted one of the Ten Best Plays of the 1971–72 season.

Megan joins Mario in a modeling career.

Mario as Deadwood Dick, his first starring role, off-off-off-Broadway. New York, 1979.

Mario, my dad, and me, the day Dad finally moved to the Big Apple. He was very proud of us all and a trouper to the end. New York, 1979.

Waltz of the Stork, a small musical, Broadway, 1982. (Grace Jones did her version of "The Apple Stretching," one of the tunes I had written for the show, and it got hot in Europe for a couple of minutes.)

THE BOOK THAT TAKES THE MYSTERY & CONFUSION OUT OF WALL STREET'S HOTTEST TRADING GAME

MELVIN VAN PEEBLES

BOLD MONEY

A NEW WAY TO PLAY THE OPTIONS MARKET
Includes the Latest Options Indexes

The dust jacket of my hardcover book on the art of options trading, the culmination of my Wall Street tenure.

My friend Richard and commuter dummies (Richard is the one on the far left). Midtown Manhattan.

My sister's second wedding. Mario, my sister Sylvia, Megan, my niece Kristen, and my younger son, Max. Altadena, California, 1986.

Chris, Mario's sidekick and body-building and acting buddy.

Isabel, pompous, opinionated, meticulous, beautiful, and, at long last, an assistant who wasn't trying to marry me or become a movie star.

Tobie, Mario's manager, who believed in him long before it was fashionable, keeping in psychological shape by riding the merry-go-round in Central Park, Manhattan.

Marsha, my crackerjack lawyer, confidante, booster, friend, and futile voice of reason.

SONNY SPOON

Mario directing an episode.

Me playing his Dad in an episode.

EXCERPTS FROM THE "NORMAL" STRIPBOARD OF *IDENTITY CRISIS*

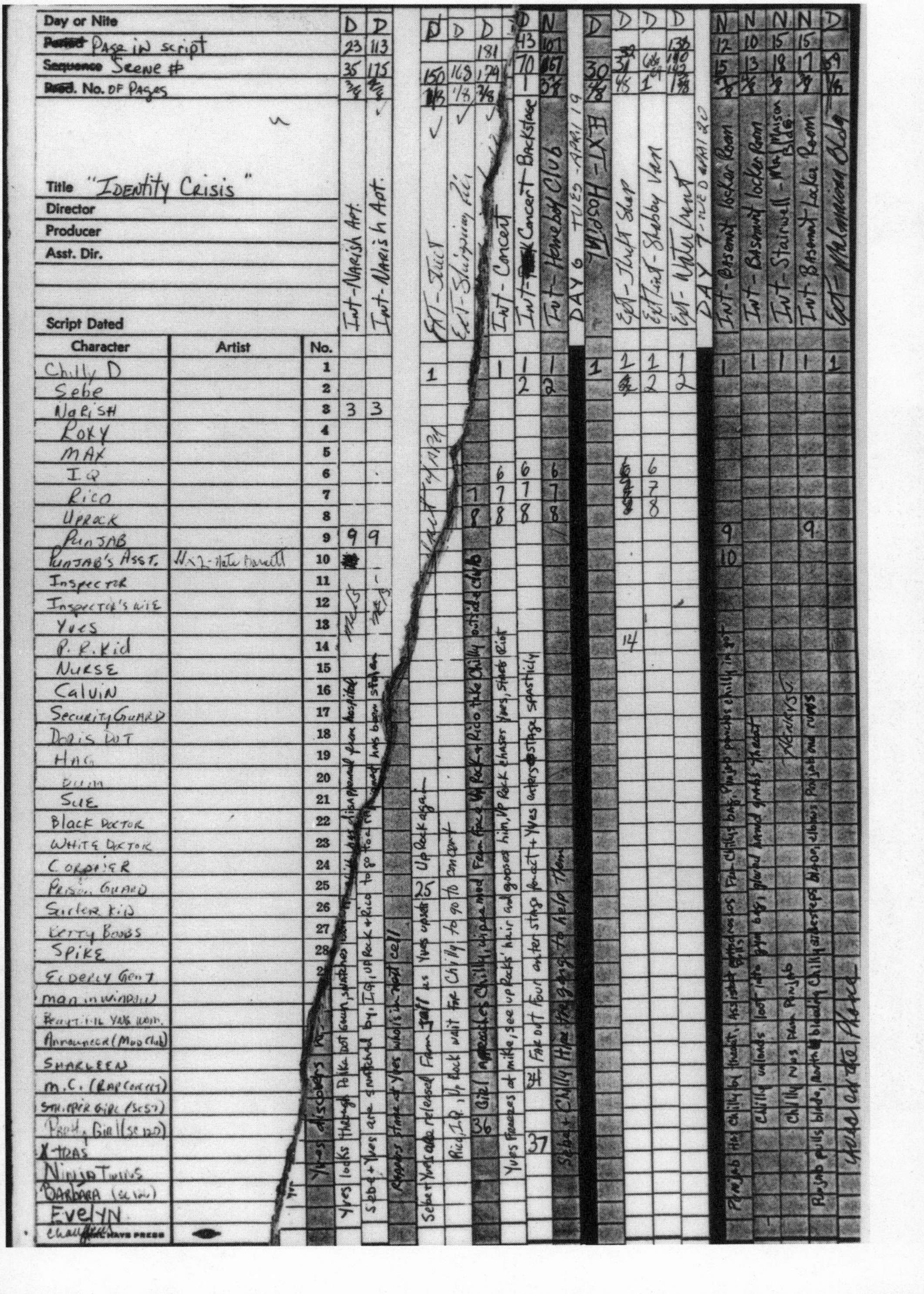

Day or Nite			D	D		D	D	D	N		D	D	D	D		N	N	N	D
Page in script			23	113			181	43	107			39	138			12	10	15	15
Sequence Scene #			35	175		150	168	124	70	167		30	37	68	110		15	13	18	1	9
No. of Pages			⅜	⅛		⅔	⅛	⅜		⅜		⅜	⅜	1	1⅜		⅜	⅜	⅜	⅜	⅛
Title "Identity Crisis"																			
Director																			
Producer																			
Asst. Dir.			Int – Narish Apt.	Int – Narish Apt.		Ext – Jail	Ext – Shipping Pier	Int – Concert	Int – Rock Concert Backstage	Int – Howard Club	DAY 6 TUES – APRIL 19	Int Hospital – IX	Ext – Thrift Shop	Ext Int – Shabby Van	Ext – Natural Agent	DAY 7 – WED APR 20	Int – Basement locker room	Int – Basement locker room	Int – Stairwell – Kin Maison BLDG	Int – Basement locker room	Ext – International club

Script Dated

Character	Artist	No.																		
Chilly D		1				1		1	1	1		1	2	1	1		1	1	1	1
Sebe		2						2	2			½2	2	2						
Narish		3	3	3																
Roxy		4																		
Max		5																		
I.Q.		6						6	6	6		6	6							
Rico		7						7	7	7		7	7							
Uprok		8						8	8	8		8	8							
Punjab		9	9	9													9		9	
Punjab's Asst.	#1,2 – Nate Harrell	10															10			
Inspector		11																		
Inspector's Wife		12																		
Yves		13																		
P.R. Kid		14												14						
Nurse		15																		
Calvin		16																		
Security Guard		17																		
Doris Lut		18																		
Hag		19																		
Bum		20																		
Sue		21																		
Black Doctor		22																		
White Doctor		23																		
Cordier		24																		
Prison Guard		25					25													
Surfer Kid		26																		
Kitty Boobs		27																		
Spike		28																		
Elderly Gent		29																		
Man in window																				
Beautiful Young Woman																				
Announcer (Mod Club)																				
Sharleen																				
M.C. (Rap Contest)																				
Stripper Girl (SC57)																				
Prod. Girl (SC 120)																				
X-tras																				
Ninja Turtles																				
Barbara (SC 120)																				
Evelyn																				

Me and Jim, my alter-ego-without-portfolio and a great director of photography, on the set of *Identity Crisis.*

Mario and Steve enjoying each other's company.

Bernard the costume designer with Coco Mitchell (Bernard is being charming and probably up to no good), circa Scene 14.

Mario, a.k.a. Chilly D., in jeopardy, circa Scene 17.

Victor, my co-editor, in a rare relaxed mood. We grew to be warm friends as we slaved to finish the film.

Bright and energetic Judy, wide-eyed and bushy-tailed as usual.

Tommy, dependable, willing, and pretty close to being a son, kidding around in an extra's costume.

Rappers in full regalia *(left to right)* Tab Thacker, Rick Aviles, Bruce Smolanoff, Ilan Mitchell-Smith, and Mario.

SOME WARDROBE POLAROIDS

Spike, Delores Garcia.

Doris Dot, Jeff Griglak.

Richard Fancy and Ilan, father and son.

Evil Uncle Max, Richard Clarke.

Archvillain Narish, Nicholas Kepros.

Nate, in a one-of-a-kind outfit.

Foul play afoot. Max, Narish, Yves, and
(back to the camera) Sebe.

Rappers doing their thing, Scene 71.

Roxy (Shelly Burch) with motorcycle and
locket.

Sebe with Roxy trying
on welder helmet,
circa Scene 65.

FATHER AND SON WORKING TOGETHER

Mario pretending to agree with an angle I have chosen.

Me pretending to agree with
Mario's suggestion.

Toiling in complete unanimity, blissful,
never-ending harmony—sorta.

Through it all, buddies, partners, and pals.

SOME CAMEOS

CRASH! Hope W. Sacharoff and Dick Ashe, Scene 45.

Larry "Bud" Melman, Scene 62.

Mario, me, August Darnell
(Kid Creole),
circa Scene 32.

Dianne Brill, Scene 107.

Olivia Brown and
Mario, Scene 120.

The barge sinking (next-to-last hurdle), Scene 189.

Nate's one-of-a-kind outfit, Scene 185.

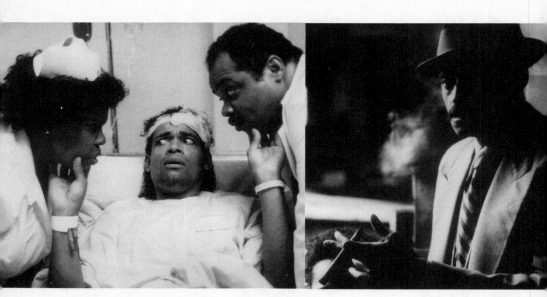

Chilly D./Yves a.k.a. Chip, son.

The Inspector a.k.a. Block, dad.

BOOK
TWO

PREPRODUCTION

ISABEL

A friend of Melvin's called from the West Coast. She didn't know me, but MVP wasn't in, so we started to chit-chat.

"What's Melvin up to? Doing a movie? Yes, that's Melvin. You're his assistant? Your first movie (she broke up laughing) and with Melvin Van Peebles?"

I said something about initiation. She said that it's called "baptism of fire." And so it was, though I didn't know it then.

The truth was that I had only been recently elevated to personal assistant, and in retrospect, it had been a peaceful time compared with what was to come. There was as much tranquillity as one might expect working around a person as dynamic as Melvin Van Peebles. With book deals here, Wall Street deals there, and various creative projects in between, the office always buzzed with excitement. When the talk of making a movie started, I was prepared to assist in any way that would be useful, not sure what that assistance might entail or if the movie would ever really come to fruition.

I read the screenplay. It was very funny.

February 18, *The New York Times* had devoted an entire article to MVP's redecorated apartment. Included were my photo and credits as interior design consultant. Still high on the article, I failed to notice that I was putting in longer hours with Melvin and additional days.

By mid-March, the two days a week I had contracted for had grown to five, and the normal eight hours had bulged to a from-dawn-to-dusk ten or twelve.

March 14. Was typical of the minimeetings, not unlike your usual male get-togethers. Jim Hinton had called in some of the men, all of whom seemed to be having an enormous amount of fun, talking junk and the technical aspects of movie making.

March 20. I heard the date April 13 repeatedly. They would begin shooting on that date. I thought I had misunderstood because this sure didn't look like the movies to me. I got a bit anxious—sure that I should know or do something brilliant in the event this project materialized. Melvin assured me there would be a lot to do—but others who were trained and experienced would handle that work. No, they would not be working here in the office—that's the last thing in the world you'd ever want to witness. I felt slighted. All of this fun would be somewhere else.

Though I had a zillion questions, the case was closed as far as MVP was concerned. Though I rarely attended the old-buddy meetings that grew both in frequency and in attendance, I overheard snatches of foreign jargon spoken by those present. I became more nervous and upset daily, being there, expected to perform—but from where? However, Jim Hinton one sunny afternoon took time to break down the very rudimentary procedures of movie making to me. He instructed me to take a sheet of paper. "Write at the top, Preproduction." Jim has a way of emphasizing words, and in this case PRE was all-important. He leaned forward, dipped his head, an action that allows him to look square at you over his eyeglasses. "The Preproduction Procedures (I added that) read as follows":

(1) Legal: Corporate papers and deal.

(2) Banking: Open account—make deposit—get checks.

(3) Insurance: Liability for persons and equipment, also employee disability.

(4) SAG and other union certification and security bonds (leave space under this, you may have to add to it).

(5) Trade Accounts: Credit-application letter, security bonds, etc., Camera Services Center film lab, Kodak film purchases.

As director of photography, he listed only equipment for that job—there would be a list for each. Payroll Service—Bon Bon. I was disappointed. I thought I'd at least get to pay the people. "I don't see much for me to do," I moaned. You can moan or complain to Jim. He'll take the time to see you through it. He quietly assured me that I'd see so much that I needn't worry about payrolls, etc., which could be very complicated.

I didn't ask about jargon this time and even now cannot fathom why my head was splitting from this tiny tidbit of information. I'll never learn all of this stuff. In parting, he said, "Make ten copies of all legal papers." At our next meeting, Jim explained the next two stages:

Production: This stage rambled on. I had lots of notes for it as well as for the postproduction stage.

I could hardly wait for an occasion to lay all of this newly acquired knowledge on my boss. In my enthusiasm, I may have sounded a little (maybe even very) pompous as I rattled it off. "Whoa, don't try to know what you don't know," he said. "Stay away from the technical stuff, all you need to be concerned with for now are . . ." and without even taking a breath to pause, he rattled off filmmaking:

(1) The development stage, which includes the search for talent (technical as well as creative), acquisitions, scouting for territories, plus the molding of the script to capitalize on preliminary observations.

(2) Preproduction, when the cooperation of authorities is sought and locations signed up. The script is revised to final form, and commitments with performers, crew, equipment, processing labs, and transportation are concluded.

(3) Principal photography (production), the actual filming of the picture with its army of cast and crew, is the most publicized, glamorous, and expensive process in the production chain.

(4) Postproduction includes editing, scoring, dubbing, sound effects, opticals, and titles.

MVP then explained that the dollar amounts and days allocated changed with every project but these basics never changed.

I looked up from my note taking to thank/admire him, but he was halfway to the elevator.

TOMMY

I was in college when GLUM, a.k.a. Good-Looking-Uncle-Mel, a.k.a. Mr. Melvin Van Peebles called me one day and said, "Son, I think I may have something that might interest you." He was talking about my playing a part in his latest endeavor . . . the making of his film *Identity Crisis*.

I was still in school, but I wanted it so badly that something, maybe only my inflated zeal, somehow allowed me to convince all my professors to let me work on the film in New York while I finished my last semester of school in Boston.

I closed up shop, so to speak, moved out of my apartment (my home for the previous four years) and was in New York working on the film inside of one week. As things worked out, I made it back to Boston just in time for my graduation, sometime after the final day of shooting on the film.

I had taken a handful of film classes in school and had worked on one film, a short, before *Identity Crisis*, but having worked with Melvin in other fields all my life I thought I knew what to expect: hard work and gratifying rewards. At times I wasn't sure, but in the end it was what came to pass.

When I arrived at his door that first day I'm not sure what I expected, but what I got was an office bustling with people and a job with never-ending things to do. Melvin knew that each person had his place, but that each person had to fight his way up the ladder to earn his right to his position. I got there and started work as production assistant, or P.A., who in real life would have to be described as that SOB whom anyone else on the set could tell to do anything, the job should have been finished before it was requested or sooner, and the only response could be some version of, Yessuh.

In the beginning I had thought that film life would be glamorous. Those first two weeks of being little more than a messenger helped me to learn the proper respect that I owed those above me on the production ladder. In between runs from one end of Manhattan to the other, I was part of the office staff and did everything from typing to filing résumés and fielding the few zealous actors who got past the doorman downstairs.

As the days went by, I was even able to eavesdrop in on a few of the conversations between the head crew members. After many of the meetings, Melvin would have me get dinner or we would run down to one of his many "dive" restaurants, where he would clue me in on the details, answer my questions, or give me my penance for the inevitable mistakes of the day. Melvin is one of the toughest men I have met and his expectations sometimes seem impossible, but he knows how far to go and when to pat you on the back. Somehow a pat on the back from him always made it all worthwhile.

Sometime during this period, I saw Mario again. I had known Mario almost as long as I'd known his father and had had some really great times with him, but I suppose I had expected him to be different as a result of his newfound success. I was pleasantly surprised. We got along as well as ever. He is great fun to be around; it may be hard to imagine how he would be in person, but it shouldn't be. Every facet of his personality that people see in his work can be found in his personal life. Mario is a real-life actor. It is sometimes hard to separate the man from his roles because they seem to come so naturally to him.

Once the crew was mostly assembled, home base became a combination of Melvin's uptown office and the Henry Street Settlement House (a historic community center near the Williamsburg Bridge) and I found myself messengering back and forth from one "home base" to the other with a multitude of stops along the way. At times it was really frustrating, since all the trekking around took me away from where the action was. I soon learned, however, that the action didn't come from the director's mouth, but had more to do with the crew's constant state of motion.

All my life I had worked every summer from the minute they kicked us out of the classroom until they forced us back in. I started working in Manhattan when I was eleven and worked in too many fields to keep count. But even my days as an electrician's assistant or in housing construction hadn't prepared me for the sixteen- to eighteen-hour days and six-day weeks that comprised my life during the filming. It was never boring though. I would miss out on some of the filming and the "whole picture," but each errand had its place and further prepared me for the coming months.

Each time I came back to Henry Street I would see the progress the rest of the "machine" had made. All of a sudden a production office had materialized and they were auditioning.

Melvin was the director/producer, and Mario was the writer/actor/second unit director, but they're not the complete story. The team continued with Preston Holmes, who was our production manager, and Jim Hinton, our director of photography. As the days went on, I saw them playing with a large portfolio-type book filled with multicolored panels. At first I had no idea what it was, but one day someone sat me down and showed me that this board was the entire film in a nutshell. It told the shooting schedule and order of the film, as well as whether scenes were day or night, what actors were needed, and everything anyone might need to know about the day-to-day or the future.

MARSHA

The now infamous dinner at Rosa's led to a series of intense meetings and phone conversations with Melvin and/or Mario about the film. Between them they divided up the work.

Lawyers and laymen alike are familiar with a legal concept known as "conflict of interest"—that certain point in a business transaction where two parties may be deemed to be conveying preferential advice to one over the other or advancing one party's interest to the other's detriment.

Working with Mario and Melvin on *Identity Crisis,* I soon learned that what they enjoyed was not conflict but rather an "identity of interests." From the outset, Mario and Melvin were wearing a number of hats in this venture of producing an independent theatrical feature film—producer, executive producer, screenwriter, director, star, and creator of the logo. I wear one hat—the lawyer for the production entity—and I like it that way. In the fourteen and a half years during which I have been practicing law, the situation of a father and son producing a feature film while each is also writing, directing, and/or starring in the film is akin to *Close Encounters of the Third Kind.* It isn't done. In my firm we do represent different generations of the same family—but not on the same project. We are very careful not to apprise Mom or Dad of their son's or daughter's legal situation.

In their legal dealings in *Identity Crisis* and despite my protests, Mario and Melvin were adamant in waving away (and waiving) any potential or perceived conflicts between them. They were right. No conflicts existed.

Mario is "Mario" or "son." Melvin is "Dad." And they have style. When it came time to review the director's and screenwriter's contracts, Mario, Melvin, and I sat in my office and reviewed each provision together. They set the pace. They got it done. Revisions were made immediately. When all were satisfied, the agreements were signed. One, two, three.

VICTOR

Jim Hinton telephoned me in March and asked if I would be interested in editing a theatrical feature. I was surprised and flattered because I had not seen Jim in a few years, and the last feature film we did together, *Ganja and Hess,* was in 1972. In recent years, I had been concentrating my efforts in documentaries and hadn't been communicating with narrative filmmakers.

NO IDENTITY CRISIS

After reading the script, I was convinced that *Identity Crisis* would not return me to dramatic features. The picture was a comedy caper, and since I had never edited anything similar—well, the old story, "Do what you have done before." I expected Melvin's first question to be, "Can I see something you've done like this?"

A more important reason for my doubts was that in general the "doc" editor continues to edit documentaries and the narrative feature editor remains in his specialty. The line is not frequently crossed.

I didn't know Melvin Van Peebles and I hadn't taken into consideration that Melvin doesn't delve into the past, doesn't believe in generalities, and crossing lines is certainly not one of his problems.

Our first meeting was at Melvin's apartment, which had been turned into the temporary production headquarters. His living room was everyone's office, secretary, production manager, assistant director, et al., and his bedroom was the conference room. We met in the "conference room," but it might as well have been in the hallway, since we were constantly interrupted by questions, deliveries, actors and actresses (casting was in progress), and one model who insisted on telling us in detail about her casting audition for a Calvin Klein commercial. She definitely had the look for jeans.

Mario entered and asked Melvin if he could join in the discussion for a few moments before the next actress showed up. Since Mario was the writer, leading star, and co-producer, I was surprised that he felt a request was necessary. Melvin's answer, "Sure, son!" set me straight.

I soon understood that Melvin and Mario would share production responsibility and respect each other's professional ability but they would also maintain a very close father-son emotional tie. There was never any awkwardness about Mario saying "Dad" and Melvin saying "son." They showed an openness that would set a comfortable mood during production.

Jim Hinton must have done a good job representing me,

because Melvin never questioned my credentials, but we did speak broadly about "film attitude." I soon realized my doubts were unfounded, since Melvin would make his decision based strictly on feelings. When the meeting ended I knew I would be supervising the postproduction, being more familiar with the New York film scene than Melvin, who had produced his other films in Los Angeles. I did not know, however, what my editing role would be. Melvin told me that he would be editing the first cut, and then my involvement would begin with the fine cut. I was not aware that Melvin had been a film editor as well as a director, and I wasn't comfortable with this situation. It's the first cut when the decisions for pacing, restructuring if necessary, emotional impact, and the general look of the film are made. More important, this is when all the mistakes of production must be solved, and the fun part of discovery begins. I realized that Melvin did not really know my abilities and was naturally being protective of his film.

CHRIS

Mario had been telling me of a project NBC had been talking to him about, and in the winter of 1987 *Sonny Spoon* got off the ground. Mario got me a job as his trainer and also managed to get me a role in a couple of episodes. During the filming of *Sonny Spoon* Mario encouraged me to learn about production in planning for the future. He was always driving home to me the concept of how almost futile it is to be an actor (and only an actor) in this business. Think about it for a minute. You have two hundred or three hundred or God knows how many hundreds of people vying for each role. And the people who get seen are only a fraction of those submitted. They're the lucky ones. It was good for me (as an actor) to see how the whole thing works, because it gave me new hope as an actor to see firsthand just how hopeless it really is if you're an actor with nothing else going for you. That's one of the reasons Mario was always harping on the importance of acquiring production skills if I planned to stay in this business, as well as the necessity of having another means of earning a living unrelated to acting.

I started to bug the assistant directors on *Sonny Spoon* every chance I got, and carried away quite a bit of production knowledge.

When Mario first mentioned *Identity Crisis* to me he had expressed his hope that I would want to help in the production of the film from behind the camera. So as soon as *Sonny Spoon* was on hiatus, we were on our way to New York to make *Identity Crisis* happen. Mario told his dad he thought I could handle the second assistant director slot, and using what I had learned from assistant directors on *Sonny Spoon*, I constructed the first production board for the film from the script.

I often thought back to how I'd met Square Head, and how far he had come in the time I'd known him. Yes indeed, it appeared that "Mr. Personality" could go about as far as his "just pumped the neighbor's cat grin" would take him.

BERNARD

Oh my God, we were running around like chickens with their heads cut off trying to get ready for the big day. It involved a whole lot of hard work and a whole lot of hustling. The way Melvin works is that he gives you a project, he squeezes you in, and he knows the right people to pull together and hold.

Actually we had within the film almost a thousand costumes, so it was serendipity, creativity, beg, borrow . . . we didn't steal. It was that kind of side show. A lot of things came out of my storage. A lot of things I dug up. I must have about three hundred items that I keep stored over at the

Sofia Brothers that I pull out whenever I need to. But then there were certain things that were bought one way and then completely redone. You know, the colors were changed. They were recut, painted, dyed, whatever.

In the movie, Mario must have had about thirty costume changes. He was playing two different characters. He was playing Chilly D., who is a home boy, a ghetto kid. And the other character was Yves Malmaison, a successful designer from France, who has a unique personality, to put it mildly. That's a nice way of saying it. He is in essence gay, but he has a son who is from the one and only time that he was married. By in essence gay I mean he was not a screaming faggot, but he is on the edge of it. He is the kind who wears different-color wigs every day and thinks it's nothing unusual. When most people put on a toupee or wig, they want you to think it's their hair, so that they can't be blond today, a brunette tomorrow, a redhead this afternoon, and have gray hair this evening. But Yves has that kind of flair and he wears everything he possibly can. Even the beginning of the film starts out in that godawful color of lavender that you have to have courage or be dead to wear. They usually either put it on folks in a casket, 'cause they can't fight back, or somebody feels that it is a great color and it appears as a dinner jacket. Of course that's not all for the dinner jacket. He has to have a clean shirt and the printed cummerbund and tie and the bugle beads and rhinestones, so that it's as theatrical as it is logical—something of a Las Vegas look.

Now Chilly D. is streetwise, macho, straight. He sometimes wakes up from his other identity and finds a wig on his head and doesn't know where the hell it came from. He is really what you would call a hunk, which of course is perfect for Mario.

As far as I am concerned, his best costume is his birthday suit, but we couldn't go that far. So when I put him in the fitted T-shirt and some jeans that I cut my hands up slashing and aging and leather-printing and goin' . . . he looked but absolutely fabulous! And then there's the place where I got him to put on a pair of silk drawers, where the woman takes

the whipped cream and sprays it all over his body ready to
. . . I guess do whatever you do after whipped cream goes on
something you like. Um, it's a lot of stuff because there are
a lot of scenes and the scenes within the film go from elegant
to high fashion to sleaze bar to low life to the wrong side of
town to the warehouse. And people, people, people . . .

Then there's Doris Dot. Doris Dot is a drag queen and a
performer. We never get to see him/her shim or whatever
. . . but Doris Dot is big and Chilly D.'s girlfriend is big, so
she borrows clothes. She borrows clothes from Chilly D.'s
girlfriend so that whenever possible it is always polka dots
so that it goes with the name Doris Dot. So we have one
particular scene, the entrance scene with Doris Dot in a pink
wig that is all fluffed out and a pink dress with the most godawful . . . they got to be the size of a fifty-cent piece . . .
polka dots and blacks you ever saw. I mean it was purposely
made to be tacky.

I made that costume myself with the help of my assistant,
George Bergeron. We did not know that Doris Dot was going
to work at nine o'clock in the morning till about nine o'clock
the night before as happens a lot in film when they have to
switch scenes around. Also because Melvin has the kind of
genius which he does, which he loves to kill all his friends
who love working for him. Well, it's the truth. It gives us
that kind of energy. I said, "Melvin, I know I could crawl out
of this hole that you dug me into, but did you have to throw
the dirt in, too?"

JIM

I think Melvin is a good businessman. I think some business
people in the industry are resentful of him for that. They are
just not prepared to deal with a creative guy on the business
side of the ledger. They really get nervous when they come
in contact with what I would call an artist-businessman.

They feel that it just isn't right for him—especially since he's Black—to have the financial understanding necessary to be a strong negotiator, bargainer, and businessman. So sometimes, I think it might be helpful for Melvin to direct somebody to carry on negotiations for him just to make it look like he's not running the show. Business people like to think of talent in a certain category. They're used to talent being confused and caving in.

Melvin originally trained as a director in Europe, and operates on the European directorial system in the United States. The director carries the most weight in European filmmaking, and the producers are just support personnel for the director. But since in the United States the producer dominates and the director handles the creative aspect, Americans who have to deal with Melvin often are confused.

Melvin's tough, but he is honest. That's why I'm with him after all these years. He keeps his word. He never says something that he does not mean, and he always keeps his word. Always keeps his word. And so you don't have to worry about compensation or credits or anything once he agrees to it. And that's a wonderful attribute. I can respect him and trust him and that's why we have remained friends over the years. The man keeps his word.

I consider Melvin and myself to be two of the best and the most cost-conscious producers in the business: first, as far as keeping cost of productions down, and second, staying within a fixed budget. I have done many productions on a fixed-cost basis and not run over, and so has Melvin.

Melvin has the uncanny ability to edit in the camera. He doesn't shoot for ninety seconds if there are only going to be sixty seconds on the screen. There are very few directors who have that much self-discipline and that much ability to previsualize in order to do that. Melvin does not shoot a million pieces of film to put 5,000 feet up on the screen. He shoots only what he needs.

BLOCK

TIME: the middle of the last week of preproduction.
LOCATION: my apartment living room.
SUBJECT: filmmaking as war . . . reflections before the battle.

I was reviewing the troops. The crew sat, squatted, and leaned, gathered at the far end of the living room. At the southern end of the room sunlight was streaming gaily in, subverting the importance of the occasion. Coffee and Danish pastries had been passed out and the crew slurped and nibbled as I passed among them.

This was the first time the entire team had been assembled and, incidentally, the last time they would all be together until the wrap party at the end of principal photography. In fact, this group of people would never be assembled again, for some would have fallen along the way: too lazy, too much ego, too little talent, and other you-name-its. I was reflecting on this as I gulped my coffee and tried to guess how each one would do, who would last and who would be history.

Whom did I trust the most to go all the way?

I looked over at Mario, recently arrived and still smelling of L.A. Number one was Mario—no—not because of the blood-is-thicker-than-water thing or because he was writer/partner/star of the film; something even better than that—integrity and the courage to hang in. That didn't mean he wouldn't be a pain in the ass, but he had plain ol' tenacity and grit, and I must admit I loved him for that. Once when we were doing a small show on Broadway, which coincidentally wasn't doing too well, Mario was taken ill with a virus. He came to me so weak he could barely speak and asked what should he do.

I gave it to him straight. "Your understudy isn't ready to go in yet, and if you go to the hospital before he is, we'll have to close the show."

He looked at me, eyes all bloodshot from the flu and said, "Your call, Dad . . . I'll do whatever you say to do."

I asked him to stay and that's exactly what he did. The show was saved, or, more precisely, its demise postponed. It folded shortly thereafter anyway, as a result of my artistic inadequacy, but that's another tale . . . *aaaAAH*, show biz.

At tie for second place in the dependability department, so close you couldn't separate them, were my veterans, Jim Hinton and Bernard Johnson. Preston would have been right up there in the dependability department too, but he was only helping out as a friend between commitments and I knew he would be leaving us shortly. Jim, as I already mentioned, was a rock, and Bernard, the costume designer, was wily, pragmatic, and pure steel. Bernard had worked with me longer than anyone in the room, since my ballet-company days back in '68. Brother Bernard, an elf, an imp, small body, big mouth . . . a brilliant mind, hidden behind, or rather buried underneath, a lifestyle of young boys and tall ballerinas. Bernard, like Jim, was a friend. The rest of the crew were munching, swallowing, slurping question marks to me. I had worked with a few peripherally or on a short-term basis. I knew a few socially, but the majority had been chosen by recommendation, favor, or hunch.

In short, I didn't know how they would react under fire. I had figured, why not indulge myself with a little guessing. It was now or never. Soon everyone would be scattered to the four winds on various assignments. The next day the phones would be connected, and we would be moving head-quarters down to the offices I had obtained for us in Lower Manhattan.

I begin to speculate. First there was my personal team, Isabel, my latest assistant, who had never worked on a film —Isabel the orderly one. How would her neatness deal with the bedlam of movie making? Would her strength and plain ol' common sense withstand the waves of production madness that would be coming at her? I thought they would.

Then how about the award-winning documentary-film-maker friend, who was recovering from a serious accident, and who wanted to learn the commercial side of the business? A large lady with a cultivated, gentle voice and a winning smile, she had worked under the most arduous conditions imaginable from filming the guerrilla war in the Sahara to clandestinely shooting a documentary inside South Africa about the government's torture of children. I had no doubt that she would do well, if only her health did not fail her.

Then there was Jim's team, which comprised the bulk of the crew. They seemed okay to me and, as it turned out, notwithstanding the time constraint he had had to work under assembling them, the best group one could possibly ask for, with one teensy-weensy exception caused by his aforementioned kindheartedness. That choice was so disastrous it almost sank our ship two days into shooting.

Evidently Jim had never heard of the Peter Principle of elevating someone to their level of incompetence. To make a long story short, Jim had let a guy talk him into hiring him for a key position that was above his capability.

Of course, disenfranchised folk are especially sensitive to the plight of anyone being held down, or not being given a shot, having been handed the dirty end of the stick on numerous occasions. Perhaps we don't see clearly who is actually overqualified (as everyone always thinks he or she is, human nature being what it is) and who when they complain about being held down and underutilized is full of shit. *Oh well, nobody ever said it would be easy.* I still believe that your altitude is more a product of your attitude than your aptitude, yet a person can be more suited to one job than another. Curious isn't it how someone can perform so brilliantly at one level and be total bust just one rung away. Startling, how, as it was in this instance, that a person efficient and motivated in one position could find a directly related promotion a total drag, abstract to the point of incomprehensibility. Oh well, that's what makes a horse race. Needless to say, Jim's near fatal choice wasn't fatal, otherwise the film wouldn't have gotten made. But it was touch and go for a minute.

Anyway, I never teased Jim about his fuckup, and a good thing too. Since, as it turned out, I made a major goof too.

That fantastic documentary filmmaker with the charming smile I had hired turned out to be bad news, a real prima donna. Maybe it was that her terrible accident had shaken her confidence so that she felt compelled to exert herself, but anyway, her overbearing manner strained the resources of an office staff already weeks behind and scurrying to catch up. She ended up being universally detested and left in the middle of preproduction.

In fact, looking back it seems that the head of each department made at least one personnel boo-boo, Mario and Bernard included, although theirs weren't as crucial as Jim's and mine. Of course, all that lay in the future, and I didn't know the specifics as I reviewed the troops, but I was sure some folks were going to rise to the occasion above and beyond the call of duty and some were going to go sour. *I just didn't know who was who.* I figured if 80 percent worked out, we would be okay. I think we ended up just around there, maybe even doing a little bit better.

Maybe life is like a balloon—you get out of it what you put in. Maybe one person's challenge is another person's nuisance. On that note, I figured, it was time to stop speculating and get my ass in gear. So I called the gathering to a halt.

As the crew was dispersing, a tall young production assistant—they are generally used throughout the industry as gofers (as in go for this, go for that), the lowest person on the moviemaking totem pole—came up to me and politely inquired if he might have a quick word with me. I was in an elder-statesman mood and said sure. He explained to me that he had already worked on several films when he was in Europe and hoped I would keep him in mind when we got to the postproduction stage, and that he had only taken this position so he could see me, a master, at work. I pride myself on being able to smell bullshit, but the kid was obviously sincere and I told him I would certainly keep him in mind come postproduction time. I even made myself a note to try and find some postproduction work for him. Plus, I gave myself a little speech about this being what it was all about, helping people to help themselves. Unfortunately, the young man was a little heavy-handed on the helping himself part. And he got himself fired his third day for stealing.

JUDY

I probably have the worst memory in the world, so most of the circumstances of my knowing Mr. Van Peebles are one big blur.

I do remember that I was just returning from London, where I had been living with a friend while on sabbatical or, as Mr. VP calls it, "dropping out of the human race" from college. I had run out of cash and had returned home to get a British work permit, when my life changed.

While in line at the British consulate, I was reading the *Daily News* and I read in Marilyn Beck's column that Mr. VP after a long absence would once again be making a feature film with his son Mario. I remembered Mr. VP's name because a couple of months back I had seen *Sophisticated Gents,* a really great television film written and starring MVP, on television and had really enjoyed it.

Well, my permit application had been rejected because of lack of employment, I couldn't afford to return to London right away, and I needed a job. I thought back to the Marilyn Beck column. What about the movie? I could pick up a few tips on filmmaking, and besides, I had nothing better to do. Needless to say, I knew nothing about the movie business.

That night I wrote MVP one of those, Dear so-and-so, I-think-you-are-great, give-me-a-job letters.

Four days later I got up the nerve to telephone him about my offer to be his Girl Friday during the production of *Identity Crisis*. His telephone number was in the phone book, of all places. I never thought that famous people had listed phone numbers but there he was, on page 5,612. So I called him up.

"Hello, Mr. Van Peebles, my name is Judith Norman and I wrote you a letter . . ."

"Uh-huh, uh-huh, tell me about yourself."

"Well, I'm looking for something interesting to do and I read about your upcoming movie and decided to see what the movie business is all about."

"Uh-huh, uh-huh, why don't you come over this afternoon."

"I'm sorry, but this is not a good day for me." (Terence Trent D'Arby, the newest pop sensation was performing at the Beacon Theater that night and, well . . .)

"Uh-huh, uh-huh, how about tomorrow? Call me in the morning and we'll arrange the time."

"Uh-huh,"—he kept saying uh-huh, uh-huh, and I was so nervous that I almost started to mock him—"okay, what time tomorrow morning?"

"Before nine."

"Okay, goodbye."

"Goodbye."

I couldn't believe my ears. He sounded so nice.

The following morning, 8:57, to be exact, I called MVP and we made an appointment for 1:00 P.M. at his place.

When I arrived at MVP's apartment, I was coolly greeted at the door by Christopher Michael, Mario's friend and ex-roommate, who would be working as a production assistant on *Identity Crisis*. Mr. VP was not in.

Besides Chris, there was a girl named Kim, an extras-casting agent, who had been waiting for MVP for about twenty minutes. She had even bought him coffee and a Danish.

Chris went into the other room, leaving Kim and me to chat. Kim drank the coffee and we both ate the Danish.

Finally, after waiting another twenty minutes, Kim decided to leave. I begged her not to go, because I did not want to be in the apartment alone with a man I did not know. (Hey, I read Jackie Collins.) She agreed to wait ten minutes more. When the ten minutes were up and I could not convince her to stay, Kim left.

I sat nervously on the couch, looking at the ceiling.

NO IDENTITY CRISIS

Fifteen minutes went by (I was counting), and the front door opened and who walked in but Mario, dressed in black sweatpants, a black turtleneck sweater, a black cowboy hat, and a pair of leopard fur shoes on his feet. Mario was much better-looking in person than in his photographs. He came over to me and extended his hand.

"Hi, I'm Mario Van Peebles. How are you?"

Somehow, I managed to say hello.

He disappeared into the other room. Boy, was I relieved. I kept hoping that he wouldn't return (Good-looking men make me silly.) No such luck. Mario came back into the room, sat down directly opposite me on the couch, picked up the telephone, and started talking sexy to some bird named Barbara. ("Hey, baby . . . yeah, I enjoyed it too . . . well, you know what they say, cleanliness is next to godliness . . . yeah, baby . . .")

I tried to ignore him, but I couldn't. He just kept talking on the phone and staring at me . . . hard.

Finally, he hung up the phone and spoke to me.

"How do you know my dad?"

"I don't."

"Oh yeah. You mean you just come into this man's house and you don't know him?"

"Yeah, I mean, yes, um, we spoke on the telephone and I'm here," I said with my voice cracking.

He just looked at me with disbelief.

After ten minutes of Mario's grilling, MVP arrived with Preston Holmes, the temporary production manager (Preston is very handsome and very intelligent and very mellow) and Jim Hinton, the director of photography (Mr. Hinton is tall, lanky, cute in a boyish sort of way, and very sweet).

Mr. Van Peebles was also much more handsome in person. He was dressed in old jeans, a blue shirt with red suspenders, and a hat. Not what I was expecting, but then again, I didn't know what I was expecting.

We went into the dining room and talked a bit. About what? Blame my memory problem.

Mr. VP said, "Okay, come down to Henry Street on Saturday, we'll be having casting auditions and maybe you could help out. Do you know where it is?"

Of course I was so nervous that I just blurted out, "Yes, don't worry about it, I'll find it." And that is just what I told myself: don't worry, Judith, you'll find it.

"Okay, I'll expect to see you at 9:00 A.M. Saturday down at Henry Street," he said as he was walking me toward the front door.

"Don't worry, I'll be there."

ISABEL

The actors were coming, seeking *their* opportunity. The word was out. The Screen Actors Guild (SAG) had posted a notice in its office that Block and Chip, Inc., Melvin and Mario Van Peebles, were making a movie. Head shots, 8 x 10 glossies, postcards with résumés, many with "choose me" letters began to appear by regular mail, via Federal Express, and under the door, some so elaborately designed they were real works of art. I wondered what we'd do with them later. Maybe people come back for their stuff. What did I know? Others enclosed ballpoint pens with their name, address, and telephone numbers. With all due respect to the senders, I was not sure if the trouble and expense helped anyone's cause, but I was thankful for the pens because someone was always lifting mine.

Other bios were brought into the office by bearers of elaborately concocted tales of their longtime friendship with MVP, or Mario. I was flabbergasted. I had never dreamed there were so many actors in the world, and half of them, it seemed, were beating a path to our door.

There was this Ruby Dee-ish looking woman, but time-worn, who with poise and perfect diction convinced the doorman, then me over the intercom that she was an old and dear friend of MVP. After I had waited a longer than normal time than was necessary for her to reach our door, I looked out in the hall and there was the actress writing a note to Martin Van Peoples. It was apparent that not only was she not near and dear, she hadn't taken the time to get his name right. This came right on the tail of MVP telling me not to believe or act upon anything unless it had been authorized or validated by him. Not that I would have, but this became our bond and probably the key to our success as working partners.

There was another meeting—MVP asked me to stay to handle the door and telephones. It was already 7:30 P.M. and I would rather have been home. However, instead of being sullen, I chose to be silly. Actually, my sense of humor was adjusting to show biz.

The doorman buzzed. My sense of humor prompted me to answer, "Casting." "There's a Mr. Dumbello down here. He says he's got a cat for a job, or something." I asked to speak with him. "Do you have a résumé?" "No, but I have a cat." "Does she have a résumé?" I thought that would really get him. Totally undaunted, he replied, "It's a he, and no, we didn't bring his résumé either. Could we come up? He really wants to work." Normally, I'd have said "Just leave your résumé with the doorman," but since they didn't have one anyway and I have a thing for cats of the meow ilk, I said, "Okay." This little balding guy came bounding out of the elevator, hand extended. "Hi, I'm Don Dumbello." He non-stopped into a spiel of thanks for letting him come up, the professionalism of his cats at foraging for garbage on cue, catching mice, and other alley-catology. Jesus, each one has a prepared speech. What does it bring to mind? I drifted a bit . . . mental recall . . . walking a mile in that kind of shoe. Each of these people has a routine, maybe what we call salesmanship in the corporate world. I softened to this guy as I remembered mine. The smile, the extended hand ready for shaking, the eye contact, brilliant conversation, and vi-brating kneecaps. I was polite, patient; he took a breath. I pounced. "Okay, okay already. Where's the cat?" Could this be a hot con to get a part in *Identity Crisis* and I fell for it? "You want to see him?" He was overjoyed, and began digging into a battered canvas satchel he was holding. We were kind of . . . he in the hall and I in the doorway not sure how MVP, who was meeting with the guys in the other room, would take to a cat's auditioning in his apartment. Out of the bag came this scrawny, pointy-faced Morris-colored animal. Its last meal was obviously its last movie, weeks—even months before. The cat, dangling from his owner's hand, looked me straight in the eye and gave a greeting—a guttural meow that probably meant, "Hi, I'm . . ." in street cat-ese and started pawing the space between us. "He likes you. Ya wanna hold him?" I did not get to answer. In an instant the cat was clinging to my sweater, rubbing his head on my shoulders, face, my arms, somewhere near my waist in some kind of spastic passion. "He likes you, he likes you!" the guy exclaimed happily. "And, ma'am," he went on solemnly, "he really wants to work." I tried to disengage myself from this purring love machine, thinking, Holy shit. I don't usually swear, but this was an extreme situation. I was hoping that once on the floor the cat wouldn't pee or worse, as I've seen overexcited dogs do. He didn't, but began an immediate eyes-closed, torrid romance with a leopard-patterned chair that happened to be in close proximity.

The guy was saying all kinds of things, like "He loves it here. He really loves it here. He wants to work . . . tonight." The cat had a leash on which I began to pull from the hall outside of the apartment where I'd joined the cat guy. The cat was pulling like crazy against me! He was trying to stay in the apartment. This animal had never been here before and was now refusing to leave. The guy was babbling. The cat dug his claws into the rug. I couldn't believe what was happening and, I was beginning to freak out, because I heard sounds like the guys breaking up their meeting . . . "Okay . . . great . . ." and I handed him the leash, did a thumb toward the elevators, the other hand on my hip. "We'll call if we need you and/or your cat." Suddenly as solemn as a judge, the guy scooped up his cat, returned him to the satchel where it went back into its play-dead routine, and turned and left. I couldn't believe what I'd just seen. The men file out of the meeting. "Did I hear you say cats?" MVP asked. "Yes," I answered casually, "ah, no—C-A-T . . . singular . . . wanted a job in *Identity Crisis*, darned good actor too," and gave him the cut from the *New York Post*. MVP gave me a curious glance—suggesting I get some sleep when I get home, because it was obvious that I must be overtired.

At that point, the cat could forget it, because it was clear to me that Melvin had no respect for any input or suggestions I offered regarding this precious thing of his called filmmaking. His attitude was, Since you've no experience at it . . . keep your mouth shut . . . your eyes and ears open . . . and learn. All well and good, but there is acquired knowledge and common sense in people that should be recognized.

Throughout the first two phases of the film this was a real bone of contention. I didn't appreciate in the least his apparent disregard of my intelligence and let him know it on more than one occasion. He'd just clam up and ignore me. Two days later he'd give me one of his this-is-why dissertations that I didn't want to hear but always learned from. Also, there was no point trying to argue it out. I am extremely deficient in that department, while Melvin is a master.

By the time we started postproduction, I had a handle on winning debates with him . . . sorry, no trade secrets . . . or maybe it wasn't so much winning as having been in the trenches together for so many weeks that a mutual respect and admiration had grown. I had learned a great deal and had much more to contribute. Our disagreements became constructive problem-solving sessions directed toward creating a better product.

No, the cat did not get into the movie, though there may be some feline special effects in the background. As for the head shots and bios, they wound up in Monday's trash! Obviously, while I was off on Sunday, the casting folks sorted through the hundreds of requests for work, separating the wheat from the chaff. I arrived in front of the building just in time to see the piles. So much for what we'd do with them . . . no deliberation . . . chop, chop . . . into the jaws of a hungry garbage truck. The elaborate tri-folio collage by the little Rabbi . . . chewed up . . . gone. He'd done a lot of work on it . . . he should have sent a stamped, self-addressed envelope with it. I would have returned it. I walked into Melvin's building amazed and a little sad. I'm so sentimental about things like this. People's hopes, so alive just days ago, now breakfast for a garbage truck.

That seems to be show biz, I mused and readied myself for the adventures of the day.

CHIP

There are times in my life when I forge ahead in my day-to-day survival, press-onward mode, like a bird flying south with some inborn homing instinct, not stopping to reflect or ponder why, just flapping its wings on a seemingly endless journey. Then, wham! Suddenly something hits me, sending me reeling, like a near miss from a Yellow cab barreling down Broadway, instantly reminding me of my own mortality. Sometimes the messenger is more subtle, like an aroma that sends me back to some cloudy place in my childhood, making me painfully aware of the passage of time. Or a park bench where I debated with a good friend I have since lost touch with. At any rate, the questions that surface are the same. Like pages in a book, I have a finite number of days. What am I doing? Why? How? Where is all this flapping of wings leading?

I really enjoy traveling with my hip little mother. Maybe because the "wild goose" took me everywhere when I was a kid, I get such a kick out of taking her on trips with me now. And it's always been a dream of mine to work with the old man. To give back to him, to both of my parents, bringing something to the family pot; not as a debt but as an honor.

150

NO IDENTITY CRISIS

Just two guys doing their thing. For some it's father and son's moving and storage, for us it was our production company, Block and Chip, Inc. I was plugging away on the detailed film preproduction stuff, flying along just like that "bird going south" analogy I just gave. When, wham! It hit me. We were going to be casting actors in six minutes! This was the real deal, man. We were going out on a limb. We were going for it, making our damn flick in the relatively short hiatus I had from doing *Sonny Spoon*. Father and son moving and storage suddenly seemed a hell of a lot safer than Block and Chip's big blunder or Melvin and Mario's new book, *How to Blow the Family Dough in Ten Easy Weeks*.

Isabel, my Dad's conscientious assistant, poked her head in the door and said nervously, "Mario, your dad's on his way down, Ann Marie is already in the casting room, and some of the actors for the role of Yves are here. What should I tell her?" Hell if I know, I thought. "Tell her I'll be right there, Weezie," I replied, trying to stay cool. Weezie is my affectionate nickname for her.

Ann Marie Kostura was casting the film. I had worked with her way back when I was acting in *One Life to Live*. She was still there and although she had moved up in the ranks, was anxious to cast a feature. Several casting directors had expressed interest, but I brought her to meet Dad personally. Although she wouldn't be able to handle the contracts and deals with the individual actors, as feature casters often do, she had a great eye for hip New York talent. I felt she would be an asset. Dad agreed and today marked our first week of casting.

I gathered up my notes and headed down the hall toward the casting office. Three distinguished gray-haired gents in sports coats sat out front waiting for me to give one of them a job. I nodded politely and went inside. As I did, I caught a glimpse of my reflection in the door. I looked young. In my jeans, sneakers, and oversized Oxford shirt, I looked more like some hip kid that would bop in delivering pizza than a writer/co-producer.

"Hi, Ann! Let's go ahead and get set up. Mel baby will be here in a minute," I said, kissing her cheek.

Ann looked sharp, the epitome of SoHo chic, with her tight black dress and spiky blond hair.

We pulled a couple of the desks around, lined up the chairs, and prepared to start auditioning the actors. Wham! In burst Dad, grinning and out of breath, like the soul version of Indiana Jones with his lizard-dad fedora.

"Okay, gang, let's do it!" he hollered, slinging his beat-up leather bag onto the floor and plopping into a chair.

Isabel escorted in the first actor—a bushy-eyebrowed brown "colonel mustard" type who reminded me of my old macro-economics professor at Columbia.

"This is Mr. Van Peebles, our director, and Mr. Van Peebles, our writer," she said. "Of course, you already know Ann Marie."

"Please have a seat," I said, the good cop or personable cop to Dad's, shall we say, observant cop. "Mind if I give him a brief plot synopsis, Dad?" I asked, establishing for the actor and all concerned that Dad was the boss. Dad and I had discussed this before and mutually agreed that it is important not to have two captains guiding our ship. He understood that as a writer, co-producer, and actor in the show, I had some particular ideas as to how it should turn out and he had expressed his trepidation. I assured him that if we came to a difference of opinion, I would definitely defer to his experienced judgment as director, producer, and dad. Now this who's-the-boss topic is a sensitive issue with lots of folks who often tried to drive an emotional "ego" wedge between us. But making a film is akin to going into battle, and if my dad, who is one bad-fighting-seasoned-in-the-trenches-brother, says duck, I'm not gonna stand there arguing. I've also been fortunate enough to have experienced directing my dad. And when I do he confers with me about everything from line readings and wardrobe to subtle shades of difference in the character's persona. On my show *Sonny Spoon* and in this situation, I am the boss. This man is as good an Indian as he is a chief. He can take what he dishes

out. No ego trip, no power trip, no star trip; the guy's okay
with me. I felt I was in a win situation. If the movie came
out good, great. If it flopped, I learned a hell of a lot. But
most important, and I stress this point, Pop and I did a movie
together. Not that this silly movie is important as anything
other than a symbol of a dream. It could have been building
a house or sailing around the world. For us it was making a
film together. "But what if you lose your shirts?" all our
concerned friends asked. Good question. If we lose our
shirts, we've both been shirtless before and I'd rather be poor
and know that when I could, I did. I got off my butt, tried
my best, and lived it with my pop while we were still both
young and able. If I live long enough to be an old geezer,
bouncing my grandchildren on my knee, I won't say, I could
have. I'll say, I did, we did, and to me that's wealth. There
is, however, a thin line between brave and foolhardy. Foolhardy we're not. As I said, for me gambling has little appeal.
This wasn't a total crapshoot. We did know something about
this flaky business and how to hedge our bets. Family-wise,
we all have been through college, and, knock wood, we're
healthy and everything's paid for. It's not exactly like gambling the last of the rent money, although it can come to
that.

At any rate, I gave the actor a brief synopsis of the plot,
and explained to him that the two roles we were considering
him for were Yves, the Liberace-esque French designer, or
his sophisticated older brother, Maximilien Malmaison. I
also told him the approximate start dates. No sense casting
actors who will be unavailable when you need them.

If there's a realistic rule for casting the right actor, I have
yet to discover it. When I was studying at Stella Adler's, one
of our fellow students was often referred to as Colonel Sand-
ers. Like the colonel who only does chicken right, this guy
gave a great audition but seemed to have zero ability to follow direction when he got the role. No burgers, no shakes,
no variations, just good old Kentucky Fried. However, I've
seen one-note actors shine in cameos where a character has
a limited time to establish himself. This places the emphasis

on clever casting not acting. When I direct, I usually try to get the actor to give me two different line readings on the same scene. This helps me get an idea of his flexibility and general ability to follow my direction.

The particular actor we were auditioning seemed to have a decent spread of credits, theatre (O'Neill and Shakespeare), television, including a soap and some film. The first thing I noted on his résumé was his theatre experience. I had started my professional acting career at the age of eleven in the theatrical production of *A Thousand Clowns*. Of the three mediums, theatre, television, and film, theatre seems to be the truest medium. Like a born-again Moonie trying to convert all who cross his path, whenever new actors confront me with the inevitable question "How should I get started?" I reply, "Theatre. Get ye to a stage."

In film or television, you shoot a scene or part of a scene, and then the director yells cut. You then wait while they futz, fiddle, reset camera and lights to do another angle. If a mistake has been made you can reshoot it, unless you're under the gun time-wise, in which case the director will try to convince you that it was a wonderful mistake that improved the moment, babe. In theatre, the actor waits for no one but his fellow thespians and cues. It is a live medium (*sans* net). No director will yell cut. No editor can save your performance.

A couple of years ago, my sister Megan, Dad, and I all worked our collective buns off doing our family Broadway musical comedy *Waltz of the Stork*. During one sequence, Megan sauntered out seductively for the Hawaiian Maiden number, complete in bouffant wig and hula garb, only this time the graceful lass had managed to hook her wig onto a corner of the set, and yes, she twisted out only in a stocking cap. Dad looked at Sis and drew a blank. Megan, not realizing anything was amiss, launched into a song. I jumped in and the audience, none the wiser, loved it. No retakes. The show must go on!

In both film and television, the camera guides the audience's eye, telling it what is important through the use of close-ups. In theatre, there are no close-ups. The thespians direct the audience's eye with their gestures and body language.

In television and film, you almost always shoot events out of story sequence. When I played Stitch Jones, the jive-assed marine in Clint Eastwood's film *Heartbreak Ridge*, we shot the end of the film with all the marines coming home to the marine base airport at the beginning of the film shoot. This was done in order to complete all scenes scheduled on the marine base before we flew to Puerto Rico for the "invasion of Grenada" sequence. My character, Stitch, starts out in the film as a raw, hip-hop, foul-mouthed marine who sees himself as Jimi Hendrix incarnate. Because of his interaction with Clint's character, Sergeant Highway, Stitch evolves into a gung-ho, albeit still foul-mouthed, marine. In order to jump out of sequence to the end and play the evolved character Stitch became, I studied the script, charting his growth in hopes that his final evolution would seem natural. Once we filmed the end, I would be committed to attaining that level of growth. I would be counting on Clint and the editors not to cut one of the character's vital growth scenes from the film, or else Stitch's evolution at the end could become totally inappropriate. Unlike the approach used in *The Cotton Club*, which I worked on for eight weeks, and where entire elaborate dance numbers and scenes ended up decorating the cutting-room floor, Clint's style of shooting seemed more akin to mine or my dad's. Shoot what you intend to use. "Lean and mean, put the money on the screen." I was pretty confident that if I committed to Stitch's film growth, the necessary steps leading up to it would remain in the movie. As it turned out, they all did, which is rare. Clint was more than generous. His one directional note was, "Keep up the energy, kid." Man, you don't have to tell me twice. He's secure enough so you don't have to make everything his idea. No politics, just "Be all that you can be." Once he realized that I wasn't just an actor trying to Bogart more lines, he let me go off! I think he got a kick out of me. After all those years of Off-Broadway and being king of the

B-movies, I was like a poor kid at a picnic, not letting a scrap of anything go to waste. Dirty Harry let me do my Improv stand-up shtik, he let me write my longtime buddy Chris Michael into the film, he let me write and perform three songs (I got a lot of requests, but I sang anyway). We worked out together (he benched 250 pounds along with me and big Chris), saw movies, and surfed (rather, he surfed, I sank). Since I was used to Dad, where when working, you shut up and don't overdo the questions (let the man think, dig?), the then mayor of Carmel even let me into the ultimate sanctuary of the editing room. In short, Mr. Eastwood made my day and my career.

But back to my original point about theatre, which I left somewhere back in the audition room. In film, the actor acts, the director directs, and the editor, hopefully under the director's supervision, edits the performance as necessary. The director/editor has final cut, but when the curtain goes up on a stage play, the director, producer, and writer can only pray that the actors have listened to their notes, remembered their lines, and deliver. From my experience in directing television, it seems to be more of a producer's medium especially in episodic series, where directors come and go like glorified house guests of the producer, who calls the overall shots. If film is a director's/editor's medium, and television a producer's medium, I'd venture to say that theatre is the actor's medium. It's no accident then that some of the finest actors have originated on and often return to the stage.

The down side, however, of just doing theatre is that the actor can appear too broad and theatrical on film. When every minute gesture is magnified thousands of times and projected onto the humongous silver screen, there is no longer a need to project so that the last row of the balcony can hear and see you. I had this problem of rechanneling, refocusing all my theatrical energy when I first made the jump into film after several years of Off-Broadway. A few years ago, one of my first C-movies was released after years of gathering dust. We shot the under-$200,000 budget movie on weekends in the South Bronx on 16-millimeter, under bare-minimum, change-clothes-in-the-car, run-'n-gun, guerrilla film conditions. The director, "Billy Z," I called him, was a gutsy young Italian editor, who lived with his grandma in the Bronx. He managed to finance the film on family loans and nerve. At the time, I had to fight, beg, and bribe him just to stay in the sucker. Now that it seemed I was becoming a Hollywood flavor-of-the-month, Bill, who had since become a comrade and co-conspirator, called me up to rib me about the "good news" of the film's long awaited release on both film and videocassette.

"Damn, should I leave the country now or later?" I joked. "Can I buy up all the prints?"

"All 'cause of you, pal, you're hot, babe," he laughed.

We had both come to view it fondly in retrospect as a valuable "learning experience" not unlike being toilet-trained. The cassette came out all right, and it read in big hide-yo'-face letters: "STARRING MARIO VAN PEEBLES OF HEARTBREAK RIDGE AND JAWS!" As if it were my latest flick, not my earliest blundering rite of passage. The thing about acting in a movie, B, C, or otherwise, is that your face is up there, captured on celluloid permanentsville. And, man, was my face up there, fresh from the theatre when we shot it. I had forgotten or, more likely, blocked out how broad I had been. Now magnified to sixty feet tall on the screen, my mug was the size of Iowa and my overly animated expressions made me look like a hyperactive Cabbage Patch doll. Mom, of course, loved the picture. She insists her friends sit through every bad movie I make. Dad, unable to suppress it, laughed his ass off. My only consolation was my sister Megan, who has since left the business to become an advertising sales executive for a magazine. Perhaps a move partially motivated by the release of this film? Now, Megan is not the nurturing, consoling type by nature, or at least not with me, in fact, *au contraire*, she and little brother Max take great pride in pointing out my cinematic blunders. But I had convinced Megan to play my sister in the film, and the child was almost as bad as I was. Let me tell you, nothing will humble you quicker than seeing two hundred people go for popcorn during your big Stanislavski breakdown scene. Dad spent opening night trying to console the director, Megan, and me with this "chalk it up to experience" stuff. Mom, meanwhile, comforted us with how magnificent it all was because at least we portrayed nice, loving people who didn't hurt animals, etc.

Although the often inane plots, nondirection, and sheer speed of shooting a soap can lead an actor into the bad habit of going for the quick or easy choices, the intricate mechanics of hitting your mark, turning naturally into your key light, and answering the phone with your right hand so that camera "B" (yes, that's the one with the red light on, dummy) can swing into position before the commercial break should not be underestimated.

During my three-month stint on *One Life to Live*, most of my scenes were with Phylicia Allen, now Phylicia Allen Rashad, or Mrs. Huxtable from *The Cosby Show*. Poised, warm, and smooth as silk, she'd give me encouraging words and help me keep my energetic self within the frames. I used to watch myself daily on the tube, pen in hand, taking notes and cringing as I consistently ducked out of my key light and missed my mark. Eventually, I mastered most of the mechanics at least well enough to forget them and just act. But, hey, by that time, I was on to bigger and better things. Coppola had discovered me and I was slated to star in *The Cotton Club*. Well, maybe he didn't quite discover me, I guess I helped him a little . . . and I didn't really star, I was featured . . . I mean I had a line . . . well, it was cut, but you'll see me if you don't blink or go for popcorn. It's still right there in black 'n white on my résumé, so it must be true.

Yeah, so enough of me, back to this actor we were auditioning for *Identity Crisis*. I gave him a synopsis, his credits seemed solid, and I was wondering if he could do the French accent well enough to play the designer, Yves, or his brother, Max. The actor said, "Well, gentlemen, what scene should I read for the audition?"

"Don't need to read anything," Dad said, grinning. "As they say in Hollywood, we'll be in touch."

"Dad, should I give him some pages to read when he comes back to audition?" I asked.

"This is the audition, son. I just want to talk with the actors, is all."

The room grew quiet. Maybe I wasn't understanding Pop correctly. I tried rephrasing. "Dad, what material should he use for his audition scene?"

"I understood you the first time, son. The answer is none," he replied with that slight edge in his voice.

I glanced at Ann Marie. No, she hadn't gotten it either and was looking at me like "hey, he's your dad, babe." Weezie was staring at her pencil with that I-ain't-getting-involved expression.

What was he trying to be, eccentric? He was joking. No, I know him, unfortunately he was not joking. Bad time to disagree with the old man, just starting the movie and all. Who was he, Gandhi? Was he telepathic, he just looked at these actors and knew who was who? It was a test, right? See if I trust him. Okay, Pop, I trust you, now cut the bull, let's find out who can do the accent. Dad says when I'm not pleased I make a very disconcerted face which in turn makes him disconcerted. Was I making that face? I was definitely not pleased. Okay, no time to argue, Mario, show family solidarity now and discuss this later. Maybe all that marathon jogging bounced his brain out of whack. Maybe old veteran Dad has gone shell-shocked on me, and what this family needs now is strong leadership, me. Now I was sounding like George Bush. Dad took over as head of the family when Grandpa got older and always said one day I'd have to do the same. Maybe this was my cue. Damn, that's a lot of responsibility, I'd rather let him do it for now just as long as he leads as I see fit. Is that what you're saying, Mario? 'Cause if so, that's not right, man. Come on, you had an agreement, remember? One captain, one ship. What happened to all that stuff? "Okay, that's all for now, thank you," I said to the actor with just the right lack of enthusiasm, enough to show I wasn't thrilled but I'd definitely stick to the agreement and back Dad up. Weezie heaved a sigh of relief, Ann Marie rolled her eyes heavenward, and I laughed inwardly. This is like a play. I must love my old lizard dad, I thought. Even if we sank this puppy, I couldn't think of a better guy with whom to hang out on the Bowery. Hell, I wanted to make him happy, see him work again. He deserved it, he'd worked so damn hard. We'll get some cheap wine and wash car windows at stoplights. No, better yet, he'll wash, I'll supervise, 'cause if we sink this puppy it's his damn fault.

There's this sort of release that comes from saying, "Okay I'll do it your way. If we blow it, it's on you." I suppose it's getting the ride without the ulcer, although I had a feeling this wouldn't be the last directorial fork in the road we'd come to and, in reality, I probably cared much too much not to get an ulcer. I've got plenty of time to win later, I thought, I want to see Dad win again now, in this lifetime. I felt a strange duality about Pop. A sense of knowing he was strong and could do it, and yet simultaneously wanting to protect him without offending him. Protect him from what? From not having another shot at the cinematic brass ring or from failing if he does? From feeling that I didn't understand him? That all this teaching was for naught, I suppose I feel a desire to protect both my parents, in a way, but again, from what? From old age? From the inevitable passing into the great void? From loneliness? From being disappointed in their offspring and what we've done with all they've given us? Maybe to protect Mom from her obvious frailties and Dad from his hidden ones. Dad's been a pioneer, out in front without many peers to talk to, to trust, to count on. He made some of the toughest unions hire minorities and women. He used his power to wedge in disenfranchised third-world folks, who often in turn let him down and forgot how they got there.

Ultimately, it seems that each generation believes it is unique. It feels it has the key, and that the volumes of experience it has acquired are "required readings" for life. Sometimes Dad gets frustrated. He seems to want me to see all that he has seen, to know what he knows. So much of his gratification, in terms of doing this film, came from teaching me—the passing of the paternal baton of knowledge to the next generation. I seem to be the heir apparent. The first-born square-headed kid. "Learn without trying to sum up the lesson too damn quickly, son," he growls. I understand. However, in some cases, like right then in that audition room I just plain disagreed. I thought we should audition the actors, not just talk to them, period. Once while I was up in the hallowed halls of Academia, an economics professor and I had our philosophical differences. It wasn't that I didn't understand him. I politely pored over the material twice to reassure him that I had understood in detail the steps he took, I simply did not agree with his deduction. But, hey, he was the teacher and I was the student. Win the war, not the battle, right? Yeah, I got an A.

Dad had taught me at an early age to "learn," to strip away what one knows or assumes one knows, set down the bulky, awkward baggage called ego, which you really don't need to lug around, and just learn. Learning is learning. Disagreeing is disagreeing (profound realization). I'd say 91 percent of what I've learned from Mel baby (cinematically) I agree with, so this not reading actors had to be part of that other 9 percent. Hey, for 9 percent what am I, an idiot? Who am I to argue with my director/producer this early in the game? Even if he is my dad, he's directing my script, right? I wrote this sucker. It's my writing credit. Look Machiavellian or not, agree, get the flick done, stupid, argue later if need be, but for now, as they say in French, *laissez passer*. Chill, bro, chill and learn from that old, shell-shocked lizard dad.

BERNARD

Well, there is one thing I could tell, relative to casting. I could tell immediately who Mario had chosen and who Melvin had chosen. Because Mario is from the fashion/modeling world, plus his background in the woods of Holly, he opted for the beautiful people. All of the soul food, all of the chitlins, all of the collard-greens characters were Melvin's. Mario chose some comics, but a lot of the comic folks I knew were Melvin's right away. I could just tell, 'cause I know Melvin's taste. I could see Melvin and I could see Mario, and the blend was fabulous.

It would never, ever have occurred to me that someday I might be working on a movie that Mario was starring in and Melvin was directing.

Mario was already acting by the time I even knew he intended to. He had actually invited Melvin to see a play, and Melvin didn't take me with him. I don't know why. Maybe I wasn't in town. Melvin thought that he had probably a small role in the thing . . . and it turned out he was doin' the lead! And this was heavy stuff. I think it was Shakespeare. And Mario broke Melvin's face by being fabulous. He had been going along with this and not troubling all of us in the business. It wouldn't have been trouble to me.

Mario was seriously thinking about acting, doing Off-Broadway things and all the while modeling for the buck. And I'm thinking all he was gonna do was model. I look up, and there are people asking me, "Well, have you seen Melvin's son?" And I said, "Which one?" 'cause Melvin's got two sons, both as handsome as sin. And I wanted to know, "doing what?" "Well, he's in this movie." There's Mario, and he's fabulous, played a killer or something. And of course the women just pee on themselves he's so gorgeous. Well, of course, he'd been gorgeous as a child. I had to go see it. I got past the gorgeous, he was doing such fabulous work that the gorgeous was incidental, although I do like the gorgeous.

NO IDENTITY CRISIS

That's why I kept tryin' to take his clothes off when costuming *Identity Crisis*. I just wanted to make sure that the women in the audience got a chance to know what was really underneath that clothing. When he did *Waltz of the Stork*, it was the first time I had had a chance to work with him on a production. He was energetic. He was cooperative. To use a hackneyed phrase, he was the quintessence of what you want a professional to be. He never complained if he was given some business to do that had to be put in very quickly without mulling it over, rehearsing it, honing it, what have you; when he had to try this or that, because Melvin is that kind of creative too—just goin' out and doin' it. Mario was always on time. I even remember him working when he had the flu. He was dedicated.

In that show he was sort of a background to Melvin's character and he and a young lady were the supporting cast, and they jumped in and out of costumes all during the performance. They were in constant motion with wigs and outfits. I find it interesting that Mario, in *Sonny Spoon* and this movie, does the same business of switching wigs and switching characters. I mean there are not that many actors who you can think of who would, or could, play, you know, cameos and keep changing voices and personalities.

STEVE

Like many aspiring actors, I have always fantasized that my big-screen motion-picture debut would be a moment of triumph . . . introducing Stephen J. Cannell in the role only he could play. The papers would herald the coming of a new star, a man whose acting talents were exceeded only by his prominent profile. A farfetched fantasy. And then the phone rang. . . .

"Steve, it's Melvin." He was calling from New York, a great film town.

"Hi, Melvin." My voice shook slightly. After all, this was Melvin Van Peebles, famous director. Oh, yeah—he's my friend, too, but maybe this was my chance. I heard he was casting a film called *Identity Crisis*. There was a long pause on the line, and then Melvin's voice shot across the monofil-ament with clarity. "Hey, Steve, I'd like you to play a part in my movie. How about it, guy?"

Oh boy! Oh boy! Oh boy! It's finally happening. Me in the movies. Okay . . . I'd done some small acting parts in the past—mostly on TV: a *Magnum* last year; a Bob Conrad Movie of the Week the year before that . . . but, come on, guys—that was just TV—this was the movies. I took a deep breath because I didn't want my voice to shake.

"Uh, well, Mel, you know I'm really busy. . . . I got my hands full right now. . . . What are the dates . . . ?" Rule No. 1: Don't lunge at anything! A big director will back away if you come on too strong or act too anxious. My mind was racing. Oh boy! Oh boy! Oh boy! Me in the movies . . . "I suppose," I continued, "depending on the quality of the role and its importance to the movie, I might be able to find the time, Melvin . . . but you know I've got my hands full editing the last episodes of *Sonny Spoon,* along with my other TV projects."

Mario Van Peebles, the star of my current NBC midseason show was, coincidentally, Mel's son. I was finishing post-production on his show. Not that I was going to let that spoil my big screen debut. Oh boy! Oh boy! Me in the movies.

Then came the bombshell. The announcement I'd been waiting for. "It's a nice little part, Steve. I'll send you the script." The use of the word "little" in connection with my feature-film debut was a little off-putting, but after all, that can be a euphemism; Zanuck could have said that to Gable: "I got a nice little part for you in *Gone With the Wind*." Yeah, that's probably it . . . yeah . . . yeah . . . that's it, of course. "Send it along, Melvin. . . . Good talking to you. . . ." And some small talk about Mario, who was quickly becoming a great friend, and who had adopted me as what he called his Hollywood Dad.

It is a truth among casting directors that if the character

doesn't have a name in the script, we are usually talking a nothing part. You don't expect a part known as Cop One to win an Academy Award. My role was on page fifty of the script and was known as The Coroner.

We all carry misconceptions about our physical attractiveness, but somehow I never saw myself as a coroner. Coroners are wizened little men who spend hours sawing up corpses. Their mouths are usually pinched, they wear bow ties; there is an essentially dorky quality to most coroners. Okay, I thought, I'll read on. This coroner may be a hero . . . a man who pumps formaldehyde into a handsome crime fighter by night. A dashing crusader for the rights of man. Yeah, that's what this guy must be . . . yeah, of course . . . and the fact that he doesn't have a name here is a writer's trick. We'll find out as we go that his real name is revealed later . . . Stephen J. Cannell, starring as Brett Eagle, the coroner. Yeah, that's gotta be it . . . read on, McDuck. . . .

A short time later, I closed the script. Well, okay, so he's just a coroner. He's got two nice little scenes. It will be a chance to hang out with Melvin and Mario for a while. See New York, catch some shows, and what the hell, maybe I can sneak in a few ad libs and improve the line count— something I had cursed other actors for pulling in my own productions.

The phone rang. It was two days later. My secretary said, "Melvin Van Peebles is on the line." Moment of truth. Here goes.

"How ya doing, Steve? You get the script?"

"Yeah, Melvin . . . it arrived."

"Whatta you think? Part's not too small, is it?"

"You kidding, Melvin? It's perfect. It's the best part in the movie. . . ."

"Are you going to bring your wife?" he asked.

"Marcia, you bet."

"Great! If we get time, maybe we can all go out to dinner."

"Good deal."

"Okay, great, Steve . . . then we'll count on you two weeks from today. We're running a tight ship, so bring your own wardrobe . . . dark suit . . . bow tie. . . ."

"Thanks, Melvin. Okay. I'll be there two weeks from today."

To my mother, who asked me, "Why are you going to New York, dear?" I answered: "Oh, you know, Mom, to star in a movie that Melvin Van Peebles is directing."

To my wife, Marcia: "I gotta go to New York. Melvin thinks I should star in his next feature."

"Really?" She looked suspicious. "What's the part? Is it important?"

"Pivotal . . . life-or-death character . . . a man who literally pumps the life juices into the veins of the other characters."

"Sounds like a coroner," she joked.

ISABEL

People often ask what's MVP like. I answer, a nice guy, understanding and supportive.

Then I ask myself, Come on, Isabel, what's he really like?

He's a sugar man. Sweet . . . as in sugar, dextrose, glucose, syrup as in corn syrup—corny, sometimes but with sugar. Sweet . . . as in the molasses that Brer Rabbit found himself stuck to.

But sugar is dangerous stuff, addictive. MVP is addictive. He becomes your habit. Your central thought. He works at it to become your habit. He's a dealer of the happy stuff. The sugar high then zap, the low as he's off on some other sweets-dispensing quest.

The addicts are many, the telephone calls, the letters, the sad, lovelorn faces, waiting, waiting. He keeps them waiting. And just when they're prepared to bolt from the line he's there again.

He's a driver and will get the best out of you. He'll push you to excel—but the sugar confuses the mind. Is your performance benefiting him or you the most? More likely the latter.

NO IDENTITY CRISIS

After the renovation of his apartment was completed, I came aboard to work as a part-time bookkeeper and gradually assumed more and more responsibilities. Melvin doesn't offer or give you chores, rather, he threatens not to. Example, if you don't get on with projects A, B, and C, I'll have to get someone else to do D. He rambles on forever about how this is in no way personal and he wouldn't have to ask you if he had a contingency or felt someone else could handle the work load with your capability. I could see the syrup but like the others got high on its sweetness. A lovable man, but not always likable.

I noted that most people were accepting of the bitter in order to savor the sweet. He was the guru for many. I must not lose myself to this person.

JUDY

My first day on the job was also the day before Easter. I had an evening flight to North Carolina to see my grandparents. Planning to go directly to the airport after work, I arrived in the city around 8:00 A.M. lugging all my stuff. Since I didn't know where I was going, I jumped in a cab. The just-off-the-boat driver didn't know where he was going either, although he had practically sworn on his mother's grave that he did. Somehow, we ended up in Brooklyn.

It was 10:00 A.M. when I finally got to Henry Street. Mario was putting up signs on the doors for the auditions. I asked him where I should go and without speaking, Mario wrote "that way fool," on the sign, but then he crossed out "fool" and replaced it with "y'all" and turned and smiled at me. I got the message.

I went crashing up the stairs, pulled myself together, then sauntered nonchalantly into the room as if I were an hour early rather than an hour late.

That day they were having casting auditions. My job was

to introduce the actors to MVP and his panel of helpers, which included Mario, Ann Marie Kostura (the casting director), and Shirley, a very well-known journalist/documentary filmmaker, whom Mr. Van Peebles had placed as her casting assistant.

I was rather intimidated by the group. They all seemed very confident. I felt totally out of place and self-conscious. I remember commenting on the lack of punctuality of a lot of actors. MVP explained that it was all psychological.

I was asked to go to the store and purchase some refreshments for the group. I wrote everything down. I didn't want to make a mistake and therefore prove correct Mario's low opinion of me.

The diet drinks were no problem. The problem came with the fruit juices. It seemed like there were a million different kinds. I was overwhelmed. I must have been in that aisle for fifteen minutes just looking and thinking, What if they don't like this or that? I finally bought brand names, apple, grape, and something else.

When I got back everyone seemed pleased and I even got an approving smile from Mario.

MVP does auditions in an unusual way. He sort of looks at actors and gets a feeling from them. He doesn't make them read sides (excerpts from the script) or do monologues about their tragic childhoods à la *Fame*. I thought this was very interesting; it takes a lot of pressure off the actor. The actor had to rely solely on his looks and personality.

At the end of the day, MVP gave me a copy of the script and very firmly said, "You were late today. You're not going to do that again (and I thought I had gotten away with something). I'll see you Monday at 9:30 A.M."

Monday morning I arrived at 9:15.

Shirley was already there having cornflakes. Shirley was very nice in the beginning. She offered lots of advice about journalism and she told me a lot about herself and her career. Shirley also asked me all kinds of loaded questions. "Have you known Melvin long? Don't you think Melvin is handsome? How did you meet him?" I guess she was feeling me out. I can't really blame her, here is this girl who just calls Melvin Van Peebles out of the blue and four days later is sitting comfortably in his living room, whereas Shirley has known him for over twenty years.

I met a lot of people that day, all of whom I still have a soft spot for in my heart.

Ironically, the three people that I grew closest to during the production—Tommy, Isabel, and Kia, a production assistant who joined the team later—were all born on the same day.

Tommy Jarecki's parents were old friends of MVP. He and I started working that Monday. Tommy and I were both going to school in Boston. Tommy was really sweet. Whenever I needed help, Tommy was there. That includes blowing up 150 balloons for the fashion-show scene, with Mario's brother Max watching and laughing.

Isabel Taylor-Helton is quite beautiful and sophisticated —and believe me—she knows it. Isabel is a great gal. We both tend to dabble in astrology and our signs are very compatible (Isabel's a Pisces and I am a Scorpio).

Bernard Johnson, the costume designer, is an absolute scream. Bernard is this little-bitty guy with a huge mouth. He is a flirt and has incredible energy and a very naughty sense of humor. (I love it!) Bernard and I had so much fun together.

Ferman "Virgo with an Aquarius rising" Lee, the Gaffer, reminded me of my grandfather. Not because he is old, because he's not, but because he has the same mischievous nature as my granddad. Although he was very serious the first day we met, once we got to know each other we had loads of fun. Ferman would always tease Kia and me by calling us "princesses" whenever we complained about something.

That Monday was just script revisions, running errands for Isabel and Shirley, meeting people and preparing for the auditions that were to be held the following morning.

The next day it was back down to Henry Street. By now I

had read the script and loved it. It was hilarious and I was very interested in seeing how it would happen.

As the actors came and went, I would mentally select whoever I thought should play this or that role.

When I first saw Shelly Burch, I knew she was going to be Roxy, the gorgeous amazonian deaf-mute. Shelly is not only beautiful, but she has a great body and a certain vulnerability, as they say in show biz. Shelly was perfect, especially after all the other model types who were also up for the role. To me, they were too ugly, too old-looking, too young-looking, or just unfeminine.

One person who auditioned was the largest female bodybuilder in the world, six feet two inches and all muscle. Chris, Mario's friend who was acting as second assistant director for a while, and I freaked out when we saw her. She came with her husband/manager who was about the size of Danny DeVito. I kept nudging Chris, who happens to be a bodybuilder. I just couldn't believe that She was not a He. Chris explained to "little me" (his nickname for me) that some women with the help of steroids could get that bulky. (Why?!) The husband kept boasting about how much money they made through various bodybuilding pageants (freak shows) and endorsements and how awful she looked before her transformation.

Another casting I got right on the nose was Sue, the sexy, Dolly Partonish secretary.

She walked in wide-eyed and fresh from a recent "nookie trip" (her words) to California. Take away Dolly's boobs and add two huge eyes and you have the actress. The real clincher came when she did her imitation of a baby crying. She actually gets paid to sound like a baby for commercials and soap operas. Her face scrunched up and she started making these baby noises. It was hilarious. Hello, Sue!

One soap-opera actress from *All My Children* was up for the part of Spike, the tough, punk-rock bartender in the sleazy bar scene. She strutted in with a shorter-than-short black miniskirt, a very low-cut white tank top, black fishnet stockings, and black pumps with four-inch heels.

NO IDENTITY CRISIS

We were talking and having a good time. I was trying to get information out of her about upcoming episodes of *All My Children* and she was trying to get information out of me about the script. Neither of us was successful.

Another girl who was up for the part was there at the same time chatting with us. Talk about opposites, she was heavy, short, not very attractive, and Puerto Rican. She was dressed in a blue unitard and a leather jacket.

Mario stepped out of the room for a breather and the first actress started squealing about how fine he was and all the things that she would do to him if she ever had him alone. To add to all of that, she called out his name, slipped her sleeves off her shoulders, making her breasts seem huge, and licked her lips. (Mario was completely oblivious to this dramatic display of lust.) When her turn came to go in, she burst through the door and barked, "I'm gonna kick your butt and I'm gonna take your shoe off to do it."

Unfortunately, that was one of the auditions I didn't get to sit in on. Chris told me that she left MVP a very erotic photograph of herself. But the second actress got the job.

Casting Yves's nerdy yuppie son was difficult for me. Everyone I liked the panel hated or vice versa. As a matter of fact, at first, I didn't like the actor who got the part. There was another guy ahead of him that I thought would be much better. Boy, was I wrong, because Ilan Mitchell-Smith, the actor who was chosen, went on to do an excellent job as Sebe, Yves's son. I liked him a lot too as a person. He was loads of fun.

By the end of the day MVP made his choices. Ann Marie went home, leaving Shirley to take care of the details of the deal memos and contracts. It was all interesting, especially the deal memos, which broke everything down in simple terms, such as transportation, meals, or any special needs that an actor had. By reading between the lines I think I learned a lot.

Lillian Pyles, the production office coordinator, was the next person that I met. When I first saw Lillian I thought that she was related to MVP. They have similar profiles. I wasn't the only person to notice the resemblance. The doorman at MVP's place asked Lillian if she was MVP's daughter. (Lillian had red hair, compliments of Dark and Lovely, and from what I've been told, MVP's daughter Megan also has red hair, except that it is natural.)

I decided that I liked Lillian. She was a lot of fun. I kind of latched myself to her for the production.

The first couple of days Lillian and I were busy setting up the production office. That meant getting files organized, putting together the Contact List (a listing of all the vendors used by the production company), starting the Staff and Crew List (names, positions, and addresses of the crew), buying supplies, etc.

By the way, MVP referred to me as an intern and was not paying me. Money is not my favorite topic of conversation. I find it embarrassing to talk about, so I just kept working, silently hoping that he'd offer to give me a couple of dollars. Then one day MVP asked to see me. Alone? (Had I done something wrong? Or was MVP upset because all of a sudden I was with Lillian all the time rather than with him?)

So, we went into a little room across the hall. I sat down. MVP stood. The conversation went something like this:

MVP: So, are you learning anything?

JN (nervously):   Oh yes, a lot. I am learning a lot about the office working with Lillian.

MVP: Uh-huh, uh-huh. (There he goes with the uh-huh, uh-huh again.) Lillian says you're a lot of help to her. Well, tell me, what are you interested in getting out of this? What do you want to do with your life? (My least favorite question!)

JN: Well, I don't know. I'm still young. Um . . . maybe I'd like to do what Shirley does, make documentaries.

MVP: Well, you know, Shirley is what you call a giant in her field.

JN: Yeah, I mean yes, I know.

There was a knock at the door. Someone to see MVP. MVP excused himself and went to meet with the person at the door.

NO IDENTITY CRISIS

I went back to work in the office with Lillian, not mentioning a word of my conversation with MVP.

Bernard stopped by and we started joking around and gossiping. He told me an interesting story about an incident that happened way- back with him and MVP. It seems that Bernard was working with MVP on *Aint Supposed to Die a Natural Death* and the cast got a little uppity with MVP. Bernard read them all the riot act and the show went on to be a hit.

Just as Bernard was finishing the story, MVP called me back into the windowless little room.

" . . . Anyway," MVP said, renewing his conversation, "I like the way you work. Someone said you mentioned wanting to be a writer, so remember, I don't want to see any gossipy articles about me, my family, or movie-making secrets! Next, you're new, so let me make it real clear, I'm the boss! My orders supersede everyone's—Lillian's, Mario's, Jim's, etc.—got that? That's the way it works. If you want a job, you got it. But if you let me down or cross me, I'm going to break both of your legs! And don't think I'm fucking around. I'm from the South Side of Chicago and I will kick your ass! So . . . what would you like to do—stay or go?"

I was horrified. I couldn't believe that this man had just threatened me. I was so shaken up that I almost started to cry, but I kept my cool.

JN (softly):   I like working with Lillian. I think I'd be good in the office.

MVP: Uh-huh, uh-huh, that's fine with me. So, now you're a production assistant.

JN (in shock):   Okay, great.

MVP: Great, huh? Well, it should be, since you're gonna start getting paid as of today.

I got up slowly and walked out of the room, looking over my shoulder as I was leaving, his blunt words still ringing in my ears.

JIM

This was my first time to work with Mario. We had spent a lot of time together, but this was the first time that we were on the set together. As it turned out, I was highly pleased with his conduct on the set. Very much impressed with his knowledge of filmmaking in general. And he was a definite asset to production in front of and behind the camera. He had a strong hand with the casting and he felt the need to stress technical standards, on which, of course, we concurred with him. Of course the relationship between Melvin and Mario had plenty of opportunity for tension. They had never really worked together as peers. I mean, there was the father directing the son and there was the son a star in his own right. Was the son going to try to usurp the powers of the director/father? Bear in mind that Mario was the writer and one of the co-producers. Plus all of this without clearly defined lines of authority and power. It could have been a disaster if each individual had not practiced rigid self-discipline, and been considerate of the other person.

This type of working relationship had great potential dangers, which for the most part never really surfaced, except for one time.

BLOCK

The embodiment of all the preparation for the actual shooting of a feature film is the strip board. The strip board is a series of about eight to ten panels, each sixteen inches tall and ten inches wide, hinged in a way to fold for convenient carrying. The inside of each panel has a ridge at the top and bottom so that "strips" of cardboard, each representing the essential information for the shooting of a specific scene can

NO IDENTITY CRISIS

easily be put in, taken out, rearranged, or what-have-you, and eventually turned over when the scene has been finally shot. In short, a strip board is a thumbnail visualization of all the weeks of preproduction.

Strip boards with their sturdy black leather covers seem immutable, as if they contain irrefutable natural laws of the universe . . . one almost tends to forget the thousands of wishy-washy, six-of-this-half-a-dozen-of-that, heads-you-win-tails-I-lose decisions that actually went into 90 percent of the Truth cast on the cardboard strips therein.

Realistically, minus the spine-stiffening hyperbole, what a well-prepared strip board boils down to is a battle plan for the shooting phase of the filmmaking process.

A strip board is a pleasant reference when you are ahead of schedule and a sullen reproach when you are behind.

Although the concept of a strip board is not difficult to understand, to prepare one (because of financial and technical considerations) is a complicated task. At first glance, even a finished strip board seems a mangled mess (which is not too far from the truth . . . strips of cardboard bearing bits of scenes chopped and rearranged into delectable, digestible bits for the filmmaking process) . . . unnecessarily complicated—*not really*—there is method in the madness.

Take *Identity Crisis*, a fairly classic case: over 150 scenes, 193, to be exact. So if you start at Scene 1, shoot it, then shoot Scene 2, then 3, and so forth, right on down the line, everything would be fine—right? . . . *Wrong!*

Suppose Scene 1 is an OUTSIDE:NIGHT shot on the West Side, and Scene 2 is an INSIDE:NIGHT shot on the East Side, and then Scene 3 is an OUTSIDE:NIGHT shot back on the West Side again. Time- and money-wise it would be suicide to shoot in sequence. Just think about it for a moment. You shoot Sebe and his dad driving down Fifth Avenue, then go across town and shoot Chilly D. walking down the hallway with his ghetto blaster, and then back outside and across town again to shoot Sebe and his dad cruising through the city. Don't forget there is a small army of technicians, equipment, and support personnel (though never seen) standing behind the camera: sound truck, lighting truck, makeup truck, food truck. The quickest way to ensure a mutiny in the film business is not to have hot coffee for the crew on a chilly night. Imagine revving everyone up, shooting that Fifth Avenue scene, then shlepping over to a corridor in some factory, setting up (which can take forever), then shooting a quick hallway shot, then rounding up the whole kit-and-caboodle and heading back out into the night again.

Obviously it would be more expedient to shoot OUT-SIDE:NIGHT Scene 3 immediately after OUTSIDE:NIGHT Scene 1, and do Scene 2 on some other occasion . . . and that, Virginia, is what a strip board is all about. It simply reflects the preproduction decisions, of which there are a zillion, all things considered, for grouping scenes, or parts of scenes into their most efficient clusters.

A strip board is an idyllic dream of how principal photography will proceed—dream, because it never seems to come out that way. In the case of *Identity Crisis,* the dream quickly deteriorated into a nightmare.

Normally the strip board is prepared by the first assistant director, first A.D., under the supervision of the director. He correlates and consolidates the preproduction decisions, then starting with the appropriately colored strip (blue for OUTSIDE:NIGHT, yellow for OUTSIDE:DAY, white for INTE-RIORS) he jots the information on the strip. Then the strips are assembled on the board in the most desirable sequence.

Because the start of principal photography was moved forward, the man Jim had talked me into promoting to first A.D. could not join the team until four days before actual shooting began, and the task of preparing the strip board fell between the cracks and landed in the lap of Chris, the temporary second A.D., a sincere guy, but also a neophyte himself, who unfortunately had insufficient training for the task, and who even more unfortunately had no way of realizing it on his own, and instead of giving him the proper supervision, I was so busy, as a result of our accelerated preproduction schedule, that the impending catastrophe completely escaped my notice. To add insult to injury, when

the first A.D. did show up, he turned out to be totally un-
suited for the position and resigned after a few days. Eventually a truly terrific first A.D. was found, a fellow named
Ed DeSisso, a hardworking, extremely competent, take-no-
shit kind of guy.

The *bad news* is that the strip board was in such poor
shape by then that even with Ed on the team it didn't get
straightened out until we were halfway through principal
photography.

The *good news* is that it wasn't the disaster it might have
been because I rarely use the damn things. In fact, the truth
is I was four days into the shooting of the film before I even
realized that the "official" strip board was out of whack.

Being self-taught moviemakingwise (my basic film education, other than watching triple features in the balcony,
consisted of a guy showing me how to "splice," glue the ends
of film together, back in the pre-Scotch-tape days) I didn't
even know that such a thing as a strip board existed until I
was on my ninth or tenth short film. For years I had managed by simply thinking through the film I was going to
shoot. Then, in my head, I would put the scenes into groups
and sequences that would make them as cheap as possible
to shoot and make my film. As my movies gradually grew
longer and more complicated the groups and the sequence
of scenes would fly out of my head during the hurly-burly of
actually making the film. My mind would go blank on me
and I could not remember what scene I had planned to do
next. Then one day the obvious solution hit upon *me* (the
solution being so obvious that I shrink from claiming that I
hit upon *it*). Write it down! *voilà*, eureka, etc. From that day
forth I never had a problem. Before I began filming, I started
(and still do) by assigning every scene in a film two numbers. The first number represents its actual chronological
position in the script. The second number represents its position in the sequence I intend to shoot.

In short I had reinvented the strip board. In fact the only
major difference between an official strip board and my device, which I dubbed "the poor man's strip board" is the

amount of information on a strip. Whereas an "official" board is a piece of cardboard with tons of pertinent information on it, all cleverly condensed through the use of colors, codes, and abbreviations, I discovered that once I knew what scene I was to shoot all the relevant material surrounding it sprang back into my head free of charge; therefore my "poor man's" board consisted of only a line describing the scene which served to remind me where I was and what was coming next. No matter how voluminous, the instant I focused on the line describing a scene, all the other essential information came rushing back to me; which actors, which props, what equipment, and so on. Although I began to keep an "official" strip board, it was mostly for the use of the other members of the crew, to enable them to stay in sync with one another.

Personally I still prefer my one-line scene descriptions, the "poor man's strip board," which translates into five or six triple-spaced sheets of regular typing paper that can be folded and handily tucked into a trouser or jacket pocket. Not so handily, however, that I'm not always losing a copy. My specific Alzheimer's antidote is to make six backup copies from the original before I begin shooting.

Anyway, that's how, like I said, it was the fourth day of shooting before I realized that we were in deep shit as far as the "official" board was concerned.

PRINCIPAL PHOTOGRAPHY

NOTES FROM PRINCIPAL PHOTOGRAPHY

The manuscript moves from some beginning to an end following a thread in the author's head. That is the story: Phase One. Once that story is chosen to be turned into a film it must pass into Phase Two, where it is disassembled and rearranged for the convenience of "principal photography" —the shooting process. Then afterward in "postproduction" —the editing process—it enters Phase Three, where it is reassembled into a fascimile of the original script, Phase One.

The journal of *Identity Crisis* follows the day-by-day chronology of principal photography—the Phase Two disassembled order of the actual shooting—rather than the natural story line. This way you get to relive the contortions of the filmmaking process. The trials and tribulations will be where they occurred in principal photography, in that aberration known as the shooting schedule. In the end, after the dust has cleared, it is the way one usually remembers an event, anyway.

IDENTITY CRISIS SYNOPSIS

Flamboyant French designer Yves Malmaison (Richard Fancy) has the world at his feet, but the lavish Manhattan opening of his new line of dresses turns out to be a setting for murder. Accompanied by his yuppie son Sebastian (Ilan Mitchell-Smith)—to whom the effeminate designer is a constant embarrassment—Malmaison heads for his glittering opening, unaware it will be his last party. On the way, he hands a crazy old bag lady a bottle of whiskey. She babbles that she is a witch, and owes him a favor.

Meanwhile, Chilly D. (Mario Van Peebles), an employee in Malmaison's firm—a young rapping Romeo of a janitor—has been stealing dresses and redesigning them for his girlfriends. Chilly D. is unaware that an international gang has been using the dresses to smuggle narcotics and that he has been giving away their loot. The thugs corner Chilly D. to force him to reveal what he has done with their fortune in drugs.

Climbing out of a window to escape the thugs, Chilly D. falls from the ledge and crashes onto the sidewalk unconscious. Just then, Yves lurches out onto the same sidewalk, gasping his last breaths. Yves cries out for help, and the old bag lady conjures a genuine spell. Amid crackling blue lightning, the spirit of the fashion designer enters Chilly D.'s body.

Malmaison wakes up in Chilly D.'s body, very confused about his identity. Yves seeks out his son Sebastian (who, at first, does not recognize him) and together they set out after the killers. But every time Chilly D. receives a blow on the head, his own personality takes over from Yves, and Sebastian has to learn to deal with both of them in one body.

The trail leads them through the "underground" clubs of Manhattan, to "rap music" concerts, where Chilly D. and his friends perform, a dismal night in jail, hilarious encounters with sexy ladies, a female mud wrestler (Shelly Burch), rough gay bars, exciting chases through Manhattan harbor, and a wild shootout of a finale. Made on location in New York City, by Melvin Van Peebles, *Identity Crisis* features dozens of offbeat, colorful characters and a hot, original music track. A fast-paced murder mystery loaded with unexpected laughs—a brilliant satirical twist on every double identity movie ever made!

IDENTITY CRISIS (POOR MAN'S STRIP BOARD)

1. EXT. STREET MALMAISON SHOWROOMS AND OFFICES NIGHT
2. EXT. STREET NIGHT
3. INT. MALMAISON OFFICE BUILDING NIGHT
4. EXT. STREET NIGHT
5. EXT. LIMO ROOF NIGHT
6. EXT. SIDEWALK NIGHT
7. EXT. ENTRANCE MALMAISON OFFICE BUILDING NIGHT
8. INT. MALMAISON BUILDING
9. INT. MALMAISON OFFICES NIGHT
10. INT. ELEVATOR
11. INT. MALMAISON OFFICES (YVES) NIGHT
12. INT. HALLWAY NIGHT
13. INT. BASEMENT LOCKER ROOM NIGHT
14. INT. SHOWROOM NIGHT
15. INT. BASEMENT LOCKER ROOM NIGHT
16. INT. SHOWROOM NIGHT
17. INT. BASEMENT LOCKER ROOM NIGHT
18. INT. STAIRWELL NIGHT
19. INT. SHOWROOM NIGHT
20. INT. HALLWAY NIGHT
21. EXT. LEDGE NIGHT
22. EXT. ENTRANCE MALMAISON BUILDING NIGHT
23. INT. ROOM ADJACENT HALLWAY NIGHT
24. EXT. BLACKNESS NIGHT

25. EXT. SIDEWALK MALMAISON BUILDING NIGHT
26. INT. GRAVE DAY
27. EXT. GRAVEYARD DAY
28. INT. GRAVE DAY
29. INT. HOSPITAL ROOM DAY
30. EXT. HOSPITAL DAY
31. EXT. GHETTO STREET DAY
32. EXT. SECONDHAND STORE DAY
33. INT. HOME BOY CLUB DAY
34. INT. SLEAZE BAR DAY
35. INT. NARISH APARTMENT DAY
36. INT. HOSPITAL CORRIDOR DAY
37. EXT. STREET HARLEM DAY
38. EXT. CENTRAL PARK TWILIGHT
39. EXT. STREET RITZY SECTION NIGHT
40. EXT. FRONT YVES'S BROWNSTONE NIGHT
41. INT. EVELYN'S MANSION NEXT DOOR NIGHT
42. INT. UPSTAIRS BEDROOM YVES'S
    BROWNSTONE NIGHT
43. EXT. FRONT YVES'S BROWNSTONE NIGHT
44. INT. UPSTAIRS BEDROOM YVES'S
    BROWNSTONE NIGHT
45. EXT. YVES POV NIGHT
46. EXT. YVES'S BROWNSTONE NIGHT
47. EXT. STREET GREENWICH NIGHT
48. EXT. HOME BOY CLUB NIGHT
49. INT. AUTO NIGHT
50. INT. BURGER SHOP NIGHT
51. EXT. HAMBURGER SHOP NIGHT
52. AND 53. EXT. GHETTO STREET AND ROOFTOP NIGHT
54. INT. CHILLY'S APARTMENT NIGHT
55. AND 56. EXT. GHETTO STREET AND
    ROOFTOP NIGHT
57. INT. CHILLY'S APARTMENT NIGHT
58. INT. MALMAISON OFFICES MORNING
59. EXT. PHONE BOOTH OUTSIDE MALMAISON
    BUILDING DAY
60. INT. LOBBY MALMAISON DAY

182

NO IDENTITY CRISIS

61. INT. MALMAISON OFFICE (YVES/NARISH) DAY
62. INT. DOCTOR'S OFFICE DAY
63. EXT. ROUGH STREET DAY
64. EXT. ALLEY DAY
65. EXT. ROUGH STREET DAY
66. EXT. CHILLY'S BUILDING (RUN-DOWN
    TENEMENT) DAY
67. INT. CHILLY'S APARTMENT DAY
68. EXT. HARLEM RIVER DRIVE DAY
69. INT. VAN DAY
70. EXT. PARK CONCERT BACKSTAGE DAY
71. EXT. CONCERT PARK DAY
72. INT. CITY JAIL CELL NIGHT
73. INT. JAIL CELL LATER NIGHT
74. INT. JAIL MORNING
75. INT. SEBASTIAN'S MOM'S APARTMENT DAY
76. INT. PARKING GARAGE DAY
77. INT. MALMAISON OFFICE DAY
78. INT. MALMAISON OFFICE (YVES/NARISH) DAY
79. EXT. MALMAISON OFFICE DAY
80. INT. MALMAISON OFFICE (YVES/NARISH) DAY
81. EXT. STREET GRAMERCY PARK DAY
82. INT. LIMO DAY
83. INT. SEBASTIAN'S OFFICE
84. INT. LIMO DAY
85. INT. MALMAISON OFFICE (YVES/NARISH) DAY
86. INT. PARKING GARAGE DAY
87. INT. MALMAISON OFFICE (YVES/NARISH) DAY
88. INT. ELEVATOR
89. INT. MALMAISON OFFICE (YVES/NARISH) DAY
90. INT. STAIRWELL DAY
91. INT. MALMAISON OFFICE (YVES/NARISH) DAY
92. INT. STAIRWELL NIGHT
93. INT. HALLWAY NIGHT
94. INT. MALMAISON OFFICE (YVES/NARISH)
    NIGHT
95. EXT. STREET NIGHT
96. INT. BAR NIGHT

97. Ext. Bar Night
98. Int. Bar Night
99. Ext. Street Night
100. Int. Sleaze Bar Night
101. Ext. Back Alley Night
102. Int. Red Porsche Night
103. Ext. Street Night
104. Int. Red Porsche Night
105. Ext. Abandoned Gas Station Night
106. Ext. Entrance to Club Night
107. Int. Makeshift Arena Night
108. Int. Sleaze Bar Night
109. Ext. Sleaze Bar Night
110. Int. Mud Pit Night
111. Ext. Mud Club Entrance Night
112. Ext. Brooklyn Street Night
113. Ext. Parking Lot Night
114. Ext. 59th Street Bridge Night
115. Ext. Converted Warehouse Night
116. Ext. Loading Ramp Night
117. Int. Corridor Night
118. Int. Roxy's Place Night
119. Ext. Home Boy Club Night
120. Int. Club
121. Ext. Trash Strewn Alleyway Night
122. Int. Roxy's Place Night
123. Int. Old Warehouse Day
124. Ext. Phone Booth Day
125. Ext. House Day
126. Ext. Living Room Evening
127. Ext. Street Night
128. Int. Living Room Night
129. Int. Night (Searching for Girl with Dress Montage)
130. Int. Night (Searching for Girl with Dress Montage)
131. Int. Night (Searching for Girl with Dress Montage)

NO IDENTITY CRISIS

132. INT. NIGHT (SEARCHING FOR GIRL WITH DRESS MONTAGE)
133. EXT. NIGHT (SEARCHING FOR GIRL WITH DRESS MONTAGE)
134. INT. NIGHT (SEARCHING FOR GIRL WITH DRESS MONTAGE)
135. INT. NIGHT (SEARCHING FOR GIRL WITH DRESS MONTAGE)
136. EXT. NIGHT (SEARCHING FOR GIRL WITH DRESS MONTAGE)
137. EXT. DAWN (SEARCHING FOR GIRL WITH DRESS MONTAGE)
138. EXT. BEACH DAY (END OF MONTAGE)
139. INT. POLICE STATION INSPECTOR CUBICLE DAY
140. EXT. BEACH DAY
141. INT. POLICE STATION INSPECTOR CUBICLE DAY
142. EXT. BEACH DAY
143. INT. NARISH/YVES OFFICE DAY
144. EXT. SLEAZE BAR DAY
145. INT. CROWDED CONFERENCE HALL DAY
146. INT. DORIS DOT'S HALLWAY DAY
147. INT. CONFERENCE ROOM DAY
148. INT. DORIS DOT'S APARTMENT DAY
149. INT. CONFERENCE ROOM DAY
150. EXT. STREET DAY
151. INT. CONFERENCE ROOM DAY
152. EXT. OFFICE BUILDING DAY
153. INT. MALMAISON OFFICES (YVES/NARISH) DAY
154. EXT. BOAT DOCK PIER 21 NIGHT
155. EXT. GRAVEYARD NIGHT
156. EXT. MAX'S YACHT NIGHT
157. INT. YACHT NIGHT
158. INT. BATHROOM NIGHT
159. INT. GALLEY NIGHT
160. EXT. YACHT NIGHT
161. EXT. WATER NIGHT
162. INT. INSPECTOR HOUSE NIGHT
163. INT. MORGUE NIGHT

IDENTITY CRISIS (POOR MAN'S STRIP BOARD)

164. INT.   INSPECTOR HOUSE   NIGHT
165. INT.   OLD WAREHOUSE   NIGHT
166. EXT.   BACK ALLEY   HOME BOY CLUB   DAY
167. INT.   HOME BOY CLUB   NIGHT
168. EXT.   SHIPPING PIER   MORNING
169. EXT.   STREET   MORNING
170. INT.   CHEVY   DAY
171. EXT.   STREET   DAY
172. INT.   VAN   DAY
173. EXT.   STREET   DAY
174. INT.   POLICE STATION   INSPECTOR CUBICLE   DAY
175. INT.   NARISH'S APARTMENT   DAY
176. INT.   BARGE BELOW DECK   DAY
177. EXT.   PIER   DAY
178. INT.   ABANDONED WAREHOUSE   DAY
179. INT.   NARISH'S LIMO   DAY
180. EXT.   PHONE BOOTH   DAY
181. INT.   NARISH'S LIMO   DAY
182. INT.   BARGE   DAY
183. EXT.   PHONE BOOTH   DAY
184. INT.   NARISH'S LIMO   DAY
185. INT.   ABANDONED WAREHOUSE   DAY
186. INT.   POLICE STATION   INSPECTOR CUBICLE   DAY
187. INT.   WAREHOUSE   DAY
188. EXT.   PIER   DAY
189. INT.   BARGE   DAY
190. INT.   WAREHOUSE   DAY
191. INT.   HOSPITAL   DAY
192. INT.   TV STUDIO   DAY
193. INT.   MALMAISON SHOWROOM   DAY

THE CAST

Chilly D. .... MARIO VAN PEEBLES
Sebe ...... ILAN MITCHELL-SMITH
Narish .... NICHOLAS KEPROS
Roxy .... SHELLY BURCH
Max .... RICHARD CLARKE
The Inspector.......... MELVIN VAN PEEBLES
El Toro .... RICK AVILES
Rock .... BRUCE SMOLANOFF
I.Q. .... TAB THACKER
Yves .... RICHARD FANCY
White Eye .... HENRY YUK
Thug #1 .... HARSH NAYYAR
Thug #2 .... GLEN ATHAIDE
Nurse .... ALYCE WEBB
Hospital Doctor .... KEN PRYMUS
Hag .... HELEN HANFT
Bum .... GARY PRATT
Doris Dot .... JEFF GRIGLAK
Sue the Secretary ... PAMELA LEWIS
The Coroner STEPHEN J. CANNELL
Domino .... OLIVIA BROWN
Thrift Shop Man AUGUST DARNELL
Rap Concert M.C. ... BOBBY RIVERS
Annette's Friend .... TATIANA THUMBTZEN
Betty Boobs.......... DIANNE BRILL
Mud Club M.C. .... COATI MUNDI
Disbelieving Doctor ... LARRY "BUD" MELMAN

Inspector's Wife .. COCO MITCHELL
Jail Guard CHRISTOPHER MICHAEL
Stockholder's Spokesman ... CLARKE BITTNER
Spike .... DELORES GARCIA
Calvin .... JOHN D. MCNALLY
Ninja Twins .... ZOIE LAM
.... LIA CHANG
Woman in Window .... HOPE W. SACHAROFF
Man in Window .... DICK ASHE
Security Guard RICHARD BASSETT
Garage Attendant...... JAKE WEBER
Girls in Limo .... WANAKEE
.... DEIRDRE MAGUIRE
1st Messenger .... MARK HOOKER
2nd Messenger ..... JAMES CARTER
Girl with Whipped Cream JENNIFER STAHL
Tickling Twins ...... MICHAEL HILL
.... JOHNNIE HILL
Karate Girl .... CHINA CHEN
Girl with Dog .. BARBARA BEDFORD
Beverly .... ADRIANA
Thug .... T. JARECKI
Weasel .... DEVRON MINION
Motorcyclist .... APU GRECIA
Thug .... NATE BARNETT

THE CREDITS

Produced & Directed by MELVIN VAN PEEBLES
Written by ... MARIO VAN PEEBLES
Director of Photography JIM HINTON
Costume Designer .... BERNARD JOHNSON
Musical Director DUNN E. PEARSON
Co-Producers .... JIM HINTON
.... MARIO VAN PEEBLES
Edited by ... MELVIN VAN PEEBLES
.... VICTOR KANEFSKY
Production Manager ...... STEVEN L. JONES
1st Assistant Director ... ED DESISSO
Office Coordinator .. LILLIAN PYLES
Camera Operators   W. J. De La CRUZ
.... LEROY BROWN
1st Assistant Camera .... KARMA STANLEY
.... STEVE KAPU
2nd Assistant Camera .. IRENE SOSA
Sound Mixer .... ROLF PARDULA
Boom Mixer .... STU DEUTSCH
Gaffer .... FERMAN LEE
Best Boy .... JOHN MITCHELL
Key Grip ...... MELVIN PUKOWSKY
Art Director LOUANNE GILLELAND
Assistant Art Director..... DEBORAH WATKINS
Set Designer.......... JUSTIN TERZI
Makeup/Hair .... DEBRA REECE
.... DAVID CARRINGTON
Assistant Makeup/Hair .... DWAYNE PERRY
Costumers..... GEORGE BERGERON
.... CELIA BRYANT
Assistants to the Producer PRESTON HOLMES, ISABEL TAYLOR-HELTON
Lead Carpenter .... MICHAEL BEAUDETTE
Carpenter .... GLEN BOWEN
Set Dresser .... KEVIN O'BRIEN
Props .... MICHAEL VACHON
Van Transportation JOHN MONROE
Second Unit Director ... MARIO VAN PEEBLES

Stunt Coordinator...... JEFF GIBSON
Casting ..... ANN MARIE KOSTURA C.S.A.
Extra Casting HYDE-HAMLET, INC.
Still Photographers .... CHARLES THOMPSON
.... JUNE TRUESDALE
Production Assistants........ JUDITH NORMAN, FRED NIELSON, II, THOMAS JARECKI, STEVE BURNETT, KIA PURIEFOY, ELDRID FOYE, SABRINA KAPPLER, THORNE MAXWELL, ELEVA SINGLETON, CRYSTAL GRIFFIN, DAVID BATISTE, JOSEPH RODMAN, RUDY MOLIERE, VINCENT ROBINSON
First Assistant Editor .... MOLLY BERNSTEIN
Assistant Editors ..... MARC COHEN
.... MARY COSTANZO
Editing Room Assistants ..... JANINE FENNICK, DENA KATZEN, MICHAEL PELUSO, DERRICK W. BOATNER
Sound Editor .... AL NAHMIAS
Assistant Sound Editor.... ELEANOR GOLDSTEIN
Post Production Services.... VALKHN FILMS, INC.
Titles and Special Effects
.... THE OPTICAL HOUSE, N.Y.
Main Title Design/Art JIM SHERMAN
Negative Matching .... L & D FILMS, INC.
Color .... PRECISION LABORATORY
Legal Counsel .... MARSHA BROOKS
Additional Music .... TREVOR GALE, KENNI HAIRSTON
Music Studio .... HIP POCKET
Engineer .... BUTCH JONES
Assistant to Mr. Pearson .. JOHN VAN EPS
Re-Recording Mixer
.... MICHAEL JORDAN, MAGNO SOUND, INC.

FIRST DAYS (SHAKEDOWN/ BREAKDOWN/ & SHAKEUP)

BLOCK

Using the old, time-tested, surefire, break-them-in-gradually formula, I started shooting in midweek, on a Wednesday, so the crew wouldn't have to work a full six days before a Sunday, their off day. I chose a static group of scenes to start with, keeping the logistical distractions down to a minimum while the crew and I got to know one another. Scene 83 was our very first shot, where the secretary, Sue, is doing her nails and chatting with Sebe.

. . . couldn't have picked a better ice-breaker in a thousand years . . . Sue and Sebe are intelligent, perky and fun . . . they set the perfect tone. I hope we can hold it for the rest of the film. . . . crew nervous at first, but still very professional . . . smooth as silk by the end of day two. We'll bite the bullet in a couple of days and try and get the first logistic hurdle, scenes circa 145, the stockholders' meeting, out of the way. The security guard warns me, for the umpteenth time, to be careful not to scratch the walls with the equipment. . . . Rumor has it that the first A.D., who should be running interference for me and handling such matters was sneaking a nap somewhere (we'll see about that).

Thanks in a large part to Mario's taking the directorial duty of coaching the actors off my shoulders, we were able to move right from scene to scene as soon as the lights were ready for the next setup.

I would have been happy if Mario had been simply fair at preparing the actors for a scene, but he surpassed my wildest hopes. He was better than good. He was excellent. But with my being a pragmatist and a disciple of the Law of Diminishing Returns, he would still get on my nerves with his suggestions—wouldn't it be nice to have just-one-more-shot-from-this-other-angle-Dad. The extras and the crew were capable, attentive, and congenial. Nonetheless I thought—if my ol' ears didn't deceive me—I detected a few clanks and pings in our filmmaking machinery.

. . . Saturday . . . No, my ears haven't deceived me . . . support team needs a tune-up. . . . A vital bit of info was not passed along and . . . shit hits the fan. The lovely little Art Deco lobby—circa Scenes 8 and 60—that we were going to shoot Saturday afternoon, is only available Saturday morning. SCRAMBLE TIME . . . send a third of the crew over to Sebe's mom's apartment, originally the first location planned for today, telling them to prelight the set. This is a stall tactic to make sure we don't lose the location. . . . Dashing down to the lobby with the rest of the team, I realize it is too short a notice to change the extras call. . . . Still need to tie the lobby in with the fashion show . . . aha, I get an idea. . . .

ISABEL

When we started the movie MVP told me to bring in some kind of evening dress and put it in the closet just in case.

"For what?" I asked, heart thumping. Of course, I knew better than to presuppose anything around MVP.

" . . . Uh . . . maybe I'll get to use you in the fashion show scene."

"Oh, Melvin, you mean I'm going to be in the movie?" Oh, wow! I don't believe it. I wasn't going to be fit to live with.

NO IDENTITY CRISIS

I pantomimed a little dance step, followed by a vampy actress look. I followed MVP to the elevator during my performance. He gave me his deadpan look. The way people look when you wave your hand in front of their eyes to bring them back to the present.

"Don't get carried away," was all he said.

You are now probably thinking, dear readers, What the hell does that mean? So was I, but his mental door was shut . . . end of subject.

Our costume designer, Bernard Johnson, whom I love dearly, had borrowed a fabulous silk three-piece outfit from Lester Hayatt for me. It hung in the closet awaiting our movie debut.

Forever came and went. At least that's the way it seemed. Actually it was only the third day, but I had given up asking anyone when my scene was. The activity was at another location, so they couldn't possibly want me today. It was fairly quiet in the office. Celia Bryant, the wardrobe mistress, was gathering garments together for a later scene and doing the whatever necessary maintenance, such as spot cleaning and mending. Debbie Reece, wig and makeup, was in the bathroom coloring Jake Weber's hair red. I overheard that the first choice for the part had refused to have his hair colored.

Finally I figured that I could get at my backlog of paperwork. Two days can produce a serious backlog around here under normal circumstances, but now when nothing is normal, two days of neglect could cause havoc. Just as I began working . . . a P.A. arrived with the command to get Isabel ready. Melvin wanted her on the set in thirty minutes. The set was ten minutes away by fast car, assuming you made all of the lights. By van . . . in Saturday matinee traffic . . . we're talking twenty-three minutes.

Celia rushed me into the Lester Hayatt outfit, while Debbie, who had left Jake's hair for the moment, attempted to create miracles with my hair and makeup. We drove very carefully (as in crawled) to the location, our driver, Eldrid, being extremely careful not to excite the wrath of police.

My big moment onscreen and I feel thrown together. But worse, I have no idea what is expected of me. Times like these make me want to succumb to the debilitating effects of anger and strangle my boss.

Melvin—no greeting . . . nothing . . . directed me to . . . "Stand here"—someone made a mark on the floor—"walk to there"—another mark on the floor—then he said, "Look in your bag as though you're looking for tickets and rushing because you're late." He demonstrated. I thought he looked weird. His knees were bent kind of like Charlie Chaplin's. I ran across in front of the cameras. He demonstrated again. Imagine Melvin trying to imitate a woman in high heels. It was hysterical. I looked around: Jim Hinton, Mario, Ferman Lee, Irene Sosa. I smiled a bit, attempted a joke about how Melvin looked. Everyone was serious. My joke died less than three breaths from my mouth. With each demonstration by Melvin, his knees seemed more bent. Obviously, this had something to do with my being too tall for the lights—my head in shadow or something else rational. Hey, this was show biz. I did as directed.

Months later at the editing room, I saw me and said, "Oh gads, I don't even walk like that." Then as the movie rolled on, we noticed that the other actors Nicholas Kepros and Henry Yuk walked the same way. It was a joke on the director that he took very well—his cast of many Charlie Chaplins.

My next scene—same dress, was edited out. It was the fashion show scene where dress designer Yves (Richard Fancy) is poisoned by Narish (Nick Kepros). After working in the office all day I went to the set to prepare for my next appearance in *Identity Crisis*. Debbie Reece was busy duplicating the makeup of the actors for scenes done days before by another makeup person, Kelly Wechter, who had quit. This must be done with extreme accuracy, because although the scenes may be photographed days apart and in another location, when the film reaches the editing room it must read as one continuous period of time. Just figure that it takes nine hundred feet of film for ten minutes of onscreen action. Should there be interior and exterior used, add more footage, hours and even days. With the aid of Polaroid stills and one's mind's eye, the makeup is re-created. Debbie was working solely from Polaroids and did a great job. I felt it really didn't matter who did me. David Carrington had replaced Kelly and proceeded to work on me. We chitchatted as Debbie told him what she had used on my face the week before, since she had been so rushed there were no Polaroids of me. I said, "Just make me young." And we all laughed. When you're fifty-five, that may not be possible without a knife. As David layered on the makeup, I began to feel as if my face was in a mask. Melvin walked past and gave me what I sensed as a dirty look. Oh, rats, he's going into one of his bags! Now, although I'm as nearsighted as a bat, I didn't bother to check myself out with my eyeglasses on. Melvin avoided me all evening, both with the camera and without it. When I finally saw myself close up, I looked like something out of *Weird World* with flying eyebrows and ten layers of war paint on my face. Makeup tip to all who don't already know: Less for more. Use much *less* makeup for the much *more* than forty years old.

BLOCK

Getting the lobby scenes took longer than expected, because someone from the support team hadn't secured permission to shut off the elevators during takes. Another bit of crucial logistics fallen through the cracks. Invariably an elevator door would open in the middle of a shot and people would pour into the lobby ruining the take. Third day of shooting and we were coming apart at the fucking seams.

When we finally finished shooting the scene in the lobby I scooted off to join the rest of the crew at the Sebe-Mom-apartment, the location we had originally planned to shoot first. As soon as I got in the door, the script girl/lady/person beckoned me aside and informed me she was quitting at the end of the day.

"Why?"

"You never even ask me for your next shot, or anything," she grumbled.

"That's because I know where I am."

"I feel useless. For example, when I suggest a shot to cover something you ignore me."

"That's because I know what I want. . . . "

" . . . All I do is keep track of length and exposures, barely even basic . . . "

"That's part of a script girl's . . . er . . . person's duties," I countered. "That 'barely basic' is essential information. This is your first feature. Maybe you oughta . . . "

" . . . Well, yes it is, but I can't help it," she cut in, "I just feel unfulfilled, and besides, the crew doesn't respect me."

Aha! The worm was about to stick its ol' head out of de apple! I could feel it!

"Jim told me I should stop pestering you with classroom junk."

Jim was absolutely right, but I wasn't sure I could find a new script girl/lady/man/person by Monday morning. "Why, that's outrageous!" I protested. "I'll straighten Jim out right after this shot."

"My mind's made up," she said, mentally crossing her arms and stamping her foot.

I said that I understood and respected her position, but I hoped that since she was such a complete professional she would give me until Monday evening to find someone to replace her. She took the bait and agreed.

After we had wrapped for the day, and gotten back to the office, there was a little farewell party for Preston, who had been such a help but who had to leave because of a previous film commitment. After we'd eaten the cake and the others had left, the three of us, Jim, Preston, and myself tracked down the source of each and every fuckup. Then we analyzed the incidents, drew up a list of the deadbeats, incompetents, and thieves, and spent the rest of the evening scrambling to find replacements for them.

I staggered to bed at some wee hour (thanking God that Sunday was our off day) and fell asleep with the light on.

HITTING OUR STRIDE (INTERIORS-R-US/ RAPPERS/& CAMEOS)

BLOCK

Monday morning, smiling faces . . . a good sign. Finish move to Henry Street, its complex of rooms to serve as quasi-soundstages. As soon as a set is prepared and dressed we shoot and move on. . . . Jim politely gives the script person a few traditional tasks to do. . . . She starts smiling and asks to withdraw her resignation. . . . What the hell, I accept . . . Discover that the art director is a genius!

The original script had a zillion locations, not just the usual handful of places pinging back and forth (which would have been difficult enough to shoot), but a zillion *different* locations. Anyway, the first thing a director usually does when he gets his hands on the script is to consolidate and trim down the number of locations to a "reasonable," "manageable" size. However, I felt that the dizzy jumble of environments created a zany, quirky, mosaic of a background that captured the essence of Lower Manhattan and provided the perfect backdrop for the plot. To make a long story short, I decided to keep all the locations.

Of course, my decision to keep all the haunts he'd thrown into the script thrilled Mario . . . theoretically at least. Clear to me, not so clear to him, was the breakneck style of shooting this would necessitate. Our major bone of contention throughout the shooting was my bim-bam treatment of a scene versus his desire to linger over every sequence . . . understandable, perhaps (after all, it was his first baby), but potentially fatal. In my opinion, if we devoted a century to every nuance, we would end up with a three-hour-plus film, which even if we weren't working on a deadline to get him back in time for the beginning of his TV show, would be an hour and a half too long for a comedy feature.

Normally a director would have the writer thrown off the set. For obvious reasons, that was a little hard to do in Mario's case. Plus, notwithstanding the fact that he could be a royal pain, he kept coming up with a lot of brilliant suggestions. Luckily we were using two cameras and luckily there was a considerable amount of second-unit stuff to do.

. . . Hope the new first assistant director works out . . . too many dire emergencies, some the real thing, some absolute bullshit, rushing at me. . . . Beginning to lose my sense of perspective . . . lacking the time to analyze, you end up treating everything as a matter of life and death just to be on the safe side.

CHIP

Ever hear the joke about the bimbette who goes to Hollywood to be a star, and is so dumb she sleeps with a writer? Although the script is the blueprint for a film, writers don't get much say in a project, but, since I was also coach, actor, co-producer, and second-unit director it was kinda tough to kick me off the set. I didn't want to abuse my opportunity and I kept my opinions to a minimum. On a few occasions however, Dad Van Peebles, ever the diplomat, felt the writer in me was having too many suggestions. He would politely tell me to shut the hell up, or better yet, he'd give me something to direct on second unit. He'd say something like, "Hey, son, take camera B and a skeleton crew and go shoot us some oncoming traffic. Yeah, and take your time. Be back in, say . . . two years."

I'd be off in a flash. Usually I'd try to grab "Steady Sticks Willy" as operator, Sabrina (the fine P.A.), and Tommy. Tommy can drive his ass off and is full of ideas. Quiet Willy can hang out back of a moving truck and make it look steady, and Sabrina keeps all the local traffic distracted with a flick of her dark mane.

BLOCK

. . . First glimpse of rappers all together in costume, delicious. . . . The construction of the special sets for the chase sequences have begun. Catch as catch can. . . . The poor man's strip board is what we're working from while the official one is being rebuilt. . . . Yep, catch as catch can. . . .

When the day's shooting is finished and the crew has been tucked in, there are notes and calls and conferences still out there pounding at the door of my mind, hollering to get in.

I catch a breather as Tommy drives me up to my other office in Midtown. Isabel answers the bell. As I cross the threshold, a stampede of emergencies real and fake rushes at me.

NEGROTHON wants personal object to auction to raise funds.

WALL STREET FIRM needs notarized signature for security bond.

A MR. MAURICE says he hears I might do a movie and what would his cut be if he finds a big investor.

LAWYER FRIEND has a girlfriend who wants to be in movies.

CELEBRITY SERVICE wants an update.

ITALY wants *Sweetback* material.

ARRANGE FOR cash to convert the crew's checks to money.

JERRY wants to know if the agent got his manuscript.

A MR. WINSTON has found just the right boat this time.

ETC., etc., etc.

BERNARD

Melvin kind of let me know at nine o'clock that Doris Dot the transvestite was working the next morning. So that meant dash, cut, and get, the kind of thing you think you can do if you've had the exerience. Knowing someone is coming in, but not necessarily knowing the specific size that they may be means, first of all, the fabric has to stretch. It's got to stretch two ways. Next, the outfit has got to be something that once it goes on will look like it was meant to be that way. Then you have to give it flair. After all, that's what you get paid for. I made it somewhat tacky so that it would look like the kind of dress an unsophisticated drag queen in show business would wear. So, I came up with the idea of the dress as this almost-flamenco thing. Actually, the cat looked great. Mr. Melvin told me he loved it and he knew I could do it. I was pleased as punch, but I still could have strangled him on the spot.

BLOCK

The crew, indoors at least, has turned into a well-oiled machine. Jim hit the jackpot. They have stamina and are congenial too. Maybe I have died and gone to heaven. . . .

The weather, which has been abominable, breaks, and I decide to shoot an outdoor scene, 31, the thrift shop, to ease the crew into the street work that will be coming. Everything goes fine, except the boss lady of the laundry next door stands in the doorway of her shop, staring into the camera, and refuses to budge unless she is given double the previously negotiated sum.

The sun stays out, so, taking advantage of our good for-

NO IDENTITY CRISIS

tune, we backtrack and shoot scene 30, the exterior of the hospital. . . . By afternoon the weather turns funky again.

CHRIS

I was perched on the stage assisting the fill-light that looked down into the orchestra pit which had been dressed as Chilly D.'s bedroom, and I was glad to be indoors and not out in the cold and rain with the second crew. Normally, thanks to Mario's pressuring Dad—I like to call MVP Dad too—I would be trying my wings as second assistant director. But we were temporarily short-handed, having split the crew because of the weather, and I ended up helping the gaffer. At first I envied Mario on the bed down below, the lucky asshole, being straddled by some scantily dressed, sexy chick with a gorgeous shape. But by the third or fourth take, it was so funky down there that the aroma had risen all the way up to me and started to make me and the lights turn green. I wondered how brother Mario could stand it down there, and I began to long for some good old rain and fresh air.

BLOCK

Surprisingly the set dresser has turned out to be level-headed, resourceful, and kind. I say surprisingly because in his job interview he was haughty, with a capital H. After announcing he was gay, he launched into a tirade about the script and said he wouldn't consider working for the production unless various homosexual references were toned down. Demeanor aside, his points made sense, so his suggestions/demands were used . . . no business like show bizness.

Speaking of that, each one of the three rappers was a trip. Their actual hipness was in inverse proportion to the amount of melanin in their skin. Bruce, the little White guy, was the most streetwise. Rick, the Puerto Rican, was often an MC at the Apollo, and Tab, the huge dark brother from the *Police Academy* movies had been the collegiate heavyweight wrestling champ. Anyone of three taken individually would stand out in a crowd, but as a team they took a quantum leap. As apprehensive as I was about the logistics of the concert, crowd control, playback, etc. I could hardly wait to get to those scenes.

BERNARD

Alec Guinness is the only actor that I can bring to mind who can, outside of Mario, be in a thing and just keep changing back and forth and convince you. It's indicative of Mario's unique talent that he can juggle in and out of character like that. Especially when you see him in the scenes where, for example, he is playing an effeminate French father of a straight young man and then go from being that character into being a macho home boy without even a change of costume to help. His overstated drag-designer routine really impressed me and depressed me too. I had not really been in touch with Mario since he had reached manhood and, you know, I was hoping against hope. Actually when he first did that routine in the movie my heart sank, because I realized that he was straight as an arrow and that there was no chance for me. You know straights do it better, play gay. I figured out why. They're not self-conscious about it and they watch all those nuances and all that people who are gay do without even realizing it. When you ask gays to do it on stage, or TV, or on film, they become self-conscious and want to hide the truth, but a straight guy can just do it. That's how I knew that man in the film *La Cage aux Folles*

—he has nine children, for God's sake—was straight; he played a gay part so well. Just like Mario, they can do it because they know it ain't so.

BLOCK

The rap concert, circa Scene 70: the cute routine Mario had worked up for the rappers turned out great. But I was a little premature on the well-oiled-crew accolades, at least office-staff-wise. The call sheet said 6:00 A.M. instead of 6:00 P.M. and a very pissed caterer showed up with dinner for the crew twelve hours early.

A number of celebrities agreed to make cameo appearances in the film. Now this was risky business, because in order to make it enticing each was given a pivotal part. However, I carefully matched the role to the person and everything worked out fine. In addition, they all turned out to be very nice people . . . not a tantrum in the bunch . . . professional, prompt . . . not even a teensy scandal in the woodpile, although I can't say the same for some of the lesser well-known employees. Ah, show biz . . .

RECEPTIONIST at jazz station wants me to read her poetry.

MR. LANDRY, Mr. Winston's friend, has got the perfect boat for the film.

SHIRLEY, my documentary filmmaker friend, wants me to know it was all a conspiracy against her.

LADY PRODUCERS I know in L.A. have a meeting coming up and need a guru—me.

REMINDER FROM MR. B., the banker, that a deposit is coming due.

FLOWERS from a New Jersey friend for profitable real estate advice.

JERRY wants to know if the agent liked his manuscript.

ETC. . . . etc. . . . etc. . . .

. . . Ed, the new first assistant director, Steve Jones, the permanent production manager, and Lillian, the office coordinator, seem to have cleared up the administrative mess. Lord, it sure would be nice to be fuck-up free from here on in. Yeah, sure, fat chance, check's in the mail. . . .

COMING AROUND THE FAR TURN (FEUDS/NIGHTS/& FIGHT)

BLOCK

. . . One of the makeup ladies quit. . . . said she felt she was worth more than her contract was paying her and that she was leaving if she didn't get bigger billing and more money . . . Told her to have a safe trip. Rumor has it that the real deal was that she was miffed about coming out on the short end of the stick in a struggle for the affections of an un-named star. . . . Must talk to unnamed star about shitting where he eats. . . . On the other hand people who have lived in a glass house, or two, should be careful with their stones. There are not many films being shot in New York at the moment, so the Screen Actors Guild, in order to give them-selves something to do, keep sending their inspectors around to check and see if we have adequate lavatories and their members have enough toilet seats per behind (I shit you not, dear diary). . . . We are running low on interiors to shoot, I hope the weather breaks soon. . . .

At the beginning of principal photography I screened the dailies. Unfortunately, this stretched the length of my days to the breaking point. Soon, unless we were going into an entirely new lighting situation, I contented myself with checking out the dailies by telephone. I would simply call the lab and ask if they had spotted any irregularities. But Jim was such a good director of photography that even though we were shooting two cameras simultaneously, there was nary a problem.

All in all, things were moving pretty smoothly. Having weathered early storms, we were feeling pretty invincible. Besides, the major thing to remember—a bit hard sometimes with all the hurly-burly that can go on behind the camera—is that it is the product in front of the camera that ultimately counts.

It was supposed to be another lousy day climatewise, but then the weather broke—luckily in time for us to notify the actors on standby to report for work—and we loaded up the trucks, vans, buses, and cars and took off, racing a threatening sky.

When we arrived at our destination we discovered we were minus a truck. The driver had decided to take what he thought was a shortcut. I passed a rule on the spot about no-deviating-from-officially-assigned-vehicular-route-without-prior-written-approval, or something like that, and rearranging the sequence of shots to accommodate the temporary disaster, we started with Scene 64.

CHIP

There are certain catchphrases that remain etched in one's psyche. Something your mother or father or perhaps some teacher verbally stung you with as a child, something that you swore you would never say. Then one day it comes flying out of your past, a psychic boomerang, nails you upside the head and spurts out your mouth.

We were shooting the alleyway sequence where Yves/ Chilly D. and Sebe search for a clue to lead them to Chilly D.'s apartment. Unbeknownst to our heroes, they had been followed by a dark, imposing figure astride a Harley-Davidson, who I as a writer imagined would suddenly drive up, engine revving menacingly, blocking the mouth of the alley. The concept being, or rather, my concept being, start with a close-up, then pan down to reveal the gorgeous Amazon in all her splendor astride the Harley. I had personally constructed her black chain-mail garb in conjunction with Bernard to give her an urban "road warrior" hipness. We added a few pink, frilly, feminine-type items to reflect her profound innocence. She was to be a sweet, deaf girl who had blossomed into a stunning woman standing six feet three, able to flatten most men at will. All right, that's all the nice, lyrical theory stuff that usually doesn't mean diddly to the guy on Times Square who asks, "That def chick wit de helmet was kicking ass, jack! Was she really dat big?" However, I found or like to believe I've found, that paying attention to even minor details—when not at the expense of the big picture, of course—pays off. That gives a character something of an offscreen back story—a personal philosophy that might reflect itself even in the minute details of wardrobe, hair, props, etc.—counts. That Joe Blow in the street, not just we in the industry who clap harder for our own screen credits than for the movie or should I say film, actually does pick up on these details.

Anyway, so back to the shoot. This alleyway sequence was to be Roxy's first appearance on the screen. I had wanted it to make a visual statement. Dad and I had both agreed on Shelly Burch to play the role of Roxy. Shelly is tall, foxy, physically imposing. I had worked with her way back when, during my long forgotten *One Life to Live* days. I had also seen her in *Nine* on Broadway with Raul Julia. A triple threat: the lady can dance, sing, act, and has chutzpah. Since the deaf-mute character of Roxy had no lines, Shelly had learned the appropriate sign language. I was concerned that she keep her facial expressions soft yet strong or intense without overcompensating for the deafness like someone talking to a friend through a store front window.

First of all, on this particular day we were doing the alley scene, it was cold, crisp, a mother of a New York day. The wind was taking no prisoners. Shelly, a real trouper, was clad only in stockings and a pink ballet tutu topped with the chain-mail jacket, so I wanted to keep her in the warmth of the van for as long as possible. Originally, we had been scheduled to shoot some other scene, but a monkey wrench in our plans forced us to fall back on the alley scene, and I had had to finish Roxy's helmet sooner than I had anticipated. As I said, I had imagined Shelly driving up and blocking the alleyway. But she couldn't drive a motorcycle.

Okay . . . so, ixnay on the driving up, we'd just have her appear at the end of the alley. Hey, it'd be more in line with the mysterious nature of her character anyway. Writers must accustom themselves to believing that kind of stuff. Now, the helmet. Dad and I had argued back and forth about her helmet. His point was, we had to put a helmet on Roxy because we'd have to double her with a stunt person for all driving sequences. Without a helmet, we would be limited to shooting her from the back, so as not to show the double's face. The writer, me, not realizing the actress cast as Roxy would probably not be able to handle the motorcycle driving convincingly, had written in that she had a long, free-flowing, thick, black mane of dreadlocks (inspired by my Bahamian *Jaws* experience). I felt strongly that dreadlocks sticking out from under a typical fishbowl motorcycle helmet crammed on Roxy's head would look stupid as hell and blow the whole look. I argued for a Roman helmet. If painted matte black, that at least would be in keeping with Roxy's urban-gladiator theme. Dad said, "To hell with her theme—we've got to cover her face! A Roman helmet has no face mask. What about a football helmet as a compromise?"

"Well, Dad," I said, trying to keep it cool, "in effect, that's no compromise at all. The football gag is the same stupid, bubbleheaded profile with dreadlocks sticking out."

"Look," he snarled, "I'm about to put the bitch's head in a paper bag 'less you got a better idea!"

Eventually, I recalled how in one of my earlier B-movies, a Cannon art film called *Exterminator II,* we had used the welding mask worn by our lead to literally mask the fact that in many scenes we used a double.

The welding mask, if done up properly, I reasoned, with bolts and paint, could look tough and metallic, hide her face entirely, and because of its open back allow her dreads to

flow freely in the wind as the writer had always intended. I
didn't mention "the writer intended" part—it just didn't
seem like the thing to say at the time, dig. I just kinda diplomatically pointed out the advantages of the welding mask.
To which he snapped, "Look, man, if you think you want to
play with some damn welding mask, fine, but I ain't in it,
and far as I concerned, if it don't work, it's paper-bag city."

So now that we were shooting this alleyway stuff ahead of
schedule, I had to pray that Bernard, the costumer, had already purchased a welding mask, and that I could spruce it
up quick, fast, and in a hurry. Okay, as luck would have it,
they had bought the mask and, yes, on the ride over from
base camp, I fixed the sucker up rather nicely, spray-painted
it, and let it dry in the cold wind.

Meanwhile, the transportation guys showed up with Rox-
y's black metallic Harley. Which turned out not to be a Harley, plus, it wasn't black. It was a funky grayish-brown. This
totally blew Roxy's pink-and-black color scheme. I grabbed
one of the transportation guys and quietly asked him what
happened with the black bike. He launched into some long-
winded explanation about this was all they had in Manhattan and to go to Jersey would have been, blah, blah, blah,
etc. So, okay, I quickly got one of the fellas in the art department and told him to cover the greenish-brown parts of the
bike with black duct tape. Quick, fast, and as I said, in a
hurry. Meanwhile, I snatched up some of the camera department's silver metallic reflector board, used to reflect
light, and going back to my papier-mâché art-class days, cut
out some cone shapes, rolled them up into horns, and taped
them to the bike's fenders like metallic dinosaur spikes to
camouflage that wimpy Suzuki look.

Just then, someone in the camera department howled,
"Who the hell snatched my black duct tape?!" The guy from
the art department yelled back, "Van Peebles told me to use
it to cover the . . . " I cut him off quickly and said, "Just cool
it and finish up fast before Mel baby starts shooting film."

"What's going on?" Pops snapped, as usual appearing out
of nowhere. I could tell by his tone of voice he was facing his

own dilemmas. Something about a semi-exposed role of film; potentially a very serious problem the gravity of which did not escape me.

"Nothing, man," I said.

"Looks like *nothing* is using up a lot of camera tape," he replied, eyeing the now mummified motorcycle.

"Hey," I said, changing the subject, "I've got your actors all ready and the mask is ready. I think you'll be happy with it." Notice I said "your" actors, making it clear I was doing him a sort of a semi-favor. Which I was, even though I loved rehearsing the actors. This saved on production time, and time was of the essence. So, I theorized that since I saved time by rehearsing the actors, what's the big deal if now and rarely then, I like needed a little extra time to make sure everything was magnifico.

"I'll be ready to shoot in two seconds," he said dryly.

"Right, me too," I replied. And then, although not wanting to overload his circuits, decided to go ahead and ask about the lighting. But too late. Lizard Dad Van Peebles had been called away on some other problem. Often it seems filmmaking is the solving of a series of logistical problems, hopefully with cinematic solutions. Maybe not, but, hey, that stuff sounds good anyway. So as not to bother the old man, I went and rapped to big Jim Hinton, our director of photography. Jim stands six feet four, moves slowly and deliberately, and chooses his words accordingly. Sure-footed, even-tempered, sturdy as hell, and a wizard with light, Jim is perpetually puffing on extra-skinny cigarettes, probably on the theory that skinny cigarettes will kill you less quickly than normal ones. I call them his "effete petite" brand and adopted them for the effeminate character of Yves. Jim's eyebrows are always up into his forehead, he has salt-and-pepper hair, bifocals low on the nose, and eyelids permanently at half-mast. He appears to be simultaneously wise and yet surprised.

"Sir Hinton," I said casually, "you gonna give me some reflected light to help throw some sparkle into foxy Roxy's eyes?"

Jim usually talks in wise minilectures, or parables, expounding on the ratio of light to dark. Father to son, film to life, etc., he's one of those guys I truly enjoy listening to and learning from and was a great Spock to my dad's Captain Kirk.

Jim took the customary light reading. By the way, the light was moving out of the alleyway at an alarming rate. But nothing shakes Big Jim. He took yet another reading, squinted up at the bashful sun, and ordered up the reflector board.

"Action!" Dad suddenly hollered out of nowhere. He occasionally did this as a threat, even though no one was manning the cameras, and the actors, including me, weren't in place. I looked over at Jim. He chuckled and gave me a knowing wink.

"All right, Mel, hold on, I'll be right there," he hollered and started one last light-meter reading as the wind began to howl.

Good, one more light reading, I thought, that gives me enough time to get Roxy in place on the motorcycle. The helmet should just about be dry, I thought, calculating the seconds in my head.

"Come on, Roxy baby, showtime," I said, trying to coax Shelly from the warmth of the van. She reluctantly stepped out as a blast of frosty downtown wind whipped through the alley, hurling my Quentin Crisp fedora down toward the camera.

"I said action, damn it!" Dad hollered again.

By now everyone was racing to man the battle stations. I grabbed the welding mask, which was as dry as it was gonna have a chance to get. The sun was going fast. The reflector board was fighting the wind, but was being held in place by an assistant. Ilan Mitchell-Smith was politely trying not to gawk at Shelly's now frozen boobs, and I was hoping that that drop of water I felt wasn't rain.

"Speed," called Rolf, the sound man, indicating that the sound department was ready, rolling tape, and not about to be accused of holding up the show. I had worked with both

Rolf and Stu, the sound team, on two prior films. Because the clouds and the sun kept playing peekaboo and the luminosity kept going up and down, Jim was trying to steal us one more next-to-last light-meter reading. Finally he decided to augment the sunlight with silver-coated boards called reflectors. I was hoping Dad wouldn't bitch about the reflectors costing us time. But naturally, he did. We kept it anyway because it did add a nice, warm supplemental light. For art, I'll suffer the slings and arrows of parental abuse.

Meanwhile, I dashed over and started trying to fix the helmet on Shelly's head.

"Ready!" Jim reluctantly hollered, pocketing his trusty light meter which was like a permanent extension to his arm.

"Rolling," shouted cameras as they slated the marks and started rolling film. It was then I realized something was definitely amiss. Roxy's dreadlock wig was so big, I couldn't get the welder's helmet over it at all. I glanced at Pop. The moment of truth: would he really put a paper bag on Roxy's head? Surely that was an idle threat, but this was not a good time to find out. He looked like he might. Damn!

"Dad," I said, fumbling for any solution, "the helmet's a little stuck, just one more second, please."

"I don't care what the hell it looks like, just shoot it!!" he hollered.

Silence. That's it, I thought, the phrase a director should NEVER say. It seemed to echo through the alleyway. One of those phrases that stay etched in my mind forever. Where art meets economics and economics cruelly triumphs.

I will never say that, I promised myself.

Suddenly, the answer to the helmet problem came to me. I tore off a long piece of duct tape from the mummified motorcycle and taped the helmet right to poor Shelly's wig.

Somehow we managed to get the necessary shots that day. It didn't rain, the paper bag was never mentioned again, the light looked fine, Ilan and I remembered our lines. In the movie the whole scene looks unhurried. The welder's mask worked fine. Then later that week, it disappeared, never to be found again. But at least it was right there when we needed it and is recorded forever in celluloid.

BLOCK

We eased into night shooting. It is easier on everyone if you arrange the schedule so as to keep the minimum spread between the start of each day; not start at noon one day and midnight the next. Which, incidentally, is against union rules. Anyway, we had a large block of night shooting to do and I figured it was time to try our highly vaunted, well-oiled machinery again. Then, figuring further, I decided that we would devote the first night to shooting a new hurdle, a logistical nightmare, the fashion show, circa 14.

. . . Under the best of circumstances it is going to be a long night . . . no mishaps, please God . . . lots of extras: expensive and complicated to reshoot. . . . The construction crew started at noon. At dusk they manage to get the canopy up . . . looks great. The red carpet goes down. I order it moved slightly to the right . . . a little more . . . HOLD IT . . . perfecto. Hooray for Hollywood! The extras start to trickle in, full of themselves, because they are in evening dress. . . .

All in all, the first night went well, although we didn't get a shot off until two hours later than planned. We were having trouble getting the runway adjusted on which the models strut their stuff. Once we finally got started we managed to catch up because everyone was so cooperative. AMEN. Normally the extras would have become restless, but they were having such a good time pretending to be blue-bloods—actors tend to take on the personality of the scene—that they were positively genteel.

We were on a roll. So I figured, Why not try another toughie?

The next night we shot 41 through 51—the rappers outside the home boy club, and in the limo, and with the cops
outside the burger shop. That went well too, except for the
limo company billing us six hundred dollars extra for a
scratch they say one of the rappers' jackets put on the hood
and a play-cop claiming he should get triple money because
the car he was in rode over a curb and the real cops gave us
a lecture about using a flashing red light without specific
authorization.

We plowed through the night sequences. The thugs had a
nice chemistry about them; comedy mixed with menace.
Drama abounded off-screen too. Nate, the tallest thug, a
gentle giant of a man, fell deathly ill and was rushed to
the hospital. Nate was my oldest friend on the film, after
Bernard. He was an excellent theatrical stage manager
as well as actor and I had known him and worked with
him since *Aint Supposed to Die,* my first Broadway
show, almost twenty years ago. I had noticed him having a
difficult time concentrating, and since Nate was Mr. Conscientious, that should have been a clue. But, I just figured he was having trouble with some new boyfriend and
let it slide.

The night we were to do circa 2 plus, the driving sequences that open the movie, it began to rain. We had
started out early so that the cameras would be in place for
the complicated traveling shots I wanted to do and so that
we could catch our breath and wait for darkness free of anxiety. The makeup car got caught in traffic on the way to
location, and fell so far behind that it was out of range of our
walkie-talkies. It didn't find us until the last minute. So
much for an anxiety-free evening.

It started to rain. At first I thought, We're done for. Then,
I checked the image through the camera lens. The city was
glistening, gorgeous. The Plaza, the park, the cars, Fifth
Avenue—everything looked so spectacular, I couldn't bear
to lose the magic and decided to shoot it that way.

The script person reminded me that this series of shots
didn't call for rain. "Now it does," I told her. She said,

"But suppose it stops, how are you going to match the shots?" I assured her that it had better not stop.

. . . Hats off to Yves (Richard Fancy) and his movie son, Sebe (Ilan Mitchell-Smith) . . . poking out of the sunroof of the limo, in the pouring rain, dashing around the city, and barreling down FDR Drive without ever dropping one line of dialogue. . . . Yves's wig blows off . . . luckily we are at the end of the shot . . . we may need it again and I am not sure the hairdresser can match it, so by walkie-talkie I send a car to pick it up. . . .

The rain stopped and started the rest of the night, but it was there every time we needed it, right on cue. The script person was happy, and me too.

Mario came over and told me everybody was calling me a genius. I told him I wasn't, but I'd take the praise, and could I give him some free advice?

"Okay," he said, "sure."

"Take any compliment you can get," I told him, "you may not deserve it, but it sure might come in handy. . . ."

CHIP

I remember it as if it were yesterday, almost. It was summer, my fifteenth.

"Megan," said the old man, "I'm gonna lay some profound info on you, kid." My stubborn little sister, as I expected, with her naturally red hair and temperament to match, bristled in anticipation of Dad's free advice. And as expected, Pops, undaunted, continued laying it on in his usual bold-ass manner. "It seems to me that women who don't start exercising when they're young often end up out of shape later. So if you want, I'm gonna pay for you to take ballet lessons."

"No, sir," Megan said, adding politely, "but thank you anyway, Daddy."

The two of us had learned to be a tad discreet when dealing with Dad so as not to end up on the wrong end of his fist, an art it would take little brother Max years to master. This whole concept of getting hit by a parent was totally foreign to us, as we had been raised by our basically nonviolent, sixties-minded mother. Dad's spare-the-slap-and-spoil-the-child doctrine came in a rather harsh juxtaposition to Mom's more lenient approach, to say the least. Now I wasn't into this hit-me stuff, because if someone hit me I'd have to plot their demise . . . well at least think about plotting their demise. I didn't take no shit from nobody unless, of course, they were bigger than me, in which case I'd be cool and pacify myself by only thinking about their aforementioned demise.

Dad strolled down to me, like Patton reviewing his troops, obviously a little annoyed at Megan's lack of enthusiasm.

"What about you, son," said Dad gruffly. "How 'bout I buy some weights? You can build yourself up some muscle!"

I stood up straight, double-checking to see if he was still taller than me. He was. I'd catch him by next year and pass him in two, but if ever I was gonna be big and strong enough to kick his ass, some weights might not be such a bad idea.

"Yeah, Dad, the weights might be a good idea, thanks," I replied. Megan rolled her eyes in disgust at me, but I just grinned.

Dad hesitated slightly . . . could he read my thoughts? Slowly he reached into his rarely opened wallet and forked over a couple of presidents.

Perhaps Dad did know something about me that I didn't. Maybe I had more ambition than ego or something. At any rate, I paid close attention to the man, even though the consensus among my peers was that it was uncool to listen to your folks. But if what you want is to succeed and someone can and is willing to show you how, why get snagged on the thorns of how they present it? I can't say I always liked him or understood him when I was fifteen, but I had a plan: learn what you have to learn and split with the knowledge.

I figured I was smarter and working on getting bigger and then if he crossed me, watch out. . . .

BLOCK

. . . Good news. Bad news. Sublimely ridiculous news. I notice a different body on the set giving orders. Ed says she's the new second A.D. That makes the fourth one. I watch her and she seems knowledgeable and forceful, probably okay. The carpenters constructing the route of Chilly's escape from the thugs have hit a snag at the ledge. I finally manage to explain what I want. @#%#&%@!!? . . . WE DIDN'T HAVE TO RUSH AFTER ALL! . . . The writers have gone on STRIKE *and Mario's* HIATUS *has been* EXTENDED IN-DEFINITELY. @#$*&!!?&%#. *Now they tell me,* A QUARTER OF A MILLION BUCKS *in overtime* plus! *Ah, show business.*

We kept plugging along on our six-day week. It would be more disruptive to try and change horses in midstream, so we decided to stick with the same schedule.

I offended the actress playing the Hag, Scene 6, by addressing her as "Ma'am" when I was giving her instructions. She said I was being too impersonal, that if I were a feeling, courteous person I would address her by her given name. I made a quick calculation and decided it would be more efficient to remember her name than fuss with her. So I got her name from the call sheet and referred to her by her Christian name for the rest of the scene, and she was as happy as a clam. *Ah, show biz . . .*

JIM

We were doing a traveling shot. Mario was in an automobile, and we had the camera truck rigged to parallel his car and get a two-shot of him and the other principal. His real name was Ilan, but in the film it was Sebe. Melvin was very nervous about this automobile because it was very, very expensive, a Maserati, lent to him personally by one of his friends. He did not want it damaged and he especially didn't want to attract unnecessary attention because we did not have a police permit for this particular street. Melvin was standing in the middle of the street so he could direct the scene better and from there gave he specific instructions to Mario to drive the car only one block, turn the corner, and come back.

We get the shot, but we couldn't turn the corner where Melvin asked us to because it was a one-way street. So we had to go two blocks instead. Mario decided that since we were there we might as well shoot a couple more takes, which we did. So we turned the corner at the second block and came back to where we were supposed to be. Melvin, with this grave look on his face, came running up to Mario, and started shoving him for not following his instructions. Mario, being a respectful son, did not attempt to retaliate. Then Melvin drew back to punch Mario's lights out, but by that time I had managed to get between them. There was a lot of yelling and shoving and carrying on, but Mario was cool. The first assistant director, Ed DeSisso, also got between them, and the evening finished with Mario getting his things together and splitting. I drove Melvin home and had a good personal talk with him.

The next day Mario didn't seem to hold a grudge against his father and the incident passed. When we finally had a chance to speak, Mario said, "It was a one-way street. What could I do?"

That's one thing about Melvin, he likes his directions followed exactly. If you deviate, he's going to jump you in the chops. On the other hand, he manages to make every dollar that goes into the production add up to five on the screen. That's because he is editing in his head while the shooting takes place. He's already three jumps in front of you. That's why he needs you to do exactly what he says—if not, it won't fit together. I think Melvin thought Mario was trying to second-guess him.

This is a good example of the father's adamance about having his directions followed to the letter. It is also a good example of Mario's commitment to the production by not allowing a personal difference like that to get in the way. In my conversation with Melvin I said, "Just treat him like you treat any other actor and don't go overboard with him. Your son took it from you once, all right, but don't do it again."

I think Melvin was concerned that Mario didn't really know what an accomplished filmmaker he is. But I believed that Mario did know. He has made certain statements to me about his father which showed me that he recognizes the true significance of his father as a film director and his place in film history. It is a fact that is glossed over by people in this country, and even Mario failed to communicate it to his father. But he is cognizant of Melvin's achievement. I was very happy to work with them both as a collaborator, as an uncle, and as a brother. It gave me a feeling of exhilaration. As a producer, I'm always trying to get projects off the ground. I will put on my producer's hat, supervise film budgets, and help pull the personnel and other elements together. But Melvin got me to direct photography again. He told me that if I acted as director of photography then he could control everything else. So I did.

VICTOR

Luckily I found time to visit the set. They were shooting the Mud Club scene. As I watched the style of directing, the double camera coverage, and the improvisational liberties afforded the actors, I became even more disappointed with my secondary role in the proposed editing plan, whereby Melvin would do the first rough edit of the film and I would only be allowed to help with the "polishing." In a tightly followed script, the editor's role is to execute the preplanned thought of others, while Melvin's style afforded a wonderful opportunity for more creative initiatives from an editor, from which I would be excluded. In fact it was for this very reason I steered my career toward documentaries, where the script is usually written in the editing room.

Melvin set up the cameras to get maximum coverage of the action and capture the mood. The shot-to-shot sequence would be decided later. There was a dialogue which maintained the narrative, but the placement of the actors could vary as the action progressed. The editor would therefore have many more exciting options than a "follow-the-line-script" technique.

Melvin directed the club scene as a cheerleader, whooping up all the extras, and as a choreographer redesigning the fight movements. When Mario was not in front of the camera, he was the second cheerleader, at times appearing where he shouldn't have (something to watch out for in the cutting room).

Watching the scene, with mud flying in every direction—no one was spared—Melvin orchestrated as the thoughts occurred to him, improvisationally directing the actors, never in the same place twice (more options to consider). The cameras were panning to keep the action framed as much as possible, no actors on their marks for a setup, and the extras were encouraged to do their own thing. Melvin allowed events to just happen. When the scene did not develop according to his expectations he would stop the action. This procedure was followed to a lesser degree throughout many sequences of the film.

I had expected to stay only for an hour, but once I got caught up in the excitement, I didn't leave until it was over. The energy level of both crew and cast was very high. If Melvin edited the way he directed, the cutting room would be one vibrant place. It was fortunate that I did stay till the conclusion because it was a good time for a second conversation with Melvin. There were some technical difficulties to be straightened out, but more important, it was a chance to share feelings. I never attempted to sell my talent, but I hoped Melvin would discover it.

CHIP

One of the advantages of being an actor who writes is that I play out the dialogue when I write it. It helps me develop a character's vocal pattern. The down side is that when some other actor comes in and actually plays the role, he often ends up playing it differently. For example, when I played out the announcer's dialogue in the Mud Club sequence in my head, I pictured him as sort of a sleazoid, à la *Wrestlemania*. The actor we cast was Coati Mundi of Kid Creole and the Coconuts, an outrageous bald ball of energy. Coati, who had just finished *Who's That Girl?* with Madonna, showed up on the day of the shoot with an inspired prop. "Hey, bro," he said, winking at me and whipping a bald doll from behind his back, "I thought I'd bring a compadre with me."

I had wardrobe put stripes on the doll's dress to match Coati's outfit. And Pop put Vaseline on the doll's head to match Coati's cranium. Coati tore the role up. The end result far surpassed what I had written, although, if some bystander had asked me I probably would have said—following Dad's free advice—that I always intended that the part be played that way.

Speaking of bystanders, I suppose to someone who didn't know us well it would seem that I missed a golden opportunity to put all that weight lifting and hard years of bodybuilding to good use by kicking my dad's ass when he started hollering and shoving me. But down deep I knew that Dad wasn't challenging me to a fight. I knew that whether he was right, or wrong, whether I agreed with him or not, he was into his Neanderthal thing, trying to tell me something.

In many situations where Dad played the guru I probably seemed like a nice, passive kid to someone observing us over the years. On the other hand, Dad would seem to be the passive one to a bystander when I ran the show. Dad can be a perfect disciple, quietly and carefully following my orders. But it's hard to believe if you don't really know him.

Once, when Granddad was still alive, I asked Dad what he would do if Granddad hit him. Dad said that on numerous occasions Granddaddy had.

"I mean now, that you're grown," I persisted, "what would you do?"

Dad said, well, that would depend. If he agreed with Granddad, he guessed he'd have to stand and take his medicine. But if he didn't agree, he'd try to get the hell out of Granddad's way—fast.

BERNARD

Melvin never said he was going to have Sebe rolling around in mud in the only suit of his that we didn't have a double for. Normally I don't rent or buy a suit unless there is a spare available for backup, but it was so perfect. It had a kind of beige stripe in the weave, such a typical executive yuppie White boy's suit, I couldn't resist. I will probably have to forgive Melvin, though, since the Mud Club scene is going to be so gorgeous. I reminded Melvin that we were going to need to use the suit in some scenes that we were going to shoot in a couple of days. But he said not to worry, he'd be careful. Melvin is brilliant at doing that, but the action got so good that Melvin just kept it going. The next thing I know the poor child is down there wallowing in the mud in the worsted suit, ruining it. My wardrobe folks said, "Well, maybe we can put it in the shower." I said, "Yes. And it'll shrink to the size of an eight-year-old. No, we better call up Ernest Winzer," one of the foremost theatrical cleaners in all of New York, maybe in the world. Anything that is soaked in water or mud gets heavier. So that mud-soaked suit had to weigh about thirty-five pounds. I call Ernest in tears from the set. I gotta do melodrama, and I said, "Pick up tonight either when you're finished picking up from Broadway, or first thing in the morning." So they picked up around midnight, and I handed them this heavy thing. I said, "It's a suit, and I gotta have it day after tomorrow." Well, it came back . . . looking like it had not been touched by human hands. They're so good.

BLOCK

When I heard that the next day's forecast was for clear weather, I made the crew call as early as legally possible. We were still shooting nights, hoping to catch a little late-afternoon light so I could shoot the Narish, the arch-villain's, headquarters, Scenes 35 and 175.

Unfortunately, whoever had been sent out the day before to search for a convenient Lower Manhattan location had not found anything suitable—or at least that's what I was told at the time. I decided to go with a contingency location.

We traveled uptown and shot in a garden that I had had my eye on—just in case—as far back as preproduction. Of course this sudden change of plans freaked out the script girl once again.

On the positive side: rush job or no, Henry Yuk's makeup looked perfect, just the right amount of cornball. Henry played the thug with the white eye.

On the negative side: it started to sprinkle in the middle of the sequence. It never poured, but those scattered drops did give us some anxious moments; also, the concierge at the park threatened to run us out of the garden because we hadn't given him enough notice.

It was dark by the time we got back down to our headquarters at Henry Street. As we were preparing to do our night-time business, I noticed that we had a new second A.D., our fifth.

All things considered, the sequences at Narish's place had gone great, and I was feeling philosophical. So I told myself, What the hell . . . what's another second A.D. or two . . . things could be worse, and all's well that ends well."

Turns out my philosophical attitude was a bit premature. Off camera the plot, as they say, was thickening by leaps and bounds. To be specific: I discovered that second A.D. number four had *not* been fired, or quit, but instead was *missing since the day before!* Not only that, she was *missing with the van* used to scout locations!

Of course, once it rains it pours. One of the support crew, who was rumored to be on dope, was spotted taking a package of cocaine from her pusher in the street behind the soundstage.

Last but not least, the script person slunk into the production office and announced that she was quitting again. I took her out in the hall and begged her to reconsider, saying that after all we were over the hump. She said her mind was made up (and she said it in that way that people do when they are fucking you over). She said that it was not because she had another movie—which she did have—but because she knew in the long run it would be better for me and the film. She said she would stay until the end of the week, which was the next day. I put on my surprised, disappointed, and hurt face. She said she was sorry and left. I went back into the office and told Steve to call up one of the other script persons I had had him put on standby way back at the beginning of the film, when this one first started acting flaky, with her "underutilized" bullshit. I may be crazy, but I ain't stupid.

Driving me home, sweet Tommy, who must have gotten wind of the days events, asked me—voice full of concern—was anything wrong.

I started laughing. When I managed to stop, I told him the truth.

"Nope . . . just show business as usual! . . ."

THE HOME STRETCH (BACK AND FORTH/IN AND OUT/& UP AND DOWN)

BLOCK

Approaching the last hunk of principal photography. Shooting has been hectic, but the shots have been excellent. . . .
All the cast members, following the exemplary lead of Mario, Ilan, the two Richards, Clarke and Fancy, Shelly Burch, Nicholas Kepros, and the other stars have been first-rate. . . . The nucleus of the crew has remained efficient and good-natured. My honest assessment is that we are in good shape. Soreheads and incompetents in the secondary ranks have come and gone. If only we had known for sure that there was going to be a writers' strike, we could have taken the necessary preproduction time to assemble a top-notch support team—not to mention that we could have had a five-day-week shooting schedule. . . . Mustn't get philosophical. Remember what happened last time. Speaking of getting philosophical, no word on the van or the missing A.D. Turns out she had a restraining order out on somebody and may be dead. . . . The cops have come by twice. . . .

There are usually some scenes that were never done when they were supposed to be—for a variety of reasons—at the end of a film. And there is a mad scramble to get all the shots finished. I assigned as much of the loose-end work as I could for Mario to direct in the second unit in order to get a jump on the situation and in keeping with my earlier conversation with Jim after the shoving incident with Mario.

JIM: I don't think Mario meant any harm. I think he was just trying to be helpful.

ME: I don't give a shit what he did or didn't mean to do, the fact is, countermanding my orders was confusing the crew.

JIM: I think you're overreacting. Besides, you have a pretty big boy there. I wouldn't try it again. I might have to pull him off you.

ME: I wouldn't count on it. . . .

JIM: Well, like I said, he just wants to help.

I agreed with Jim. So here was another opportunity for me to allow him to help. . . . Soundstages are finally ready. We'll do the ledge, some chase pickups, and then move on to the morgue. . . .

STEVE

I arrived in New York on April 28. My wife Marcia and I had taken a suite in the Park Lane Hotel. There was a message when I arrived to call Steve in the Production Office. I picked up the phone and dialed the number.

"Hi, Steve, it's Steve Cannell."

There was a pause on the other end of the line. I turned my back so Marcia, who was unloading her cosmetics in the bathroom, couldn't hear.

"The coroner," I whispered to remind him of my role in the film.

"Oh, yeah . . . sorry. How was the flight?"

"Real good . . . I was just checking in." I gave him my number so the production office could reach me, and he told me he'd call me tomorrow, but it looked like my shooting call would be at five the following evening. "You'll probably be working all night," he added.

Movie companies operate like no other business in the world. They work at all hours, often you get a five o'clock makeup call for a six o'clock shoot and work until six the following morning. That old dog Melvin had me on nights. Never told me. Oh well . . . I had my part down. I had even come up with a few choice one-line ad-libs. I was going to be brilliant. Who was it that said there are no small parts only small actors . . . ? Was it Mickey Rooney?

Marcia and I finished unpacking and went out for dinner.

Eleven o'clock the next morning, the phone rang, blasting me out of a dream—a good dream actually. I was Brett Eagle, Coroner. I had just rescued Michele Pfeiffer from certain death. What a coroner I was. Stopping the bodies before they hit the morgue. You don't get that kind of service at most big-city morgues. Still asleep, I fumbled the phone off the cradle. I heard Mario's sunny voice on the line.

"How's my Hollywood dad? You know your lines yet, Pop . . . ?"

"Look out, Michele," I croaked. "It is I, Brett Eagle . . . I'm on my way."

"Is this Steve Cannell's room . . . ?" Mario asked hesitantly.

I sat up and shot the last remnants of Brett Eagle out of my head and went for one of those totally awake voices.

"Hi, guy. How's it going?" I chirped.

"Did I wake you?"

"You kidding? I already had a three-mile run in the park."

"Oh," Mario said, sounding doubtful. "Look, I have to scout locations this morning, so I won't be able to catch you till later, but I'll meet you at lunch . . . for the press conference," he said.

"Sounds good to me."

"Who's Brett Eagle?" he asked.

"Oh, he's my New York publicity man," I fumbled. "We were just going over some stuff. See you tonight."

I hung up and looked around for Marcia and found a note.

She had gone out shopping and would meet me at the luncheon I was having for the New York press to introduce my shows for the upcoming season.

The press conference went well. I got a chance to talk about my shows. Mario and Melvin showed for a while, and I was told to be in wardrobe and down at the set by ten o'clock that night. My call had been pushed back.

That afternoon, as the travel agents say, was spent at leisure . . . meaning I was in my room memorizing my lines, changing a few, adding jokes.

Mario had changed a few lines in my script, I reasoned. So I figured he wouldn't squawk too loud if I changed a few in his. I wish he had given this coroner a name—even just a first name, anything but The Coroner. Oh well.

I arrived at the set in my taxi at ten sharp. The crew was a well-oiled machine. Like most independent productions, this one was fast-moving and close to the ground . . . a no-frills operation, with very friendly people. I got into makeup and wardrobe . . . talked the wardrobe lady out of the bow tie, walked upstairs in the three-story community center that was the headquarters for the movie, and found Melvin, who was directing a scene.

The rest of the night went smoothly. I finally did my work around midnight and continued on until five. It was a big party scene. I got a chance to talk to the crew, who treated me great. Mario and Melvin and I had dinner together. Lasagne, baked beans, and cole slaw, and choice of beverage as long as it was Coke. This will not go down as one of the great culinary experiences in my life, but it was certainly one of the friendliest. We chatted about the picture and the production schedules, etc. I got a chance to meet other members of the cast. This picture definitely had a team spirit.

I got home as the sun was coming up over the Big Apple. I pulled the drapes in my hotel room, tried not to wake Marcia, and crawled into bed, immediately falling asleep. I did not dream. I was too tired.

The following day, I woke up at noon and talked to Melvin

at one. We agreed we would go to the set together at five. I had a limo, so I told him I would take him.

That evening at four-thirty, I swung by Melvin's apartment to pick him up. He was shaving when I got to his flat . . . a beautiful set of rooms overlooking the river. We talked while he finished getting ready, and then jumped in my car and headed back to the Lower East Side and the location. Tonight I had most of my scenes, and most of them were with Melvin, who, aside from being the director, was also one of the actors.

"*Identity Crisis*—Scene 95, Take One," the slate man said, and then whacked the slate shut. Two cameras rolling . . . I did my scene with Melvin, sitting at a desk in the production office that had been redressed as a police set. Mel printed the first take. The crew was impressed: "One Take Cannell," "Old Reliable," "Who is that coroner?" . . . "Why, it's Steve Cannell." "Too bad they didn't name this character," I whined.

I was in front of the camera for the rest of the night. Brett Eagle couldn't have been more heroic. I was making chopped liver of this scene or that one . . . no kidding. What a performance. Who would have thought a coroner could be so complex, so likable, so undorky?

The sun was coming up as I got home. My wife was asleep as I crawled under the covers again. This time I didn't go right to sleep. I thought about Melvin and Mario and the movie.

One of the things that makes show business so much fun is the people who inhabit it.

I had met Mario only one year before and Melvin months after that and yet, in this short time, I had made two friends I would have for a lifetime. I was glad I had done the movie. It was fun to be working for Mel and Mario and Block and Chip Productions. I put Brett Eagle away for good. Who needs him? A character without a name can be charming, fun to play, and creatively rewarding. I was real tired, so I went to sleep. Michele Pfeiffer was in trouble. I rushed to help her. "I'm coming! . . . It's Brett! . . . Hold on! . . ."

"Shut up," my wife said and kicked me as she turned over and went back to sleep.

BLOCK

Yesterday the soundstage was a madhouse. Among other things we shot the "searching montage," circa 126 to 137 . . . asked the new script how she was doing and if everything was okay. . . . She said she was having a ball. The cops called (real ones). They had checked the hospitals and morgues, but there was still no sign of the fourth ex-second A.D. All the police floating around these days are making our resident dope fiend nervous. . . . I think she thinks it's all a narc ruse to catch her. This afternoon we shot the hospital, Scene 29, and Yves's house, circa 42, back to back. Since the scenes are autonomous, the gags were immediately understandable. Everybody was laughing so hard it was difficult for the actors to keep a straight face. Mario started clowning. Since we were ahead of schedule, I threw in a little comedy myself and started yelling my orders with a German U-boat commander accent. The cops found the van gutted and abandoned . . . under some bridge, I think. Naturally, the walkie-talkie and the second A.D. were missing.

So there we were finally turning toward shore, in the middle of the Hudson River, in the middle of the night, two or three in the morning, four or five hours behind schedule, at an astronomical rate, and, nevertheless, I was in a very good mood. This was the next to the last hurdle, it was almost finished, but it had been a bitch. Getting the right boat, getting the right place in the river . . . getting the right time, etc. . . .

But, never mind all that. I was happy. It had gone fabulously, from finding the right angles in the cramped quarters

NO IDENTITY CRISIS

—I had even considered building a breakaway cabin on the soundstage, but vetoed that in the interest of authenticity— to Max's (Richard Clarke's) dying confession, Scene 159, to Chilly D. and Sebe leaping overboard, Scene 160. . . .

CHIP

Ilan and I were on the back of the boat, toweling off and cracking dubious jokes about our night of adventure on the high seas. We had stayed above deck so we could watch the Manhattan skyline grow closer and closer as we headed back to the Seventy-Ninth Street boat basin to tie up. I didn't hear the first splash, but I sure heard the second. They were just tying the boat up to the pier when someone yelled, "Man overboard!"

Hell, I thought to myself, I knew the evening had been too perfect. Even Dad had seemed pleased.

The boat's captain, a wizened old codger who looked like he had come out of central casting, had let his mangy old dog—kept locked in a closet during the filming—loose. Furthermore, it turned out that the hound, smelling home port, had decided he couldn't wait for us to dock, opting to take what he thought was a faster route via the river. Unfortunately for Fido, there were no ramps leading from the water to the walkway. The hound, who must have been about ninety years old in dog years, was going down for the final count when one of the camera crew happened to spot him.

The big splash was the ancient captain, who seemed about as decrepit as his dog, diving overboard. We fished them out. The dog was almost a goner, but Martin, the captain, who kept massaging and pleading to the dog not to die, finally managed to bring him around. There wasn't a dry eye in the crowd, as they say, and the evening (or rather morning, it was dawn by then) ended on a happy note.

BLOCK

I turned my attention to the last location: a huge complex of abandoned factories on the Upper East Side of Manhattan that we had simply dubbed "the warehouse." Once I focused on the sequences that were to be shot in and around the warehouse, I quickly realized that instead of having one last hurdle to go, I had three: (1) the alley when the thugs try to run down Chilly D., (2) the sinking of the barge, and (3) the shootout.

In the meantime they had found the fourth second A.D. She was alive—sort of—sleeping in doorways and panhandling in the streets. She had had a mental breakdown or something and was just hanging around near a bar where a guy who had been beating her up worked. He was the one against whom she had had a restraining order issued. We never did get the walkie-talkie back.

TOMMY

I was living close to MVP and since I decided to keep my car in town I drove him back and forth from work. I really enjoyed those times. Melvin demanded the respect that the hierarchy of movie making required, but still remained surprisingly accessible to even the lowest members of the production staff, including me. The drive in the morning was one of silence as he mapped out the day in his head. In the evening, it started the same way, but about halfway home, I would get a signal and would talk his ears off with my questions and criticisms of the day.

Melvin had been in the business a lot longer than anyone in the cast and crew, but everyone believed that they knew a way to do it better or knew that Melvin was doing it wrong or that it just "wouldn't work." Everyone, that is, of course, except those who had worked with Mel and knew that it would all work out and that it would be as good or better than the textbook way—plus cheaper and/or easier.

It's odd how when you're involved you can be so sure that everything is wrong and then have all your theories and high-and-mighty views torn down by the one sentence that Melvin would use to explain to me why the way "it" was done ("it" being whatever I was complaining about) actually made more sense than the way I had presumed to be better. Every once in a while, one of my comments would have some measure of validity. When it did he would sit quietly for a while and then tell me the pros and cons. On a few occasions he even used my ideas. That was a real high.

As filming progressed, I began to get a real idea of what it all meant. Each evening the crew would get a call sheet that would tell them everything from the time to be in, to where to meet, to crew responsibilities, and finally, which scenes would be shot. Once you got called, you had to help the various departments get all their equipment out and ready so that by the time the actors arrived everything conceivable was ready and available to shoot.

I was glad that for the most part I was involved on the set rather than in the office. On the set I was able to see first-hand how this would all develop into a complete work. I was one of a number of P.A.s who got all the equipment from where it was stored the night before to the set proper. Once the shooting got under way and the director said "action" it was the job of all of the P.A.s to keep the set quiet and free of pedestrians and distractions. It might seem like this would become boring, but between each take—several minutes at best—there was a multitude of requests and needs that each P.A. could get verbally or over his walkie-talkie to respond to.

One of the jobs I "acquired' early on was the honor of bringing the film to the lab. At least that was how it was presented to me. I was thrilled, of course, as it was explained to me that normally only the production manager was entrusted with the in-the-can product. All of this was, I am still told, true, but in any case, what it really meant was that I was always the last one off the set. I had to stop uptown to deliver this precious and valuable commodity before I could end my night at about ten o'clock and climb into bed for the 6 o'clock call the next morning.

I enjoyed the film because of the excitement of the production and the satisfaction of seeing jobs well done. But, what really made it for me was the people. First there was Melvin and Mario; the fiercely detemined duo. Then there was the cast and crew, in no time at all we were a family and grew very close, very fast. Of course there was the occasional squabble, and the girls were all fighting over Mario's affections. But all in all, I found it amazing how quickly so many individualists were able to buckle down and work together closely.

I found it amazing to watch the actors work. There were very few mistakes. The older veterans actually studied their lines and it seemed to be an effort made. But for Mario and the actor who played Sebe, Ilan Mitchell-Smith, it seemed almost too easy. Mario impressed me the most. His transition between his characters seemed so natural, it went beyond any question of believing or not. My second-favorite actor was Bruce, a Jewish kid from Brooklyn, who played one of the guys in the Funky Four rap group. Bruce could outrap, outdance, and out-home-boy every home boy there. His style didn't end there, though. One day when they sent me to go get him and take him to makeup, I found him standing on the sidewalk surrounded by neighborhood kids doing magic tricks. I walked up, and he finished his act by pulling a three-inch-wide dime out from behind one of my ears, to squeals of astonishment and delight from me and the kids.

When I first heard that we would be finishing up principal photography on the site of an abandoned factory up in Harlem, I had concerns, but endless flights of stairs weren't among them.

When we got there with our three big trucks stuffed full of equipment, I was told that the first shot was to take place on the fourth floor. I looked around the devastated shell of a building and suddenly realized that the only way up was up a steep, badly worn set of stairs. Over the course of the next few days we shot scenes in every section of the huge warehouse. The shooting order started at the first floor and went up to the fourth and back down to the first and finally to the fourth floor of a building across the street. (At the time it almost seemed deliberate. You get paranoid at times like these and begin to think that someone deliberately planned this hardship just for you.) At the end of each day all the material had to be reloaded in the trucks and locked up even if the last scene of the day and the first scene the next morning were up on the fourth floor. As we, the P.A.s *cum* mules, passed one another on the steps we would nod. In fact, that's how production assistants have commiserated with one another since time immemorial.

BLOCK

We were down to the last hurdle. The other two of the infamous warehouse obstacles were now history. The alley sequence, Scene 121, where the thugs try to run down Chilly D., was done. Scenes circa 176, where the barge filled with the captured gangsters and Chilly D.'s army had been built and sunk were over. We were down to the final shot— *Maybe*.

It had been a day filled with snags. The special-effects man was a major dud, as were about two-thirds of his explosions which sizzled and sputtered, and refused to detonate on command. Three retakes per shot, with about forty-five minutes in between for him to rewire, was about our norm, and the sun was sinking fast.

A momentous occasion, the last day, the last shot of the film . . . if we hurried, that is. It should have been my moment of glory, instead I was sweating blood.

"We only got time for one more," I told the special-effects

guy. "This has gotta work," I reminded him, as he rigged a charge under a villain's brocaded dashiki so that it would erupt and squirt blood on cue.

"Well, I can only guarantee to make it work if I put in a stiff charge," he said.

"Will it be dangerous to the actor?" I asked.

"No . . ."

". . . Well, shit, do it, then!"

". . . But it might tear the fabric on this whatchamacallit he's wearing," he explained, "and it looks like a pretty expensive outfit to me. Plus, speaking of that, I can't guarantee that all the blood will wash out. Maybe you better put some cheaper outfit on him."

I scrutinized the actor's outfit, an elaborate Pakistani whatchamacallit with delicate gold brocade and matching pants.

"We can't change him. He's been wearing it throughout the entire scene. It's a close-up and it won't match."

I yelled to wardrobe to check and see if they had any identical backup for him.

"No, sir," wardrobe replied, "nothing even close . . . it's one of a kind."

"Where did it come from?"

"It's on loan . . . sorta."

"What the hell does that mean?!!"

"It belongs to Nate," Bernard said, stepping in. He went on to explain that since Nate was so vain he had wanted to wear his own costume and that besides Nate was so proud of the fact that he had gotten it while on a world tour— he thought it was when he was with *Porgy and Bess*— and loved to show it off, that he, Bernard didn't have the heart to refuse. When Nate got sick he put it on the actor replacing him to create the illusion that it was the same person.

I admitted that it all sounded logical to me. On the other hand, we were losing daylight, and the news on Nate from the hospital didn't sound like he'd be needing it. So, I told the explosives guy to go ahead and make it a stiff charge and yelled to Jim to stop fucking around with his light meter because we were going to roll.

The shot was perfect.

Yes, it ripped a little bit, but it didn't ruin the outfit. The movie blood all washed out and we added some brocade to hide the hole. But Nate died a couple of weeks later anyway.

POSTPRODUCTION
(The heat's off . . .
WHEW . . . sorta)

ISABEL

The new buzzword is "wrap party." Wrap, as in end of the day: "We've got a wrap" or "That's it, looks like a wrap to me." Through the mail, brochures and letters came pouring in from lofts, discos, and restaurants soliciting our wrap party. One restaurant sent a photo all pink-and-black Art Deco with tablecloths. MVP said no way, the crew would want to let their hair down and would probably end up wrecking the place. As it turned out, we had the party—to be on the safe side—in somebody's loft.

One of the joys of the wrap party was getting to know Mario better. Before the movie started Mario had been in town on several occasions during and after my work on his dad's apartment, though Dad never saw fit for us to meet. Not that I had asked or really cared to meet the young man. Initial meetings I've had with celebrities can be weird— many of them anticipate that everyone will be the proverbial adoring groupie.

Only once during shooting of the film did we have occasion to be alone. One night we were walking back to an equipment truck. I mentioned enjoying him in *Heartbreak Ridge*. He brightened to full smile, said thanks and spoke of the fun he had had doing it. Then, after a long pause, he asked pointedly, "How long have you known my dad?" Writing it here, it sounds harmless enough. But it was a very direct query, almost an accusation. I told him some months or whatever it was and that was that. Strike one.

In honesty, I must add that owing to his father's admitted

reputation as a ladies' man, Mario may have assumed the reason for my presence, which could be transient, so why develop any friendship? Melvin's sexually promiscuous behavior was his business and not mine. Though I must confess that I find womanizers superficial creatures of habit and terribly boring. I prefer to ignore that side of Melvin if it exists. I sensed that Mario, who, like his dad doesn't expose the sum total of his feelings, was more than just a sex symbol and would prefer the traditional love life that so many Hollywood stars find elusive.

During most of the making of *Identity Crisis,* Mario remained aloof from me. The only other thing I knew was that, like his dad, he was willing to use his own professional position to help underdogs who might otherwise be passed over.

My breakthrough with Mario came while Melvin and I were dancing at the wrap party. Melvin and I both love to dance and being of the same vintage know the same steps. Mario joined us in an off-time, do-your-own-thing number. Then the DJ changed to a slow drag. We three embraced in one fluid motion and danced a minute that way. Melvin eased himself away. After a few minutes, Mario broke the silence by telling me how much he appreciated all I had done for the film and for his father. It was a beautiful moment and we had at last become friends.

A wrap party is something akin to a high school graduation party . . . with everybody getting dressed up and boogying down . . . a lot of hugging and kissing . . . most sincere, some phony. Everybody goes over to MVP and says they "knew we" (meaning themselves and MVP) could do it.

The next week a skeleton crew and myself began the serious process of mopping-up the studio space we had used down at Henry Street. MVP, in his usual charming manner, had issued terse instruction before moving on, "Don't let things drag, finish fast! Kick ass if you have to and call me if they try and kick yours." A few weeks ago, I couldn't even find my way to Henry Street and now . . . anyway, having worked at the grueling principal-photography pace for so long I found the abrupt stop brought instant inertia, but time in this case was definitely money, so I became a female Simon Legree. (Although the work load is lighter, the pay remains the same and the pay for the member of a movie crew is pretty high.)

In the meantime Melvin had set up his tent at Valkhn, Inc. to begin editing. The new names are Victor, Molly, Mark, and others. There was a new telephone number to speak with him and new address at which to find him. I didn't have to call him, but I did have to prod and push the weary workers until everything was tallied, copied, packed, and delivered, and accounts settled, which meant not only making sure everyone got every dime coming to them, but that we got back every penny of every refund or deposit that was due us too. Incidentally, the loft where we had the wrap party may have been wreckproof, but they claimed someone stole a bundle of children's clothes—expensive children's clothing of course—that had been stored in a corner and we settled with them at two hundred dollars.

TOMMY

As the wrap-up party wound to a close I looked around the loft at my friends. I thought back fondly to the time we had spent together and then to the choices spread out before me. Preston Holmes, the production manager who before he had to go to another assignment had helped Melvin at the beginning, had heard about the good work I had done and called me to ask if I wanted to come and work on another movie. I had other commitments, but the offer was tempting and made me feel very happy.

A wrap party is mostly just crew. Maybe, if all the crew— which was half Black, half White—had all been invited, I would have thought about it again. In all the time I had been working on *Identity Crisis,* it hadn't occurred to me that the crew was, with very few exceptions, Black. There had been the occasional comment about my being the token White, and aside from half of the actors, I was greatly in the minority.

I didn't take the job Preston offered me and that probably will not be the path my life will take, anyway. Besides, without the Van Peebles gang, it wouldn't be the same.

Now that it is all over, when I go to the movies and check the credits—after all, we had some real talent on *Identity Crisis*—I never see anyone I know. Now I realize the plight of these people. The best thing *Identity Crisis* did was to provide jobs for some people in the movie business, to whom a feature film credit is rare. I think I now understand the fierce determination of the MVPs better.

VICTOR

When the last shot of the production was canned, Melvin took two days off and then immediately put himself and the editing assistants on a tight schedule. He was hoping for a first cut in two months.

I watched his first three days of editing while I finished a previous project and we discussed some of the dailies. I must have made some impression because Melvin changed his plan. Whereas he would rough-cut the entire movie alone and then bring me on to fine-tune it with him, we opened another cutting room and I started to cut my first sequence. His only dictum before I started was that I should use all the camera angles, maintain the energy level, and be sure to tell the story. A strong story line was essential, but a montage type of editing was permissible and advantageous. In other words, use as many edits as possible. Melvin screened the dailies with me, pointing out his preferred takes, but allowed me to select the exact section of each shot. I was given as much freedom to improvise as he had allowed his actors.

The same openness that Melvin and Mario showed one another pervaded the cutting room and although the pace was forced, the attitude was relaxed.

Melvin screened my first sequence, made suggestions, told me not to stop but to execute the suggestions later. I started my next sequence. Melvin and I leapfrogged the script—I would get some pages, he would start later pages, and whoever finished first would move ahead. We didn't exactly race one another, but I will admit to lengthening my editing day in order to do as many scenes as possible. I tend to edit very intensely in short bursts. Melvin never stops. His attitude in the cutting room is "enjoy yourself, but get the work done and do it fast." Interruptions were held to a minimum and my lunch diet consisted of yogurt, nuts, and tea. I don't know if Melvin was a nut-eater before this film, but as we shared the editing, we shared the nuts.

Mario was a frequent visitor to the cutting room and would comment on whatever was ready or almost ready to be screened. At the time, Melvin appeared to listen and then ignore his criticisms. As I began to understand Melvin's behavior better, I realized that Mario's opinions were not being discounted but merely postponed. Melvin very seldom responds to a new idea without analyzing all the options and then executing those that fit the style of the film. Although Melvin is extremely opinionated, I always found him to be accessible to new approaches, and in the final edit almost all of Mario's suggestions were incorporated into the film.

Melvin didn't take the time, during or after production, to screen all the dailies. He would screen the footage for the first time in the cutting room and then plunge right in. That happens to be my preferred mode of editing as well. I dislike studying the footage because my initial ideas are usually my best and most audacious. My second thoughts tend to be more conservative. This film was definitely suited to my first approach. At times, I would start cutting before Melvin screened the scene. His only admonition was "Can't I see any footage the way I shot it? You want to cut before I screen."

NO IDENTITY CRISIS

When Melvin asked me to edit the Mud Club sequence, I knew his confidence in my ability had solidified. The key to editing, in order to satisfy the spirit of the scene, was controlled chaos. No editing rules should be followed and a slightly abstract feeling should permeate the flow of the action. The dialogue, of course, had to secure the scene within the context of the plot. It was important that the scene didn't appear to be a film within a film. The dialogue had to be the anchor.

My first cut ran ten minutes, or about twice as long as the film could sustain. I tried to cut it down, but my success was minimal. I became attached to many abstract touches I discovered in the material and used in the edit. Melvin suggested we put the scene aside and re-edit later with a more objective point of view. I never did regain my objectivity and Melvin finally cut it to its proper length. The long version had good impact within itself and although I still miss the small nuances that the scene contained at ten minutes, the final five-minute cut did fit the film.

Melvin's attempt to meet his desired deadline for completion led to my only crisis. He worked the Fourth of July weekend—alone. The entire staff, including me, elected to holiday. Working alone in a cutting room can cause feelings of insecurity. Editing requires deep concentration and being alone, even in a large cutting room with a window, can alienate anyone.

When I returned on Tuesday at my usual starting time, one hour later than Melvin's, he greeted me calmly, but announced that he would finish the film alone. He liked my work, but felt the backup support for a difficult schedule was lacking. I don't react negatively to surprise situations and prefer to adopt a wait-and-see attitude, which helped me in this situation. I didn't appreciate his decision, but I tried to understand his mood.

We agreed to continue through the end of the week and then shift personnel. As quickly as Melvin's negativism had appeared, his positive approach to the film reappeared, and by the end of the week, it was obvious I would continue editing with him with no interruption of process, nor loss of momentum. Melvin merely said, "Forget our discussion and see you Monday!"

The issue of backup support was never raised again and I believe this near schism in our relationship led to even better communication and a sharper analysis of the film as we continued.

The picture was photographed at locations throughout the city, creating a rich atmosphere. The sequences were short and designed to be almost a collage of images, but never at the expense of an audience's understanding. Each scene was self-contained, so we didn't have to edit in continuity. Each scene was also paced differently and, although the scenes played well within themselves, I did have second thoughts about what the finished movie would look like. Would it appear as many short pieces spliced together, or would it be a strong, continuous film?

When editing sequences exist as units within themselves, I find it difficult to judge the flow of the entire film. Melvin seemed singularly unperturbed by this possibility. Melvin kept saying "No problem," claiming he carried the whole thing in his head. Well, he had called all the other shots pretty close, so I had to go along, but it did seem a bit much.

Most films are designed with transition shots to try to blend one scene into the next. It is the transitions which bridge the plot twists and help an audience follow the flow. *Identity Crisis* was designed as separate sequences, creating variety in action, mood, and pace. The combinations and cumulative impact would deliver the emotion.

As an editor, this kept me off balance. It was very late in the final cutting when we decided to add wipe effects. These wipes delineated the pace changes and clarified the time progression. I admit that only with the addition of these effects did I feel comfortable with the film as a cohesive whole.

The freedom to create, criticize, change and then re-create stimulated Melvin, myself, and the assistant editors—a staff of three—to be imaginative. The assistants also had to be resourceful in changing established editing-room procedure to accommodate the whims and sometimes whimsy of two editors who believe that consistency is not necessarily a virtue.

As our collaboration grew more intimate, we started re-editing each other's work. Melvin had always suggested changes and then I would accomplish them. Now, Melvin would physically take my sequences and execute the revisions personally. I, in turn, not only criticized Melvin's scenes and cuts, but put them under the splicing block and re-edited them my way. Very seldom was either of us unhappy with the alternate vision of how a scene would play.

As we exchanged opinions, we were able to reanalyze structure. This led to the creation of one parallel action sequence, intercutting three segments—originally written to play separately—into one. This not only created dynamic movement, but also added suspense before the chase/shoot-out conclusion.

BLOCK

After a couple of days, or was it seconds, at the editing table all the old feelings came rushing back to me.

The truth is I flat-out unequivocally love postproduction, and when the raw material that you have to work with is what you had hoped it would be—and it was in this case—it can even be heavenly. I love each and every phase: the feel of the film, the sight of it whizzing through the gates as it snakes along the editing table, the piecing together of the takes to build a scene, dealing with the technicians at the lab, the Rube Goldberg machinery at the optical house, then later on, selecting noise with the sound man, or deciding the tempo of a tune for a scene with the music guy . . . everything. The incessant problem-solving nature of editing, the anticipation and challenge of each new sequence never causes me anxiety; on the contrary, it soothes me. It is the closest thing to what the preachers call a state of Grace, that I have ever known. Plus, for the first time, everything else was ideal, God bless Jim. Valkhn was the perfect postproduction house for me.

Victor, the boss of Valkhn, who became co-editor, genuinely loved film and the editing process. Victor had managed to infuse that love into generations of fledgling editors down through the years. At any given moment of the night or day the various rooms at Valkhn resounded with screams from some sound track of somebody's horror film, the disembodied voice of a narrator explaining the various metals used in racing-car construction for some publicity, or maybe tom-toms out of Africa for a PBS series.

Molly, Victor's selection for my assistant, was an eager, cheerful, handsome, redheaded young lady, who always looked as if she had just stepped out of a Thomas Hardy novel. We had our own room, along with whatever extra hands were needed at a given moment. Eventually, after the rough cut, we were joined by the sound man, Al, and his assistant, his terrific wife. Victor, with Marc, who was his assistant, were in similar digs on the diagonal across the hall.

One day, for the hell of it, I got down the book I had published about the making of *Sweetback* and browsed through what I had written to myself about editing. My sentiments haven't changed an iota . . . whatever that means. . . .

> Don't understand the film too quickly. Be a good parent, but don't be too possessive to the movie. The film has a life of its own, in there somewhere, find it and nurture it. That's what editing is all about. . . .

> Don't worry, be happy—Christ was nothing but a carpenter in his own home town . . .

> Solitude, just you and the film and the equipment. . . .
> [Remember] . . . Freud defined creating as opening the

floodgates of the mind and letting all possibilities and impossibilities rush in—the wild, the rational, the irrational, the fantastic—then sifting the sluice . . . the moment when the floodgates are thrown open is that super-vulnerable point in creating. Your general state should be as neutral as possible; any impurity takes on immense proportion. . . .

Anyway, to make a long story short, just as back then, I was happy in my work.

TOBIE

I knew Mario loved acting, but I also knew he was interested in writing, directing, producing, and playing a bigger part in the entire movie-making process. When I first read *Identity Crisis* I was very much impressed, and I knew the project would afford Mario and Melvin the opportunity to pool their talents and create together.

Actually getting a film project off the ground, though, is a very difficult thing. But, the next thing I know I am visiting them on the set of the movie with crews from news media like the *Today* show and CNN in tow. Then, Mario gets his breakthrough directing assignment and I track him down in the editing room and rush over to give him the good news in person. He and his dad are delighted. They say they have more big news, the rough cut of the first half of the film is ready, and the next thing I know I am being ushered into the screening room for a look. I should have known that it wouldn't take the Van Peebleses very long to turn a dream into a reality.

VICTOR

At last . . . the final-cut of the film. No doubt about it . . . it worked just as Melvin always said it would! It had been a wonderful experience and immediately I started to look forward to co-editing Melvin's next film.

Mario ran over to his dad, gave him a big hug, and told him it looked great.

". . . Un-huh . . . goddamn right, son," Melvin replied, "of course it does."

ISABEL

Rough cut, first cut, sound mix, music mix, polish, final mix . . . terms I'd overheard as the editing progressed, and now the film was finished. It was over. Hard to believe, but there it stood, on the floor in the middle of MVP's living room, all the months of blood, sweat, and tears simmered down to five great circles of film, tightly packed inside a large cardboard box. MVP, having replaced his movie-making cap with his salesman's hat, was in his den packing papers, getting ready to go off to Los Angeles to show the film. The ease with which he can divorce himself from one phase and glide into the next never ceases to amaze me.

Divorce is exactly the right word, because watching the making of *Identity Crisis* was akin to witnessing a rapid succession of marriages and divorces with MVP always the groom—marriages of teamwork and love. During preproduction, principal photography, and the postproduction stage with all its facets (editing, music, special effects, opticals and the mix), I saw these relationships develop and run their respective courses.

People adore MVP and the MVP experience of it all. They

stretch for him, and he stretches for the cause. He's the pe-
rennial drill sergeant who runs farther, climbs faster, shoots
straighter, yet also performs the menial tasks, thus giving
importance to the mundane. And while his troops slumber,
he plots and plans. There's always a yellow pad and pencil
at his bedside to log ideas, should his muse decide to inter-
rupt his sleep. The stamina of this man seems endless.

The marriages are purely metaphoric here, allowing that
the brides are both males and females. The coming together
and the parting. Seasoned professionals, as were most of the
cast and crew, took the separation pretty much in stride.
These "brides" accepted the inevitable and were already out
seeking their next "mate."

It was the same thing with the postproduction crew, only
sadder. Valkhn had been MVP's second home for five
months, and everyone had become like family. No one escaped Melvin's gruff magic, not even Dunn, Trevor, and
Kenny, the brilliant young men brought in toward the end to
work on the music. The morning of the final screening,
Molly and Marc, numbed by the reality that divorce was
imminent, followed MVP around like puppies. If he had re-
versed gears, he would have run over them.

Charming or not, the Great One can be pretty unpredict-
able and can really tick me off. Case in point—a next-door
neighbor upon eviction decided to leave without the hassle
of taking his seven-foot sofa that had had to be carried down
ten flights because it couldn't fit in the elevator. He asked
MVP if he could leave it in his office over the weekend, until
one of the porters, who was purchasing it for a hundred dollars, could retrieve it on Monday. Two weeks later the contemporary monster of a sofa was still there. In the meantime
I had learned from the porters that no one wanted to buy the
sofa and in fact, they wanted a hundred dollars to take it
down the ten flights of stairs.

So, as I said, two weeks later it was still there cluttering
up the office. And then forty minutes before he had to leave
with the film to catch his plane Melvin appeared in the doorway and announced he was through with his packing. One

would have thought it was a perfect time for reflection and solitude—right? Wrong!

Not only was the telephone ringing itself to death, with every friend, fan, divorcee, etc., wanting to be anointed before he left, but the Great One suddenly decided it would be a great occasion to get rid of the sofa.

"It's too heavy for you to carry down the steps," I said, hoping to dissuade him.

"I don't intend to." He winked. "The truth has suddenly been revealed to me," he said, stealing a line from the film. "Get the saw and shit. . . ."

I came back with a saw, kitchen knife, hammer, pliers, and a screwdriver. I couldn't figure out who was crazier—he or I. Anyway Melvin stabbed the sofa dead center and made a beautiful incision down the back, and we started pulling away the batting—fingers searching for the wooden frame. More stabbing, ripping, and peeling revealed the frame. Melvin sawed through it with agility and speed. (Can the S.O.B. do everything?) Then, we put the halves into the elevator and took them down to the garbage dump in the basement.

I asked him what he was thinking. "Nothing," he said and shrugged. So I sent him off to his important public. The telephone wailed as we made our way out the door. MVP waved to me from the taxi. For one fleeting moment, with his face framed in the taxi window, I saw a man who had traveled ahead of himself and was already 3,000 miles from home. Then he was gone into the night.

BLOCK

Isabel had asked me what I was thinking as we rode down on the elevator and I had said, "Nothing." Actually I lied. Maybe I'll apologize some day, but self-preservation begins at home, and nothing is more dangerous than giving a sum-mary before its time. What I mean is, I had been assessing my future moves toward marketing the film, something I never permitted myself before, for fear of polluting my creative decisions, and my strategy hadn't fully crystallized.

I suppose I sighed at the road ahead of me, I can't rightly remember. Then I decided to give myself a rest for the duration of the trip to the airport. About halfway to the plane I began to wonder if I was letting Mario, Jim, Bernard, Victor, Isabel, the NAACP, the Independent Film Makers of the Universe and the rest of the home team down by taking a break. So I pulled myself together and started plotting my sales pitch.

CHIP

I directed my first show, an hour television project, right after *Identity Crisis* was in the can. It went well and I was on to my second assignment. My director of photography, Jack Whitman, a level-headed, well-seasoned vet of the film business, reminded me a lot of Jim Hinton. Maybe all D.P.s are built like that to last, or rather, the ones that last are built like that.

Anyway, we were filming a big-money night shoot-out sequence on a rooftop. The special-effects crew was working double time trying to pump steam through several false chimneys I had ordered constructed to create a mysterious, surrealistic ambiance.

The L.A. police showed up suddenly to notify us that there couldn't be any explosions or gunfire after ten o'clock sharp, or they would close us down. It was 9:45 already! The entire frigging sequence was gunfire and it was supposed to take all night to film. Then one of the producers came over and told me that one of the major actors was a minor and that we could only use him until ten.

I raced through my shot list and set up camera B to pop off

all shots of the kid while I did as many absolutely necessary gunshots as possible with camera A. I knew that if the actors mime the non-pertinent gunshots, I could always dub in the gunfire sounds later. My trusty first assistant worriedly looked at his watch. Six more minutes before no kid, no guns. Even my loyal buddy big Chris, who has a personality like a hard wooden chair, looked doubtful.

In my mind I could already hear the producers sneering, "What, you didn't make your day!"

Okay, fine, I'd finish the gunfire sequence, or at least all that I could. Jack quickly set up camera A to do the big scene where the kid first ventures out onto the smoky roof. "Four minutes to go," said the first A.D., trying not to press me.

The effects men were fighting with one of the chimneys that just wouldn't work; it sputtered, coughed, belched one cloud of dust, but refused to smoke.

Then, just as in a bad B-movie, I was peering hopefully at the pitiful grains of dust and my mind tripped and flashed back. . . . back to our motorcycle venture across the desert years ago . . . when the storm had tossed my narrow butt into the pit alongside Dad and I had jokingly suggested we do a flick together someday. I didn't realize then what a mammoth-mother undertaking that would be. I thought about Mom and how she had encouraged me and put up her nest egg for the film. I thought about my sister Megan, a tiny redheaded thing, always asking me for a story, and how, years later, for two hours straight I had laid out the whole story for the film to brother Max on the Bahamian sand. I thought about the first showing of the final cut and how I had been so nervous I couldn't decide where to take a seat. I finally chose the back row. I glanced back at Pops, all legs and no torso. Built like spiders, we sat real low in our chairs. Dad had all but vanished there . . . I could barely make out his face. With his shades and hat he looked like some Mexican low-rider cruising Hollywood Boulevard. I had seen the footage in the editing room time after time, in bits and pieces, but never assembled. I wondered if Dad shared any of my prescreening jitters. I could have saved myself the anxiety, because the flick was wonderful. I even started to think about Dad and his mouth full of oxtail as I told him I was going to quit my safe job as a budget analyst and that if he acted now he could be the first to help me get back into show business. I remember watching him trudge off into the snow and suddenly realizing that maybe it had been a hard thing for him to do, to turn his back on me. . . . Sometimes I guess you are lucky if someone loves you enough to let you do it on your own. The Chinese say, "He who is carried does not know how long the road is"—and it had been a long road.

"Just a few more seconds," the effects guy yelled out, snapping me back to my whereabouts. He was still futzing with the pipe.

"Two minutes to go," the first A.D. whispered, resigned to our fate. This will look bad for him too if we don't get off our master shot. The boys in the front office don't want to hear about our troubles.

Suddenly . . . out of nowhere, a voice boomed out loud and clear, "I don't care what the hell it looks like, just shoot it!"

Who the hell was that?! Was Dad somewhere . . . ?! No, the old man was back in New York. *Holy shit*, it wasn't DAD, it was ME!

My God, I had said that horrible phrase! That sacrilegious sentence, that cinematic no-no. Even worse, I *meant it*. I meant every word . . . thank you, but shoot the sucker now. Forget the extra chimney smoke!

"Okay . . . action!" I bellowed.

The effects man ducked, the kid walked out beautifully onto the spooky roof just as it was all supposed to be. Los Angeles twinkled majestically in the background as if on cue, and we made our shots that night. The producers loved the dailies and I went home and slept like a baby. I laughed as I thought of my curse . . . the Curse of the Lizard Dad.

INDEX